T0344867

Empowered Enterprise Risk Management

Empowered Enterprise Risk Management

Theory and Practice

HÅKAN JANKENSGÅRD
PETTER KAPSTAD

This edition first published 2021

© 2021 John Wiley & Sons, Ltd

Registered office
John Wiley & Sons Ltd, The Atrium, Southern Gate, Chichester, West Sussex, PO19 8SQ,

United Kingdom

For details of our global editorial offices, for customer services and for information about how to apply for permission to reuse the copyright material in this book please see our website at www.wiley.com.

Wiley publishes in a variety of print and electronic formats and by print-on-demand. Some material included with standard print versions of this book may not be included in e-books or in print-on-demand. If this book refers to media such as a CD or DVD that is not included in the version you purchased, you may download this material at http://booksupport.wiley.com. For more information about Wiley products, visit www.wiley.com.

Designations used by companies to distinguish their products are often claimed as trademarks. All brand names and product names used in this book are trade names, service marks, trademarks or registered trademarks of their respective owners. The publisher is not associated with any product or vendor mentioned in this book.

Limit of Liability/Disclaimer of Warranty: While the publisher and author have used their best efforts in preparing this book, they make no representations or warranties with respect to the accuracy or completeness of the contents of this book and specifically disclaim any implied warranties of merchantability or fitness for a particular purpose. It is sold on the understanding that the publisher is not engaged in rendering professional services and neither the publisher nor the author shall be liable for damages arising herefrom. If professional advice or other expert assistance is required, the services of a competent professional should be sought.

Library of Congress Cataloging-in-Publication Data

Names: Jankensgård, Håkan, author. | Kapstad, Petter, author.
Title: Empowered enterprise risk management : theory and practice / Håkan Jankensgård, Petter Kapstad.
Description: First Edition. | Hoboken : Wiley, 2021. | Series: Wiley corporate F&A | Includes index.

Identifiers: LCCN 2020035534 (print) | LCCN 2020035535 (ebook) | ISBN 9781119700159 (hardback) | ISBN 9781119700180 (adobe pdf) | ISBN 9781119700203 (epub)

Subjects: LCSH: Risk management. | Organizational effectiveness.
Classification: LCC HD61 .J356 2020 (print) | LCC HD61 (ebook) | DDC 658.15/5--dc23

LC record available at https://lccn.loc.gov/2020035534
LC ebook record available at https://lccn.loc.gov/2020035535

Cover Design: Wiley
Cover Images: © kool99/Getty Images, © Ascent Xmedia/Getty Images

Set in 10/12pt, SabonLTStd by SPi Global, Chennai, India.
Printed and bound by CPI Group (UK) Ltd, Croydon, CR0 4YY

10 9 8 7 6 5 4 3 2 1

For August and Wilma – HJ

Many thanks to Tone, Lotte, and Kaja for their support and inspiration – PK

Contents

Preface

I N THIS BOOK, WE ARE INTERESTED in how firms should organize themselves to deal with risks affecting their performance, as well as the process of risk-taking itself. When enterprise risk management (ERM) arrived on the scene in the 1990s, it presented itself as a framework that allows firms to deal with precisely these questions. ERM brought novel ideas to bear on the risk management process, such as the involvement of the board of directors and taking an integrated perspective on the firm's various risks. Ideas like these set corporate risk management on a whole new path, and the response has been massive among practitioners as much as academics. Today, ERM is a rapidly expanding field that has become the new benchmark for how to think about risk management in firms.

Our interest in principles means that we will take a tour of the theories of risk management in search of insights. Theory, as we will argue in the first chapter of the book, is not only of interest for its own sake. It can often be a powerful guide to action, as it articulates the problems to be solved and identifies the mechanisms whereby value can be created. In an eclectic and sprawling field such as ERM, which has proven to be an endlessly malleable concept, we feel that such a return-to-fundamentals approach has many benefits.

Our goal is to draw up a vision of an empowered version of ERM that fully leverages these value-creating mechanisms and makes a real difference. But theory can only get you so far. ERM challenges the status quo in organizations and is sometimes met with raised eyebrows or even disinterest. Consequently, in some cases ERM is reduced to an uninspired activity far below potential: a box-ticking exercise that does just enough to meet outside expectations. The stakes are high, because empowered ERM will interact with several important decision-making processes in the firm.

The second theme of this book is that if we want to tap into ERM's full potential, we need to harness lessons learnt from practice as well. Our quest will lead us to explore the experiences of Equinor, a Norwegian energy company, where risk management has reached the status of core value in the sense of being *expected* by every employee. The firm's culture and governance structures have been profoundly influenced by ERM since its humble beginnings over two decades ago. The hard-won lessons learnt by Equinor over many years give us valuable insights into how ERM can deepen its impact.

This book is organized into twelve chapters that chart out something akin to a journey. In the first chapters, we create a foundation on which to build further, identifying theories and principles that can guide action (Chapters 1–3). From there we move on to consider the basic building blocks and tools of ERM (Chapters 4–7), onto what might be considered more advanced issues at the frontier of ERM (Chapters 8–10). Then follows a case study based on the lessons learnt from the implementation of ERM in Equinor (Chapter 11). The final chapter (Chapter 12) integrates the previous chapters and concludes the book. Below follows a brief description of the individual chapters.

Chapter 1 traces out the origins and ideas behind organized forms of risk management, and shows how ERM sprung out of an increasingly felt need to improve risk governance in firms. We also elaborate on the roles of theory and lessons to be learnt from practice in arriving at an empowered and more impactful version of ERM.

Chapter 2 discusses how risk can be defined and how that connects with the value-creation process. We establish increasing long-term value and living up to the standards of good corporate citizenship as the twin goals of companies, and by extension of ERM, arguing that these goals are not mutually exclusive.

Chapter 3 identifies the distinguishing features of ERM and compares that to traditional forms of risk management. In developing a theory of ERM, we focus on coordination and cost efficiency problems resulting from decentralized risk management, and on information and incentive problems that are also created by the existence of such risk management 'silos'.

Chapter 4 discusses risk culture: how it can be understood, the benefits it brings, and what stands in its way. We emphasize the role of short-termism in creating its opposite, a risk-prone culture, and highlight the importance of clarifying expectations and desired behaviours with respect to risk management to create a culture that contributes towards successful risk management.

Chapter 5 takes on the subject of risk governance, which refers to the formal processes and protocols in the risk management process. An important part of this is clarifying responsibilities with respect to risk management, which brings us to the crucial concept of risk ownership. The risk oversight by the board of directors as well as centralized and decentralized models of risk ownership are extensively discussed.

Chapter 6 explains important aspects of the most visible output of most ERM programmes today: the risk register. We look at the principles for creating consistent and useful inventories of risks that connect with the decision-making process and highlight several pitfalls that commonly arise in this process.

Chapter 7 deals with the risk response, that is, how managers choose to respond to a risk that has been identified and assessed. We place special importance on understanding the costs of the three broad types of response: mitigation, transfer, and retention. The goal is to control downside risk in a cost-efficient way, while keeping as much of the upside potential as possible intact.

Chapter 8 discusses risk appetite, a concept presently touted by many in the risk management community. We take the view that it is a useful point of entry for certain kinds of discussions about risk, but that it comes with several flaws that can turn it into a curse more than anything else. We also outline the concept of risk capacity, understood as a buffer of financial resources that allow the firm to absorb losses without serious consequences.

Chapter 9 introduces risk budgeting, which refers to an analysis of risk in the context of financial performance and strategic decision-making. We see risk budgeting as a way for ERM to increase its impact, allowing for a satisfactory assessment of the risk of the firm as a whole and how that is affected by corporate policies.

Chapter 10 contains a discussion of the strategic role of ERM, which many see as its 'next frontier'. We show that ERM potentially contributes to many stages of the strategy process. A more well-informed approach to integrating risk into decision-making is key to playing this role, as is maintaining a dynamic view of contingent risks and hidden opportunities.

Chapter 11 contains an empirical case study based on Equinor. We survey its origins and development over time. We also review many of its applications and give examples of how practice has changed as a result of ERM. Above all, though, we search for insights as to how risk management arrived in a position where it is considered one of the firm's core values, and how it came to diffuse the culture of the company.

Chapter 12 provides some concluding remarks and seeks to integrate the preceding chapters into a set of takeaways with respect to empowered ERM.

CHAPTER ONE

Introduction to Empowered Enterprise Risk Management

A CLEAR SIGN THAT YOU are a helicopter parent, according to online sources, is developing a bad back from constantly stooping down and following your toddler's every step. Helicopter parents are, as it were, those constantly trying to identify and remove threats to their child's safety. They hover above the playground, ready to interfere at a moment's notice, and generally put a variety of restrictions on the child's activities to remove any notion of danger. Such a highly regimented style of parenting is in sharp contrast with the much more relaxed approach that was common not too long ago. As recently as the 1980s, even in that epitome of the safety-first approach, in Sweden it was not uncommon to see small children standing up between the front seats of the car while the car was being driven. Their parents would not necessarily have been viewed as irresponsible by other adults or reflected much themselves on the possibility that they might have been taking unacceptable risks.

The helicopter parent is just one caricature describing a broader current in society, namely a desire towards identifying and controlling risks that might affect our well-being. Sociologists have even referred to our modern world as a 'risk society', meaning a society that is increasingly preoccupied with the future and any risks that it might bring (Beck, 1992). It turns out that modernity has ushered in a wide variety of man-made risks on top of the natural hazards that have always threatened societies. The complexity of the systems that support modern life, and the degree of their interconnectivity, have generated a whole range of new risks. At the same time, there has been a veritable explosion in the availability of information, making us ever more aware about potential threats. New norms emerging over time have gradually come to present an attitude of caution as a necessity.

The growing focus on risks has been accompanied by a belief that not only should they be managed but *can* be. As Peter Bernstein's epic story of risk shows, over the millennia we have gone through a series of intellectual revolutions, from being 'passive before the gods' – that is, largely resigned to fate – to claiming mastery over risk (Bernstein, 1996). The premise seems to be that science and our expanding knowledge can be used to assist us in more safely navigating the world. This premise has given rise to an entirely new profession: risk management. In its early applications, the position of risk manager typically referred to a highly specific area of expertise. However, ideas about risk management have reached further and further up the corporate hierarchy, infiltrating even top management teams and boards of directors. Power (2007) writes:

> In a relatively short period of time, in a number of different countries, hospitals, schools, universities, and many other public organizations, including the very highest levels of central government, have all been transformed to varying degrees by discourses about risk and its possible management.

Risk management, in this view, has gone from being a specialized subfield to being a source of principles for organizing and managing in general. To put it another way, there has been a shift from risk analysis, a technical discipline, to the *governance* of risk in organizations.

Interest in risk governance took a giant leap in the early 1990s with the publication of two reports that were to become highly influential: The Cadbury Code, published in the UK in 1992, and the COSO framework for internal control, also published in 1992.[1] These reports contain a set of recommendations for achieving sound governance in organizations, and to generally improve oversight over vital processes. The background for both reports was a string

---

[1]COSO (Committee of Sponsoring Organizations of the Treadway Commission) is an 'umbrella organization' consisting of the following five organizations: Institute of Internal Auditors; the Association of Accountants and Finance Professionals in Business; Financial Executives International; American Institute of CPAs; and American Accounting Association.

of corporate failures that were deemed to have been triggered not so much by exogenous risks or flawed analysis, but rather failures of governance. In other words, there was a systematic lack of checks and balances in organizations that left them too vulnerable to fraud and other misbehaviours. To improve this situation, boards of directors were encouraged to, among other things, put in place systems designed to increase control. This led to the codification of what is known as 'internal control', defined in COSO (1992) as follows:

> Internal control is a process effected by an entity's board of directors, management and other personnel designed to provide reasonable assurance of the achievement of objectives in the following categories:
>
> Operational Effectiveness and Efficiency
> Financial Reporting Reliability
> Applicable Laws and Regulations Compliance

Internal control can be viewed as an effort to address the control problems that afflict organizations without adding new and costly external regulations (Power, 2007). Instead, risk control was to be achieved from within, through 'self-discovery and reporting'. To this end, new functions like internal audit and compliance were set up in many firms, in no small measures boosted by the arrival of the Sarbanes–Oxley Act in 2002. Taking stock some thirty years later, the focus on internal control can certainly be said to have had a lasting impact on business practices. True, the application of the concept has been varied and frequently modified to reflect firms' specific needs and capabilities, but the core idea of maintaining an independent function to safeguard the integrity of important processes has stood the test of time.

The introduction of new functions related to internal control was a major leap in the broader trend towards organized forms of risk management. One of the five pillars of COSO's framework is that internal control should be 'risk based', which is to say, it should be preceded by an inventory and assessment of the risks that could pose a threat to the entity's objectives. However, the reach and impact of risk management ideas has continued unabated. Contributing to this development was the fact that internal control was found to be lacking in two main respects. One was that it was not perceived as holistic, or enterprise wide, enough. The risks that fall within its scope are only a subset of all the different kinds of risk that businesses face. There are market risks, reputation risk, business disruption risk, and so on, in an almost endless variety. The second factor that spurred on further development was the feeling that risk management ought to provide more active support to business decisions, thereby working closer with management and 'adding value'.

Functions dedicated to internal control are held back in such pursuits by their pledge to remain independent vis-à-vis management. Internal control, at its core, chiefly seeks to contain threats. A different set of ideas would be needed to realize the vision of an enterprise-wide form of risk management that supports business strategies. The principles behind holistic risk management were first developed in the mid-1990s by the people behind the Australian risk management standard (AS/NZ 4360) with later additions by their Canadian counterparts. But again, it was COSO that delivered the blueprint that was to shape much of the field's future development. In 2004 the Enterprise Risk Management (ERM): Integrated Framework was published. It defines ERM as follows:

> Enterprise risk management is a process, effected by an entity's board of directors, management and other personnel, applied in strategy setting and across the enterprise, designed to identify potential events that may affect the entity, and manage risk to be within its risk appetite, to provide reasonable assurance regarding the achievement of entity objectives.

In this definition the ambitious agenda of ERM is plain to see. It is no longer just about risk control, but it shall support decision-making in a 'strategic setting'. Risk management is now to be carried out across the enterprise and is not limited to compliance, financial reporting, and operating hazards. Another game changer was the introduction of the term 'risk appetite', which signalled that some level of risk can be tolerated. In fact, the COSO (2004) text makes explicit mention of the concept of 'capitalising on opportunities', a perspective that is absent in the world of internal control. In 2017, COSO published, jointly with consulting firm PWC, an updated version of its framework that emphasized even more strongly the connection between strategy and ERM. The other main risk management standard, ISO 31000, issued by the International Organization for Standardization, shows a similar trajectory towards a strategic agenda involving senior management.

For all these advances in the thinking about the role of risk management in firms, it is significant that its most cited blueprint grew out of the world of internal control. Lest nobody mistakes where it came from, COSO (2004) even states that ERM builds on, and completely encompasses, the internal control framework. This has meant that the ethos of internal control, with its emphasis on risk control rather than balancing risk and return in a pursuit of value, has come to have a disproportionate effect on the implementation of ERM. Power (2009) makes a key point: 'The ERM model is strongly, if not exclusively, influenced by accounting and auditing norms of control, with an emphasis on process description and evidence.' He goes on to comment on the proliferation of detailed processes for risk management based on rules and prescriptions: 'Accounting ideals of internal control are embedded in the design itself, resulting in a style of risk management practice with wide and seductively expansive reach – the risk management of everything.'

This leads to a question that is still not fully resolved. Is ERM supposed to be 'just another control function', or an in-house advisory that works closely with the executive team on matters of strategic importance? Many managers indeed seem to associate ERM more with controlling risk than anything else, and therefore seem content to just produce a risk map, check risk management off the list, and carry on as before. As a result, ERM could amount to what Power (2009) refers to as 'the risk management of nothing': a superficial effort that fails to drill deep into the interconnected nature of risks. Any feeling of safety afforded by it is therefore an illusion, or even worse, misleading, because it largely fails to articulate and comprehend critical risks.

In fact, puzzles and paradoxes abound in the COSO definition of ERM. Another example of an unresolved issue is that of the real meaning of risk appetite. The core questions we may ask are:

How much risk can we tolerate?
How exactly is risk supposed to be traded off against upside potential?

The latter balancing act is the dimension that risk appetite is supposed to bring much-needed attention to when compared a framework geared towards risk control. But as so often with these frameworks, they only establish certain basic guiding principles and leave much of the interpretation open to the organizations doing the implementation. Truth be told, however, there are probably few concepts in business that have generated similar levels of confusion as risk appetite. Risk appetite as a concept seems to be almost perfectly designed to do so by appealing to the subjective nature of risk rather than to an analytical, fact-based approach, and for being something of a contradiction in terms. Yet it pervades the discourse on risk management today. And yes, we do need a way to impose a limit on risk-taking and put that in the context of business opportunities. So, how is this dilemma to be resolved?

Another paradox in ERM concerns the role of objectives in determining risk management strategies. In the main frameworks, COSO and ISO 31000, the achievement of objectives is put on a high pedestal. In practice, many firms have taken this to mean protecting short-term targets, or the so-called key performance indicators (KPIs) that are widely used by firms to measure progress. While protecting targets sounds fair enough, this leaves ample room for behaviours that are inconsistent with the higher-level objective of creating value. In fact, it is not hard to illustrate situations where spending resources to increase the probability of target achievement is detrimental to long-term firm value. And to completely flip the perspective, there is growing evidence that the targets themselves may be a *source* of risk. The performance pressure induced by such targets has been known to cause reckless behaviour and gambling on a scale that can lead to firms getting into serious trouble. The Deepwater Horizon disaster, under the watch of BP, and the fall from grace of US bank Wells Fargo are only two examples of target-chasing as generators of risk.

And what happened to firm value as a higher-level objective anyway? Here is yet another paradox. Most managers find it self-evident that they are in business to generate profits, and ultimately dividends for their shareholders. Treatises on ERM often do speak about shareholder value, but on the whole the emphasis is not that strong. In fact, the ERM frameworks seem to be embedded, to a fair extent, in the *stakeholder* value paradigm. The first line in COSO's executive summary (2004) reads as follows: 'The underlying premise of enterprise risk management is that every entity exists to provide value for its *stakeholders*' (emphasis added). In stakeholder theory, firms exist to satisfy the interests of their many stakeholders, such as employees, customers, the state, and so on. Shareholders are just one of many stakeholders and have no special privilege when it comes to setting the firm's objectives. When business units, the very risk management 'silos' that ERM was meant to integrate, discuss their risk appetite, from a stakeholder perspective, with respect to the risk of failing to meet short-run targets, we have a pretty confused situation.

The paradoxes do not end here. We have also observed, among ERM practitioners, a curious reluctance to quantify and perform financial analysis. Another observation is that often the responsibility for a risk is simply delegated to the person who is already working in that part of the business. With the result that some sort of governance of risk has taken place, at least on paper, but nothing of substance seems to be elevated to a *centralized* form of management, as defined in the portfolio view of risk underpinning ERM. What is more, for all the talk about holistic, enterprise-wide risk management, ERM programmes seem generally incapable of addressing questions related to total risk. Any notion of what the risk of the firm is as a whole continues to elude firms that implement ERM, to the extent that this perspective is not even brought up at all.

Amidst all these paradoxes and puzzles of ERM, there is the nagging concern that, for a framework that loves to emphasize the need to use risk management as a tool in the pursuit of upside and business opportunities, there seems to be a lot of 'covering your back' going on. Is it possible that the result of all the governance taking place, and the processes needed to support it, is that firms are more anxious and slower to respond to new opportunities? Formal risk appetite statements written into policy documents, for example, do have a whiff of corporate bureaucracy attached to them. Just like helicopter parents may be accused of stifling their children's autonomy and independent judgement, could the apparatus around ERM contribute to the dulling of the entrepreneurial spirit in firms? Do people become so worried about making errors that they consistently prefer to stay within their comfort zones instead of venturing out into new and risky, but also potentially very lucrative, projects? This is certainly not the intended meaning of either the internal control or risk management frameworks. But it suggests that how such organized forms of risk management present themselves – their 'vibe' – is quite important. Is it going to be another round of control and compliance, or is it a partner in business, an enabler that that helps the firm compete, succeed, and create value? In this book, we support the latter version of ERM. While more difficult to achieve, the benefits are also far greater.

WHY A THEORETICAL PERSPECTIVE?

ERM has obviously moved on since the COSO (2004) document was published. ERM is sometimes described as an evolving phenomenon, which may take many years before it becomes codified and practised in a consistent way. In this view there is an ongoing search for best practices that eventually will settle into a body of concepts and practices that will constitute ERM. The idea is that best practices will evolve, in a Darwinian-like manner, if given enough time. Along these lines, Mikes and Kaplan (2015) argue that there is no one universal form of ERM that will be right for all firms. Rather, each firm chooses from the available design parameters to obtain an 'ERM-mix' that is suitable to its particular circumstances.

While there is certainly something to be said for letting robust practices evolve by proving their usefulness in actual practice, we also take a somewhat different view. We believe that ERM stands to benefit from a more rigorous description, at the theoretical level, of the problems it is supposed to solve in the first place. The definitions of ERM provided by the frameworks are just that – definitions. And definitions are not theory, except by accident.

They are more like opinions, descriptions of how one sees the world or would like things to be. Reflecting the endless malleability of ERM, there are indeed definitions aplenty on offer, not just in the frameworks but from large numbers of authors who have their own take on ERM. Theory, in contrast, draws attention to the root causes of the problems afflicting practice, and can therefore point to the appropriate solutions. It provides focus and structure to the design of ERM. We are not just 'doing risk management', but rather addressing certain well-defined problems with the goal of improving decision-making in pursuit of a defined higher-level objective. ERM, in this more theoretical approach, is derived from a set of first principles instead of just conjured up from definitions.

A more theoretical view of risk management in firms starts with some basic premises about what is being optimized – the ultimate goal. This is usually taken to mean firm value. In the classic theory of corporate finance by Modigliani and Miller (1958), however, capital structure (and risk management by implication) turns out to be irrelevant. The reason underlying this somewhat disturbing result is that the authors make several very strong assumptions – such as no taxes, a fixed investment opportunity set, and equally distributed information. Much of the theory since this seminal work has progressed by investigating what happens to optimal corporate policy if one or more of these assumptions *fail* to hold. In fact, almost none of the assumptions bear scrutiny in the real world. Obviously, it is fairly indisputable that taxes and bankruptcy costs exist in the real world. But we also know that decision makers suffer from behavioural biases, conflicts of interest, and lack of complete information.

The optimal corporate policy is, broadly speaking, the one that minimizes the impact of all these imperfections on firm value. The use of financial derivatives to manage risk ('hedging') and insurance are two of the policies that have been investigated from the perspective of minimizing the impact of these frictions. These strands of research amount to what could be referred to as 'classic' risk management theory, which has delivered many important insights that we will come back to numerous times in this book. Hedging to reduce expected costs of bankruptcy, for example, is a long-standing example of how the use of derivatives can increase firm value.

In these academic models, the firm itself is characterized as a *unified entity* interacting with providers of financing who know less about the company's prospects (information asymmetries) and suspect that managers have hidden agendas (conflicts of interest). Just like in classic economic theory in general, it is usually taken for granted that whoever sets policy in the firm has access to full information, and that it is the ones on the outside that struggle with lack of information. If there is a conflict of interest, it is between the firm's managers and the investors in the company, not between different layers of the firm.

Reality overwhelmingly suggests, however, that firms are not unified entities. Even if the executive team's interests have been aligned with those of shareholders (which we take to mean maximizing firm value), there remains the issue of how risk management can be applied for this purpose in an enterprise consisting of several business units with decentralized decision-making, for whom firm value is a distant and abstract concept. History is also replete with examples of executives and directors who were not able to understand the firm's exposures to risk and were taken by surprise when something bad happened. In surveys, executives regularly point to challenges in aggregating information about exposures, and in increasing the 'visibility' of certain risks.

In our analysis of ERM we shift the attention to how some of the aforementioned imperfections operate *within the firm*. ERM is much more about the risk management *process* than any specific risk management *strategy*. It belongs in the realm of corporate governance and management control, both needed to govern decision-making processes that are at least partly decentralized. The focus will be on behavioural biases, conflicts of interest, and information asymmetries as they play out on multiple levels in a firm with decentralized decision-making. ERM thus takes place at the interface between the board of directors, the executive team, and multiple business units and corporate functions. Does the board of directors really have access to full information about the main risks? Do business unit managers really use risk management to maximize value or do they pursue other agendas? Are business units too optimistic and willing to pursue ventures that imply too much risk? In contrast to the view that ERM is an evolving set of techniques, to be chosen by each firm from some kind of smorgasbord, these behavioural, agency, and information issues are themes that should guide the design of risk management in any firm.

Theory, then, is useful because it articulates with greater clarity the problems that ERM is meant to solve, pointing us to the root causes of inferior risk management execution. Our interest lies in using theoretical perspectives to understand the problems at hand, because we believe doing so simultaneously points to the most effective solution. In this book the reader will therefore find no complicated math or excessive jargon for its own sake. To us, theory is basically only a set of well-supported ideas about how the world works. We strongly believe in keeping things simple, and that the real point is to improve thought processes (and by extension decision-making). While our exposé covers some fairly advanced topics, our basic message is that most of the benefits can be reaped through a few relatively simple changes in mindsets and practices that are well within the reach of all organizations, whether small or large and regardless of industry.

 ## LESSONS FROM PRACTICE

However, as we pointed out in the Preface, theory is not enough. We also need to better understand how risk management principles can be embedded in organizations and achieve impact. ERM wants to make a difference in practice, yet often comes up against powerful forces that seek to limit its influence. ERM calls on people, at least to some degree, to change their way of thinking and how they do things, and anyone who has worked in an organization knows that this is no small task. Therefore, ERM initiatives often have an element of change management to them. ERM in our case company, Equinor, has even been described by company insiders as a 'culture project' as much as being about specific tools and techniques.

What we can learn from studying practice is, above all, what the keys to successful implementation are (and the traps to avoid). What are the things that need to be said and done to overcome the obstacles and resistance to change? What resonates with people at different levels in an organization and motivates them to take on ERM? What makes them strive together towards a common goal rather than be stuck in opposition? All in all, we want to find out about what really works and what helps unlock the potential of ERM. Theory cannot inform us a lot about these things. One has to get out in the midst of organizational life and the constant to and fro of different ideas, trends, power struggles, individual quirks, and so on. But for all the variety and richness of this setting, certain patterns are more likely to be associated with success than others. Thus, we hope and believe that many of the keys and success factors uncovered in our empirical material are generally applicable.

What is a good case company for an in-depth exploration of ERM in practice? We believe that the answer to that question is a company where ERM has demonstrably been impactful and where it has been practised for many years, interlocking ever more deeply with decision-making processes. Equinor meets these two criteria. It was one of the early adopters, launching an ERM programme in 1996. ERM has been continuously used and refined since then, from an initial focus on market risks to a fully enterprise-wide effort that actively engages the board of directors as well as smaller operating segments. Equinor has indeed reached the point where risk management is considered a core value, or 'a way of life', as it is sometimes called. It is not merely a technical exercise by specialists in the risk management function. Understanding and managing risk is something that is practised by – indeed expected from – each employee.

A case study on how Equinor got to this point holds the promise of offering insights into how ERM can be best approached in practice. We have tried to refine into a compact and accessible format all that Equinor has learnt the long and hard way. The ambition is to make the journey for someone just starting out quicker and more direct to the desired destination. What awaits at the end of that journey is empowered ERM, which occurs when the organization commits to risk management and elevates it to a core value, central to its way of doing things and how it defines itself. As a result of this commitment to proactive risk management, there will be better information and conversations around risk; clearer responsibilities; a unified language and methodology; and improved business decision-making that takes due account of risk.

CHAPTER 2

Risk Defined

W HEN ONE SETS OUT to systematically manage risk in a firm it helps to have a clear idea about what one means by 'risk', and what it is one hopes to achieve by its management. It also helps if this way of thinking about risk and risk management is widely shared by people across the organization, paving the way for a unified and enterprise-wide mindset. In this chapter we review the foundations of risk management in firms. Despite the highly subjective nature of risk, to make progress we need to establish some 'rock bottom' tenets according to which we can operate.

Most people would agree with us when we say that risk has to do with the possibility of something bad happening. Bad is usually taken to mean a failure, accident, loss, damage, or something similarly negative. But there is also a sense in which risk is a very personal and subjective thing. What you think is bad may not be bad to me. If I plan to go to the beach tomorrow, a bad outcome would be if it rains by the time I arrive there. But to a person who is anxious to have his garden watered, a downpour could be a blessing. Risk, as it has been said, lies in the eye of the beholder, and consequently needs to be defined in each specific context. There is no off-the-shelf version that can be applied everywhere and by everyone.

The subjectivity of risk, or that each of us has our own perception of risk, is not an issue as long as we are talking about individuals. In a free society, each of us may have our own beliefs and priorities, and manage risk accordingly. But in an organization, such as a firm, it becomes a problem if we cannot agree on what risk is, at least if we are looking to manage it with a specific purpose in mind. Effective risk management in an organization requires a shared view of what constitutes risk. Only then can we attempt to measure it and start integrating it into our work processes. Here we immediately run in to the subjectivity issue: not only does an organization consist of different individuals, it is also the case that how people view risk depends on their place in it. One part of the firm can view the world quite differently from the rest of it, and consequently they will not have the same ideas or preferences about risk. There are at least four layers in the company where risk preferences can systematically diverge: the corporate (headquarters), business unit, project, and individual levels. Depending on which perspective you take, risk can be understood in different ways. This tends to happen because the related goals and aspirations are not necessarily the same, despite the fact that they all belong within the same firm. Of all the parameters affecting what you think of as risk, the goal you have is often one of the most powerful. This means that whenever goals are different, as they often are throughout an organization, there is a potential conflict of interest with respect to risk management as well.

VALUE-CREATING RISK MANAGEMENT

The subjective nature of risk just described presents a problem for anyone who wishes to manage corporate risk. What we would like is a unified framework with clear definitions that can guide actions regardless of the decision situation at hand. To achieve that, we need to establish what kind of overarching purpose risk management really serves. In this book, we propose that the principal objective of risk management is to increase firm value in the long run. There are, as we shall see, some fairly convincing arguments to support this position. These days, there is additionally a lot of emphasis on corporate social responsibility, which would suggest that the scorecard is more multifaceted than just long-term value. The relationship between the pursuit of value and social responsibility is an important question that will be discussed at length both later in this chapter and in Chapter 4.

For now, we posit that risk management should primarily make sound business sense for the firm taken as a whole. This means that we can approach risk management the way we would any other business decision: by simply asking whether the advantages outweigh the disadvantages. With this in mind, we suggest analysing risk management in terms of its impact on the **expected value of cash flow** – or expected cash flow for short. This metric ensures compatibility with long-term firm value, because according to economic theory the value of a business is the sum of the surplus cash flows it expects to generate in the future, discounted back to present value. As will become clear in the pages that follow, expected cash flow offers a clear yardstick for how to evaluate proposals to mitigate risk.

Expected cash flow can be thought of as the probability-weighted forecast of cash flow. Consider a contract that promises a payment of $100 one year hence. But there is also a risk: a 10% probability that the counterpart fails to make good on his promise to pay the full amount. In this scenario we only get $50. The *forecasted* value of cash flow, which is the most likely outcome, and the point estimate that would appear in a spreadsheet, is still $100. The *expected value* of cash flow, however, is less: 90% × $100 + 10% × $50 = $95.

The fundamental observation that drives much of the analysis in this book is that risk costs money. The meaning of the statement 'risk costs money' is that, all else being equal, we are willing to pay less for an asset that is risky compared to one that is safe. This is already apparent from the difference between the forecasted and expected value of cash flow. The latter decreases when a risky outcome is introduced, whereas the point estimate is unaffected. But according to financial theory, transiting from an estimate of cash flow to a measure of value means that we also have to consider the discount rate. A discount rate is what converts a future dollar into a present value, reflecting the fact that a dollar to be received in the future is not equivalent in value to one here and now. In a one-period model,[1] we can write the relationship between cash flow and value as follows (where k is the discount rate):

$$VALUE_{t=0} = EXPECTED\,CASH\,FLOW_{t+1} / (1+k)$$

If we for now assume that the discount rate is zero, the value is equal to the expected cash flow of $95 in our simple example. Due to the presence of risk, an investor would then be prepared to pay only $95 rather than the forecasted value of $100. This is the essence of saying that 'risk costs' even when there is no payment related to it to be made here and now. The general principle is therefore clear: the presence of risky outcomes reduces the expected value of cash flow, and by extension value. To understand the impact of risk

---

[1]The formula for firm value is usually depicted as a summation of future cash flows extending into perpetuity, each discounted with a time-adjusted discount rate. We do not need this feature for our discussion here, as we are only interested in the role of the discount rate itself in the value-creation process.

on long-term value we would just repeat this analysis in a model consisting of multiple cash flows stretching many years into the future, rather than just one as in the simplified one-period model in our example above.

At this point it should be noted that risk finds its way into the formula for firm value also through the discount rate. According to financial theory, the discount rate compensates first for the passage of time, meaning a real interest rate plus the effect of inflation. These are factors that erode the value of a future cash flow that has a certain fixed nominal value. One dollar today does not buy the same amount of goods and services as it did in, say, the 1970s, simply because of inflation. But the discount rate also contains a risk premium, which is not driven by idiosyncratic events like the risk of a non-payment (the loss of $50 in our example). Instead, the size of the risk premium is, according to the most widely used theory, supposed to be in proportion to the investment risk associated with the asset – capital asset pricing model (CAPM). Investment risk is understood in a very specific sense here, namely as the degree to which the return from investing in the asset changes with the return on a broad portfolio of assets, the so-called market portfolio. This sensitivity to the market return is referred to as the asset's beta coefficient: the higher the beta, the higher the risk-adjusted discount rate. The beta can be said to capture the extent to which the return on the investment is cyclical and co-varies with the broad swings in the economy. According to the theory, this kind of risk warrants a premium because it cannot be diversified away, no matter how many different stocks are added to the investor's portfolio.

We will not go into the theory behind the determinants of the discount rate in any further detail here. Our message is instead that firms should not concern themselves with this risk premium or try to use it as a way to legitimize an effort to manage risk. It is an excessively abstract and hard-to-measure concept, and it is a futile exercise to try to manage it. No solid argument exists that this could be a source of value creation anyway. Lowering the beta coefficient automatically means that the expected return is reduced too, because the theory assumes a linear relation between the two.

This is not to say that there are no possible benefits from risk management in terms of reducing the cost of capital. Debtholders, for example, may lower the interest rate they charge if they consider a firm to have made a credible commitment to manage its risks. The lower interest rate means that shareholders capture more of the surplus cash flows (operating cash flows less interest payments). Debtholders view risk management in a favourable light for a simple reason: it makes the claim they hold safer. The credit rating agency Standard & Poor's has even gone on record as saying that it considers enterprise risk management (ERM) programmes as a positive in their evaluation of creditworthiness. There are also more subtle ways that risk management can influence the cost of capital. Raising capital is a confidence game. If the capital markets generally trust a management team and give it the benefit the of doubt, the company will enjoy a lower cost of capital and therefore a higher valuation. A well-thought-out effort at managing risk can help build the impression that the managers are capable and responsible stewards of the company. Finally, the CAPM may not hold. It is based on several assumptions that stretch the imagination. One assumption that may not hold is that investors generally have diversified portfolios. Empirical research has indeed shown that this often fails to be the case, and that firm-specific volatility in fact appears to be priced according to some empirical studies (in the sense that it is associated with higher realized returns.)

Such effects on cost of capital are elusive, however, and best thought of as an indirect benefit of risk management that comes in addition to other, more concrete, benefits. They may materialize down the road if and when the firm's risk management is judged to be credible and effective enough. But any practical effort to manage risk on the corporate level needs to be guided by other types of arguments, and as per the formula for value, there is only one place left to look: expected cash flow. A case can be made for managing corporate risk if it can be shown to reduce the **cost of risk**, which will consequently have a central role in this book. But what determines the cost of risk? It follows from the earlier example that the cost of risk has two dimensions: the probability and loss associated with a negative event. Probability is straightforward in the example (given as 10%). As regards the loss, it is measured in units of currency (as opposed to any notion of individual utility or regret). The loss should be measured as a deviation from the forecasted value if we want to express the cost of risk. In this case, the deviation is $100 - 50 = \$50$ if the negative event occurs. The cost of risk is the product of the probability and the loss thus defined: $10\% \times \$50 = \$5$. It can be noted, moreover, that the cost of risk is identical to the difference between the forecasted and expected value of cash flow. For brevity, we will refer here to the monetary loss relative to the forecasted value simply as 'impact'. We arrive at the following definition of risk:

$$\text{Cost of risk} = \text{Probability} \times \text{Impact}$$

This is a 'complete' measure of risk in that it takes into account both the gravity of the potential (negative) outcome *and* the likelihood that it happens. Focusing on either probability or impact, to the exclusion of the other, is bound to lead to mistakes in decision-making. We do not see firms spending a great deal of resources on preparing for the consequences of a major meteor hitting earth, despite the devastating consequences of such an event. The reason for this is obviously that, on our present knowledge, the probability of this occurring in our lifetime is extremely low. There is no risk so great that it must be eliminated at any cost, because it would imply the self-defeating strategy of directing all the firm's resources towards mitigating the risk. By contrast, there may be a fairly high probability that the price of oranges goes up in the next quarter. But if oranges are just a tiny part of our expenses from the weekly fruit basket, we may not be overly bothered by it (i.e. the impact is small). Just because something is almost sure to introduce randomness in our results does not mean it has to be considered as a risk worthy of attention.

RISK MANAGEMENT

Because risk costs we are often willing to consider doing something about it when that option is available. It follows from the definition that the cost of risk can be reduced by lowering the probability of a negative event or by reducing its consequence if it were to happen. If we have identified equipment failure as a significant risk, for example, we can reduce the cost of risk either by using a material that reduces the frequency of equipment failure (i.e. reduce probability), or by spending money on developing a continuity plan that allows us to operate even if there is an equipment failure (i.e. reduce impact.)

While risk management carries the benefit of reducing the cost of risk, in most cases it comes at an additional cost. There is thus a trade-off involved: it is usually hard to reduce risk meaningfully without spending anything to get there. A standard example of paying money to be rid of a specific risk is the insurance premium. Insurance is a contract stipulating that the insurance holder will be compensated by the insurance company if the bad event happens. Yet the insurance company will obviously not agree to take on this risk unless they get something in return. Hence, an upfront premium must be paid for the privilege of being protected against the negative outcome.

The storyline of much of this book is that risk management efforts should be proportionate to the cost of risk.[2] In many ways this is one of the first principles of risk management. We should not spend resources that obviously exceed any tangible benefits we can hope to achieve from it, nor should we omit to

---

[2]As we emphasize throughout the book, though, certain risks, such as those affecting safety, health, and the environment, are exempt from this rule of thumb for ethical reasons. For these categories of risks, firms are expected to do all that they reasonably can to ensure minimum impact.

take action when they are available at a reasonable expense. While people often worry about too little risk management being done, the opposite – overspending on it – is a clear possibility as well. People may be willing to shell out substantially on some vague notion that 'risk is bad' and 'something needs to be done'. Our instinctive risk aversion could lead us to jump on risk management strategies that are simply too expensive when evaluated in the cold light of day (as captured by our best estimate of probability and impact). Just because a risk is there, and would be undeniably bad if it occurred, does not mean that it is automatically justified to spend large amounts of resources on dealing with it.

The probability and impact numbers always relate to a specific **risk factor**. Ultimately, there is something *causing* corporate performance to fall below the forecasted level. We will use the term 'risk factor' to signify any random (uncertain) variable that affects corporate performance. In the above example, the risk factor is credit risk, that is, the failure of the counterpart to pay.[3] Any effort at managing risk has to identify these underlying sources of variability in performance. Firms are exposed to a multitude of such risk factors simply as a result of doing business, and an important part of the risk manager's task is to map out them and create transparency about their impact.

Frequently risk factors could equally well be called 'value drivers' because they are so tightly linked to the value-creation process in firms. For example, a strong reputation supports sales, making it a value driver. If people think highly of a firm, they may use that kind of trust to short-cut the cumbersome process of evaluating different decision alternatives against each other. For the very same reason, 'loss of reputation' will be a risk factor because it suggests that, once a reputation has been impaired, customers will choose *not* to buy that company's product. This in turn implies a loss in revenue and lower performance.

 ## DOWNSIDE RISK VERSUS UPSIDE POTENTIAL

A framework for risk management built around long-term value has many attractive features. First, one has a clear metric that indicates the appropriate course of action, and how to choose among competing alternatives. By

---

[3]In this book, we sometimes refer to 'a risk' when we really have a risk factor in mind in the sense of a random variable affecting performance. Also, when we say that 'a risk happens', or 'materializes', we mean that the actual outcome for the risk factor in question is one that would be considered bad or undesirable beforehand, i.e. a negative deviation from the expected. In the case of credit risk, this would be that the customer ends up not actually paying. This simpler terminology is preferred for ease of exposition.

consciously trading off the cost of risk management against the cost of risk, opportunities to increase expected cash flow and therefore value can be identified. Having an estimate of the cost of risk indicates how much money can be spent on risk management while still expecting to create value. That is, the principle of proportionality can be maintained more easily when we know the 'budget' we have for risk management. Second, the value framework naturally leads to a state of mind where upside potential is balanced against downside risk.[4] Upside potential enters the assessment identically because it affects the expected value of cash flow in the same way (probability times impact, except that deviations are now on the upside). If there had been a 10% chance also of receiving $300 in our example, there is an upside potential of 300 − 100 = $200. This would add a benefit of an upside potential of 10% × $200 = $20 to expected cash flow, which is now $115 (100 × 80% + 300 × 10% + 50 × 10%). Risk and upside are therefore naturally linked in this framework, which aligns with our intuition. After all, many risks that can affect performance negatively may also turn out for the better, which should inform decision-making as well.

The same natural balance between upside potential and downside risk is not true for a framework that centres on intermediate goals, or targets. As will be discussed extensively in this book, firms operate by breaking higher-level, long-term objectives down into more practical targets that managers strive to achieve in the short to medium term. The pursuit of such targets modifies how risk and upside potential are perceived, however, with many important practical consequences. One is that somebody going after a target will usually be content to *only just* achieve it, a behaviour that has been referred to as 'satisficing'. This term was introduced by the American researcher and Nobel laureate Herbert Simon in 1956 (Simon, 1956). It refers to a decision-making strategy that seeks to achieve an acceptable outcome, as opposed to the optimal outcome, which requires expending more time and effort. In a business context, the acceptable outcome is to meet the target, which produces a different focus compared to finding the value-maximizing decision.

Another reason in favour of a value-centric form of risk management is that it reduces the extent to which decisions are driven by the instincts and gut feelings of the decision-makers involved. The latter approach brings all sorts of biases and questionable incentives to bear on risk management

---

[4]Rather than the terminology 'downside risk' versus 'upside potential', some would prefer to label the latter 'risk upside' to indicate more clearly that it is the risk that creates the upside. At the end of the day, what is important is that, terminology aside, there is also some possibility of better-than-expected outcomes that affect the decision-making situation.

decisions. As will become clear throughout this book, individuals and groups of people alike have numerous biases that predispose them to make errors in a risk management setting. In the words of risk management expert Gary S. Lynch (2008):

> I have found that in most instances of risk failure the final decision was based on the individual's instinct – or worse – their incentives, rather than a disciplined risk philosophy and approach [. . .] It is far too easy in today's busy world . . . to quickly conclude, based on one's gut reaction, what risk should or should not be managed.

A more rigorous approach structured around the concept of the cost of risk helps keep these tendencies in check. It increases the chances that the firm takes calculated and well-judged risks and that the principle of proportionality is upheld, meaning the firm spends neither too much nor too little on risk management. This, in our view, should be the cornerstone of a risk management philosophy.

SUBJECTIVE PROBABILITIES

One of the first objections raised to a model of decision-making based on probability and impact is that probabilities cannot be quantified (or impact for that matter.) We agree on the point that probabilities in the real world are rarely known with any degree of certainty. We disagree, however, that this observation changes the basic approach. Risk is and remains a function of probability and impact, and whatever practical difficulties we may have in arriving at estimates does not change that. Rather than giving up, we should seek to create processes in which the best minds of the organization can come up with unbiased and fact-checked estimates, and accept those as the best we can do.

The concept of uncertainty is an important one when debating the issue of quantification. In the usage of the term proposed by the economist Frank Knight in 1921, 'uncertainty' applies when the odds cannot be calculated with certainty, and are therefore not susceptible to exact measurement. The bad news for corporate risk managers is that they are rarely ever dealing with known odds. The world is almost exclusively characterized by uncertainty, a point that was brought home forcefully by Nassim Taleb (2007) in his book *The Black Swan*. He offers an insightful example of how the world is ruled by what he at one point refers to as 'wild' uncertainty. The example is about a Las Vegas casino, which might seem to have a justifiable case for approaching risk as something quantifiable. After all, the probabilities of the various out-comes in all games are precisely known, and the casino has sophisticated tech-nology and surveillance to aid its managers. However, within the space of a few years a string of misfortunes befell the casino. One of its irreplaceable star performers was maimed by a tiger during a show. A disgruntled contractor that had been injured attempted to blow up the casino. An employee had neglected to send in required tax documents to the IFS, leading to fines for the company. The daughter of a casino manager was kidnapped, prompting the distressed father to steal money from the casino to pay her ransom. So much for thinking that the job was about controlling the odds!

Taleb goes on to argue that the world is at the mercy of so-called Black Swans, defined as events with a massive and transformative impact but that are highly improbable (unpredictable) before they occur. The processes that determine outcomes are non-linear and complex, with large discontinuities as inherent features. Shocks like geopolitical crises, disruptive technologies, and other extreme events are what really matter for understanding how econ-omies and markets develop. Think of the invention of the Internet, the 9/11 attacks, the fall of the Soviet Union, or, more recently, the Covid-19 pandemic.[5] According to Taleb: 'Our world is dominated by the extreme, the unknown, and the very improbable [. . .] while we spend our time in small talk, focusing on the known, and the repeated.'

Where does all of this leave any attempts at quantifying probability and impact? If Taleb is right, probabilities in the conventional sense appear doomed. Taleb himself repeatedly lashes out against what he refers to as 'platonic' attempts at describing the world and managing risk using calculus, calling them not only intellectual failures but outright dangerous. One of his favourite examples are the professors in financial economics involved in the spectacular downfall of the LTCM hedge fund in 2001 – a crash that nearly brought down the financial system. The hubris that these academics displayed as a result of their misguided faith in quantitative methods was, according to Taleb, a recipe for disaster. It is deluded to think that the world will repeat itself so neatly that it can be described by the probability distributions assumed by these models.

It is clear enough that the default mode of the world is uncertainty rather than known odds, and that there are massive discontinuities in the form of

---

[5]One might say that because pandemics are a known phenomenon, Covid-19 was not really a Black Swan. It is true that Black Swans are always measured relative to a priori knowledge and expectations, or a 'sucker's game' as Taleb calls it. But the ferocity of the virus, and the associated lockdowns and destruction in the economy, has shocked most of us and far exceeded anything we could have imagined.

Black Swans. It would be a mistake, however, to infer that probability estimates have no place in the corporate decision-making process. Even in an uncertain situation, the amount of resources we are willing to spend on risk management will depend on how likely we think certain outcomes are and how grave their consequences would be. The key to resolving this dilemma is to recognize that we are dealing with subjective rather than objective probabilities. Subjective probabilities can be thought of as our best guess as to what the odds really are. Obviously, being subjective, different people will come up with different estimates and have varying degrees of confidence in them.

Subjective probabilities are, despite all of this, every bit as valid for decision-making as objective ones. We simply need to strive to make them as free of biases and errors as possible, and to engage the most suitable people for the task (more on this later in Chapter 3). It remains true that risk is a function of likelihood and impact even under conditions of uncertainty. How likely we think an event or scenario is does matter for decision-making, even if we find it hard to put a precise number on it. We may disagree about the details, but it is often obvious that two outcomes have very different likelihoods and therefore should be attached different weights in our decision. Just thinking in terms of probabilities and impact leads the thinking in the relevant direction, and we might be able to obtain a reasonably accurate idea of the amount of resources we could justifiably spend on risk management.

Then there are obviously the 'unknown unknowns', those potential events that we fail to even imagine and thus cannot assess even with subjective probabilities. Those make for the truest of Black Swans: outcomes that we could not even grant the possibility of. The goal is of course to turn many of these possibilities into 'known risks' by increasing our knowledge and using the imagination. But ultimately, here we run into some limitations in terms of our ability to visualize future contingencies, and have to switch to generic strategies like keeping a loss-absorbing buffer of cash or increasing our flexibility (i.e. our capacity to change as circumstances change). Using such broad strategies, we make ourselves not only more robust to undefined calamities but perhaps even what Taleb (2012) has called 'antifragile', which means to gain or advance one's position when a disruptive event strikes. In any case, that we can presuppose the existence of unknown unknowns does not provide an excuse for not assessing the likelihood and consequences of risks that we have been able to identify, and for not trying to expand our line of sight to identify more of the ones that can materially affect us.

While speaking of probability and impact, another qualifier is in order. It should be said that a good number of the benefits of risk management can be had even without quantifying things to any particular degree. The most important ones come in the form of increased risk awareness, and the creation of roles and responsibilities. According to risk expert John Fraser (2014), the conversations triggered by proactively identifying and addressing risks constitute the real value of a risk management programme. Taken-for-granted assumptions are challenged and new insights generated, all of which leads to better prioritizations, better ways of doing things. So, the emphasis here on probability and impact is not meant to suggest that no significant benefits can be obtained without quantification. At least in the early phases of a risk management programme the focus should be on the more qualitative aspects of awareness and responsibilities. As firms gain traction, they can gradually shift the focus towards obtaining more precise estimates of the cost of risk (and risk management) to support decision-making. Lynch (2008) summarizes this point: 'Risk management begins with behaviours, awareness, and incentives. [But] the analytics are required. One must be able to price, allocate, hedge, finance, and measure risk.' All of the things listed in the last sentence are predicated on some attempt at quantification.

IS VALUE THE RIGHT METRIC?

The other main objection that might be raised to a value-centric model of risk management is whether it is appropriate that decisions are made in pursuit of firm value, which most people equate with shareholder value. This is an important question, because the leading ERM frameworks are, to a significant degree, embedded in the stakeholder value paradigm. According to stakeholder theory, the firm exists to satisfy the needs of all its different constituents, such as employees, creditors, suppliers, and society at large. As noted earlier, while references to shareholder value are often found in treatises on ERM, this emphasis is not very strong overall. This begs the question of whose interests a risk management programme is in fact supposed to serve.

We argue that shareholder value needs to remain an overarching goal when managing risk, but that it is subject to the constraint of being a good corporate citizen. By behaving fairly and responsibly towards its stakeholders, a firm reduces risk and creates long-term value. The core of our argument is that too narrow a focus on the near-term share price is counterproductive and drives up the risk that something disruptive and highly damaging will happen further down the road, which wipes out significant amounts of long-term value. To take just one example, between 2011 and 2015 US firm Valeant

Pharmaceuticals pursued a strategy of buying up companies, slashing R&D, and aggressively increasing the price of the medicines in its portfolio. This endeavour involved a host of practices that were either illegal or immoral, or both. Stock market investors, however, saw one of the things they cherish most: rapid revenue growth. So, in the short term, the stock went up, but long-term value was systematically undermined by neglecting product development and incurring the outrage of politicians and the public alike. Eventually the stock market caught up on the risks, and from 2015 Valeant's share price collapsed.

The example of Valeant serves to illustrate the important principle that the stock price and long-term firm value are not necessarily the same thing. The stock market appears ill equipped to price in certain kinds of risks, and is too easily dazzled by spectacular, but ultimately unsustainable, growth. The divergence between the two tends to be at its largest when the short-term growth is fuelled by taking significant risks, which the firm's managers are able to temporarily hide from view, as in the case of Valeant. Maximizing the share price in the short run by deploying various tricks and tactics is not what the shareholder value model is about. What shareholder value really means is summed up by Rappaport (2011): 'Managing for [. . .] value means focusing on cash flow, not earnings; it means managing for the long term and not the short term; and it means that managers must take risk into account.' What the shareholder value model suggests is basically that managers should invest in projects that generate cash flows at a rate that exceeds the rate of return expected by shareholders given the level of risk they are taking. When managers act according to this principle, the economy's resources are directed towards their most productive uses, and managers get a clear metric for judging which decision is the better choice.

Contrary to what many seem to believe, then, the shareholder value model is inherently long term in its outlook. No matter how far out in time they are expected to occur, forecasted cash flows are discounted back to the present using a risk-adjusted discount rate. The sum of these discounted present values, over the lifetime of the project, is then compared to the expenditure the project would involve. The net present value rule holds that, if the net is positive, managers should go ahead with the project. This clearly illustrates why the shareholder value model is, at its core, long term in nature.

As noted, most businesspeople find it self-evident that firms, to a certain degree, are in the business of making profits. In fact, they have a fiduciary duty vis-à-vis shareholders to run the firm in the their best interests, a key feature of corporate law around the world. Much as one may agree with Richard Branson's motto that 'a business is just a bunch of people trying to improve peoples' lives', the reality is that, at the end of the day, firms are judged by the rate at which they are able to generate profits (and the quality of those profits). If the investors in companies find that the custodians of their assets have anything but their interests in mind, financing for new ventures will soon dry up, a situation from which society at large stands to lose.

Despite all of this, the shareholder value model has been blamed and castigated for all sorts of ills afflicting the planet. People have come to associate it with things like grossly outsized compensation plans, excessive use of leverage, widespread job-cutting, and an obsession with meeting quarterly earnings targets. The case of Valeant Pharmaceuticals, for example, contained most of these elements. How the original and quite reasonable version of the shareholder value model could ever be blamed for corporate practices that are so controversial is a long story that we return to in Chapter 4. But to make a long story short: shareholder value is not and cannot be the culprit, because it is defined in terms that run completely counter to these practices. For culprits, we have to look elsewhere.

We subscribe to the emerging consensus that shareholder value and stakeholder value need not be in conflict – but you have to start at the right end. Creating value for customers and taking good care of employees are typical examples of actions that ultimately lead to shareholder value creation over the longer haul. According to this argument, shareholder value follows when one builds a fine company that operates on healthy principles. This view is sometimes summed up in slogans like 'Being good is good for business', or 'Doing good by doing well'. It might in fact be truer than ever that being good is good for business, because good corporate citizenship is in demand. Customers and investors are increasingly asking of companies to show evidence of ethical conduct and that they are doing as little damage as possible to the environment. One could take this analysis one step further, which we will do in Chapter 4, and say that ending up being perceived by the public as a wrongdoer is becoming one of the most significant risks of the twenty-first century.

RISKS VERSUS RISK-TAKING

The final distinction we would like to make in this chapter is between exposure to risk and risk-taking. By risk-taking we mean a conscious act of pursuing some kind of upside potential that simultaneously creates, or entails, new risk exposures. These are risks that must be accepted for the sake of being able to carry out the business plan. It takes place primarily in the context of implementing new strategies and acting on investment opportunities. While not always very clear-cut, there is a distinction between risk-taking and risk-bearing. Risk-taking involves executing an investment and thereby bringing certain risks into existence (as well as the upside potential of course.) When a strategy has been implemented, and the investments made, we *bear* the risks for the remainder of the lifetime of the venture.

  While risk arguably is related to a bad outcome, however defined, it is not the same thing as saying that risk-taking is bad. On the contrary, risk-taking is fundamental to individuals and firms alike. Without risk-taking there is no chance of success either. As individuals and as a society we would stagnate without it. For example, the risk of an incident can be minimized by staying in bed when the alarm rings in the morning. But that is just short-term risk avoidance, and can only lead to boredom, lost opportunities, and a lack of development. Inherent in risk-taking is one of the central themes of this book, that it carries with it the promise of reward. A more productive approach is therefore to look for the kind of risk-taking that maximizes value given one's interests and capabilities. Value is a broad, and somewhat hard-to-define concept, but it encompasses all the current and future net benefits from an activity. For an individual, that can be a combination of pleasure, pride, fulfilment, monetary rewards, and similar positive experiences. For a firm, as we have seen, value is usually understood in a financial sense: it is derived from an estimate of the surplus cash flows that its operations are expected to generate in the future.

  Risk-taking and risk-bearing are both important and will be part of our story: risk management embraces both. They represent two different decision-making situations: one dealing with the management of exposures to specific risk factors (risk-bearing), and the other dealing with expansion and the creation of new risks (risk-taking). In consequence, the trade-off between risk and reward plays out on two different levels. When risks are taken, the upside is the increase in firm value that the investment or strategy promise to bring. For specific risks, in contrast, such as a weakness in a supply chain, the upside is understood as a reduction in the cost of risk, as given by probability and impact.

  In this book, the goal is not risk avoidance, or risk minimization, but rather well-informed risk-taking of the right sort. An important concept in risk theory is 'comparative advantage in risk-taking', which essentially translates into taking the kinds of risks that the firm is uniquely well-suited to deal with, given the skills and resources that set it apart from others (Stulz, 1996). A classic example is an oil drilling company, which possesses a clear relative advantage in taking the risk of exploring for new oil fields. This is a good kind of risk-taking since it relates to how the firm is supposed to create value, the very reason it exists. Drilling for oil is what it does better that nearly everyone else, translating into opportunities for its stakeholders. But in the process of taking that kind of risk, it will expose itself to and bear various risks in the sense of potential 'bad outcomes': it may cause an environmental accident; its key employees may leave the firm; it may not reach break-even; and so on. By managing the impact of possible negative outcomes, the process of productive and value-creating risk-taking can continue undisturbed. We fully agree with Culp (2001), who wrote that risk management can be thought of as the process by which a firm ensures that it is exposed to the risks it *thinks* it is exposed to and *wants* to be exposed to in the pursuit of value.

KEY CHAPTER TAKEAWAYS

- On an intuitive level, risk refers to the possibility of harm, damage, loss, or other negative consequences.
- Risk is a highly subjective notion, and its definition often follows the goal of the individual or organizational unit.
- Successfully managing risk in an organization is facilitated by a common definition of risk that can be consistently applied.
- A formal definition of risk is probability x impact (here referred to as the 'cost of risk'), where impact is understood as negative deviations from the forecasted outcome.
- Defining risk in terms of only one of these dimensions, while ignoring the other, often leads to mistakes in decision-making.
- Risk management can contribute to firm value by raising the expected level of cash flow, the numerator in the formula for firm value.
- Risk management raises the expected level of cash flow as long as its cost is proportionate to (lower than) the cost of risk.
- 'Uncertainty' is the term used to signify that the odds of an outcome cannot be calculated with certainty or exactness.
- The world is characterized by uncertainty and hardly ever by situations involving known odds like the roll of a die.
- According to the Black Swan argument, the world we live in is driven by high-impact events that were highly unlikely before they happened, such as the 9/11 attacks or the rise of the Internet.
- Due to the prevalence of genuine uncertainty, probability and impact must be based on subjective estimates.

(Continued)

- Subjective probabilities and impact estimates are still valid inputs for decision-making provided that they are unbiased, fact-checked, and calculated based on the relevant expertise and experience.
- Not quantifying probability and impact means that the cost of risk is not fully understood, which increases the chances of poor decision-making.
- The view taken in this book is that the overarching goal of corporate management, including risk management, is to contribute to firm value while remaining a good corporate citizen.
- As customers and investors demand socially responsible and environmentally friendly behaviour, there is increasingly less conflict between the idea of maximizing shareholder value and that of pursuing a more balanced scorecard ('stakeholder value').
- In keeping with this view, failing to act as a good corporate citizen, thereby damaging the firm's reputation, is emerging as one of the key corporate risks in the twenty-first century.
- While the term 'risk' generally refers to something 'bad', risk-taking itself is necessary and desirable to create value and avoid stagnation.
- A firm should strive to maximize exposures to those risks it has a comparative advantage in bearing by way of a combination of unique skills and resources ('good risks') but limit its exposure to other risks.
- The idea behind risk management is to maximize upside potential by taking the right kind of risks, while managing downside risk sufficiently to allow this process to continue without any harmful disruptions.

CHAPTER THREE

Risk Theory

I N THE PREVIOUS CHAPTER we established some principles of risk and risk management. As such, they are valid for any type of effort at managing risk that aims at value maximization. Now we turn our attention to enterprise risk management (ERM) itself. Our aim is to explore and understand the defining features that set it apart from other ways of doing risk management, and to develop a theory of ERM. Our message in this chapter is that ERM can be seen as a solution to certain general risk management problems that result from a model of decentralized decision-making (the so-called 'silos').

We will use the definition provided by COSO (2004), given in Chapter 2, as a point of reference, because it contains several concepts we will return to throughout this book. But we believe the core of ERM is better captured by the following, more parsimonious, definition, inspired by Gates (2006):

> Enterprise risk management is a board-supervised process for integrated risk management across the enterprise.

Here we are able to pin down more clearly the three features of ERM that differentiate it from past attempts at managing risk. First, it is *integrated*, referring to a high degree of coordination of risk management activities at the corporate level. Second, it is supervised by the *board of directors*, suggesting an involvement of senior decision-makers that was previously missing. Third, it is *enterprise-wide* in scope, which means that the effort to manage risk comprises all business units and corporate functions.

So, whatever risk management came before ERM was not integrated, board supervised, nor enterprise-wide in scope. That type of risk management is often referred to as 'silo-based' risk management. Risk management, in that approach, is carried out by different business units without much involvement from headquarters, or delegated to specialized corporate functions. Unfortunately, as we will argue in this chapter, organizing risk management in this way leads to decisions that are not value maximizing for the firm. From a theoretical point of view, ERM can be understood as a set of mechanisms aimed at reducing the negative impact of silos on risk management in firms.

SILOS AND THEIR CONSEQUENCES

According to dictionaries, the term 'silo' refers to something like a tall tower or pit on a farm used to store grain. Its original Greek meaning was simply 'corn pit'. In business, it has come to represent something that operates in isolation from other parts of the organization. For our purposes, a silo will be used to signify business units and corporate functions that operate with some measure of autonomy vis-à-vis the executive team. Silos can refer to business areas, divisions, or subsidiaries, depending on the firm's organizational structure, or even specific projects and teams within any of these larger units. In addition, there is a host of corporate functions that exist to carry out specific tasks related to the administration of the firm, such as accounting, finance, and IT.

Silos have acquired a somewhat negative connotation in business. But contrary to a widely held belief, silos are not inherently bad. In fact, the fundamental reason most silos exist is to gain from the benefits of specialization. Concentrating the competence and resources necessary for a task into a specific unit usually makes good sense. When a person or organizational unit is allowed to focus on a limited number of tasks, efficiency gains tend to follow. Silos are also good for us in that they impose a sense of order and structure in a complex world. If we cannot put things into a reasonably small number of mental boxes, life gets too complicated. In the words of Gillian Tett (2015): 'Silos help us to tidy up the world, classify and arrange our lives, economies, and institutions. They encourage accountability.'

Silos are certainly ubiquitous in the business world. One enduring idea in business is that efficiency and performance can be enhanced by arranging the firm into separate business units. Being to some degree autonomous, the thinking goes, managers feel more empowered and motivated than they would as cogs in a giant corporate wheel. As a way to monitor their performance, and guide the allocation of resources, the units are assigned their own profit and loss accounts (P&Ls). The P&Ls, besides increasing the accountability of these units, make it possible to devise schemes that incentivize them to strive for performance improvements. This management model, sometimes referred to as management by objectives (MBO), was popularized by management thinker Peter Drucker in 1954. It holds that one should lead a decentralized organization by establishing clearly defined targets and expectations, which are then followed up on and connected to compensation schemes. MBO enables executives to exercise control over the business units despite delegating many important aspects of the decision-making.

Unfortunately, silos have an inherent tendency to isolate themselves over time, leading to a fragmentation that may cause the performance of the organization to deteriorate. Silos can become entrenched and start promoting their own interests. Tett (2015) recounts several fascinating examples of silo effects that have afflicted well-known companies. Famously, in 1999 Sony presented two digital Walkman devices based on mutually incompatible technology. They had been developed independently by two highly competitive departments that were disinclined to cooperate and therefore lacked insight into the other's product development.

It turns out that creating business units with separate P&Ls is a fairly sure way of generating distinct 'tribes', or subcultures, within the firm. The units play to our natural tendency to form and operate in relatively small groups that we can relate to and that make sense to us. The instincts that drive fragmentation are powerful, and companies that wish to keep them at bay can expect an ongoing struggle. Tett mentions Apple as a company that has chosen to keep a single corporate P&L. This has held back the tribalism and competitive silos that comes from having various separate P&Ls, and keeps employees focused at all times on what is best for the company. Facebook is cited as another example of a firm that promotes various silo-battling practices, with the ultimate purpose being to keep ideas and technologies flowing across the company rather than getting stuck on organizational lines. These practices include rotating employees across different teams on a regular basis and holding sessions that involve meeting people from other teams to share ideas and update each other on the progress made in various projects.

 ## THE SILO EFFECT ON RISK MANAGEMENT

The problems that firms like Apple and Facebook are trying to deal with primarily have to do with how a silo structure prevents the sharing of ideas and information in the company. Such frictions in turn keep the company's ability to innovate and compete below its real potential. The silos, however, also create negative effects in terms of their influence on risk management decisions, which is our focus in this chapter. Just as Apple and Facebook engage in silo-battling practices aimed at maximizing their ability to innovate, ERM is a search for practices that hold the silos at bay in the context of developing risk management strategies that maximize firm value.

How can silos lead to risk management decisions that are not optimal for the firm? The most straightforward argument is that there will be a **duplication of costly risk management activities** in the firm. Each of the silos has to maintain its own administration, systems, and competence related to risk management. Obviously, this adds a layer of costs. The other commonly heard argument is that **risk management will be uncoordinated**. When the silos are left to choose policies for themselves a reasonable net exposure from the point of view of the firm may not result. What makes sense for each business unit does not necessarily add up to the right overall net exposure for the firm.

The classic example of duplication and lack of coordination is foreign exchange risk management. Imagine a situation in which one business unit has sales in a foreign currency and wishes to hedge the resulting transaction risk using some financial derivative with an offsetting exposure. At the same time, another unit is purchasing some of its raw materials in that currency. It too wants to use a derivative that hedges its transaction risk. But because one exposure is on sales, and the other on purchases, the preferred action from a corporate perspective is not to hedge at all, or hedge only the net number. With silo-based risk management we instead get two actions aimed at managing risk that add to costs without any compensating benefit. In fact, silo risk management may only make the situation worse. If one unit decides to hedge, and the other not, risk actually *increases* because the financial hedge effectively destroys the so-called 'natural hedge' that the firm has through the offsetting exposures (when the exposures on sales and purchases partly or fully cancel each other out). This situation is illustrated in Figure 3.1.

Another coordination failure occurs when there is a case for determining FX policy jointly with the policies concerning other risk factors the firm is exposed to. This is because optimal risk management strategies need to be informed by the degree to which risk factors correlate. A correlation means that two risks tend to move together in predictable ways. Energy prices, for example, are known to strongly co-vary with certain exchange rates, creating potentially large risk-reducing (or risk-enhancing) effects for firms exposed to both. In a silo approach, correlations like these are ignored, and different risks are managed on a standalone basis. Another layer of silos therefore arises

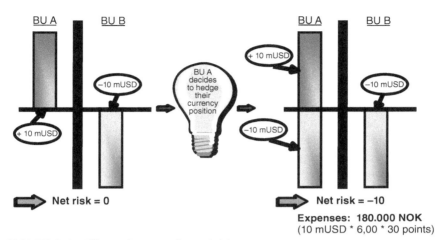

FIGURE 3.1   Effect of uncoordinated risk management

when risk factors are managed by different teams within the same organizational unit. It is quite typical for, say, insurance risks to be dealt with by a separate group of people who do not work together with those focusing on other types of risk exposures.

Maximum fragmentation of risk management is illustrated in Table 3.1. A firm with six silos, each with an exposure to the same six risk factors, can theoretically get as many as 6 × 6 = 36 risk management efforts working independently of each other. In the marked box, business unit 4 manages its exposure to risk factor 2 without taking into consideration a) other risk exposures in this unit or b) other units' exposure to risk factor 2. There is a

TABLE 3.1   Fragmentation of risk management

	Risk Factor 1	Risk Factor 2	Risk Factor 3	Risk Factor 4	Risk Factor 5	Risk Factor 6
Business unit 1						
Business unit 2						
Business unit 3						
Business unit 4		X				
Business unit 5						
Business unit 6						

complete lack of coordination, leading to the underutilization of correlations and natural hedges.

The essence of integrated risk management is that exposures in the various business units are first netted out, thus utilizing any natural hedges, and that the correlations between the risk factors are then taken into account when deciding risk management policy. These tenets follow from portfolio theory, the famous analysis of the relationship between risk and return in a portfolio of financial assets (Markowitz, 1952). The analogy from investment portfolios transfers over quite well in that a firm can be viewed as a portfolio of cash flow generating assets that are exposed to correlated risk factors. It also follows from portfolio theory that it is the *corporate* risk-return profile that is in focus when deciding policies. Targeting the risk-return characteristics of the different *parts* of the portfolio leads to suboptimization, because natural hedges and correlations are ignored. Integrated risk management is obtained when the firm focuses on corporate performance by managing net exposures and utilizing correlations where they exist. These components of integrated risk management are summed up in Figure 3.2. If any of these three components is missing, risk management is not fully integrated.

A THEORY OF ERM

The silo effect on risk management does not end with the failure to utilize natural hedges and correlations. The earlier emphasis on corporate performance points to two more dimensions that need to be considered. The first has to do with the way silos **hamper the flow of risk information in the firm**. Think back to

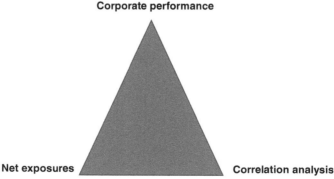

FIGURE 3.2 Integrated risk management

the Sony example. The units were not interested in sharing information with either rival departments or the executive team, leading to inferior strategy execution. Similarly, silos may withhold information about important risk exposures, or simply lack the ability to deliver it. Consequently, headquarters are unable to aggregate high-quality data about risk centrally in the organization and in a timely way, which leads to less-than-optimal risk management execution. We will call this the information problem of corporate risk management.

The second dimension refers to how the existence of silos leads to **risk management decisions that are made to maximize locally set goals and ambitions** other than for the greater good of the firm. Again, consider Sony. The units' primary motivation seems to have been bolstering their own prestige and success, rather than working together to maximize the long-term value of company. For Sony as a whole, these priorities led to a suboptimal outcome. On the same logic, the best outcome for the firm may not be achieved when risk management decisions are made to address risks that are mostly of relevance in a silo context. That is, the risk preferences of business units, or even corporate functions, may not be aligned with those of the firm as a whole. We will refer to this as the agency problem of corporate risk management.

In the theory of Jankensgård (2019), ERM is seen as a solution to the information and agency problems of risk management. These problems arise uniquely in a business model with silos and delegated decision-making, so here we arrive at the core of what ERM represents. It is a set of mechanisms created to reduce the impact that silos (decentralized decision-making) have on the firm's optimal risk management strategy.

The information and agency problems of risk management are quite general and likely to be present in any organization where there is a silo structure in place. These problems increase in importance the more autonomous the business units are vis-à-vis headquarters, and the more of them there are. In small and unified firms with a single P&L these particular kinds of risk management problems are likely to be less of a concern. Firstly, there is a much smaller information gap with respect to important risk exposures when the executive team is more hands-on and involved in all aspects of running the firm. Secondly, there is less chance of a conflict of interest if there is only one P&L that everyone directly depends on. But even in this kind of firm the problems discussed here are still relevant, because the board of directors may remain at an information disadvantage and therefore be unable to carry out risk oversight properly. Just as silos might manage risk based on preferences that are not wholly aligned with the best interests of shareholders in the long run, so can the individuals in the executive team (more on this in Chapter 4).

In the rest of this chapter we discuss the agency and information problems in greater detail. It is important to understand their sources to come up with correct solutions. When discussing the agency problem, we quite often find that the source is not a conflict of interest per se but rather behavioural biases that lead away from the optimal outcome. One could therefore speak of a 'behavioural bias problem of risk management', but we have nonetheless chosen to group these issues under the broader agency problem to facilitate the exposition.

THE INFORMATION PROBLEM OF RISK MANAGEMENT

The information problem of corporate risk management refers to the problem of collecting information about risk exposures in a timely, intelligible, and relevant format, to support centralized decision-making as it relates to risk management. Simply put, to be able to make the value-maximizing trade-off between risk and return, the executive team and board of directors need to operate on a platform of high-quality information about risk.

The information problem is often overlooked by academic theories and textbooks, which take full knowledge of exposures for granted. However, there is much evidence to suggest that firms struggle to understand and quantify their own exposures. That is, the executive team and directors often find it difficult to know, at any given point in time, what the firm's exposures to risk are. Again, we can take foreign exchange rate risk as an example. In surveys, executives regularly cite 'lack of visibility' of FX exposures as a major challenge standing in the way of effective risk management. Interpretation: they wish they knew what their exposures really were!

Aggregating risk information at the top level is widely acknowledged as one of the main risk-related challenges facing organizations today. The consequences of a lack of relevant information have often proven to be severe. It is considered to have been a contributing factor behind some of the disasters that befell financial institutions during the financial crisis that erupted in 2007. In the words of the Basel Committee of Banking Supervision (2013):

> Many banks lacked the ability to aggregate risk exposures and identify concentrations quickly and accurately [. . .] across business lines and between legal entities. Some banks were unable to manage their risks properly because of weak risk data aggregation capabilities [. . .]

This sentiment is echoed in reports and surveys by numerous professional organizations. For example, the European Central Bank (2018) concludes that firms continue to struggle with establishing satisfactory systems and procedures for risk data aggregation:

> One key lesson from the financial crisis was the need for more information on risk in order to make sound business decisions. IT, data architecture and related business processes were not sufficient to support the broad management of [. . .] risks.

The reports investigating the sources of the financial crisis reveal that firms had an especially hard time dealing with the accelerating rate of change that so often plays out during turbulent times. Even systems that were thought to be first-rate struggled to generate an adequate bigger-picture view of risk. What this tells us is that lacking capabilities in risk aggregation is a key feature of the information problem of risk management. If data systems and analytical tools are not up to the job, risk-related information often fails to flow upward in a timely manner. On top of weak capabilities to aggregate information, scores of academic studies have documented that managers, all else being equal, prefer to disclose less rather than more. This propensity helps explain the information asymmetries that complicate the relationship between a firm and participants in the capital markets. The point we emphasize in this book is that information asymmetries exist also *within* firms. The operating units in a decentralized business model have access to information that is not available to the executive team unless somebody makes a deliberate effort. The executive team, in turn, has an information advantage relative to the board of directors, and can in many cases control what information ultimately reaches the directors.

Why do people choose to hold on to information instead of letting it flow freely within the organization they work for? On one level, information is power. It is gratifying to be privy to an exclusive and important piece of information that few others get to see. Another and more fundamental reason behind data hoarding is that by disclosing less, a silo maintains more freedom to act according to its own preferences. A lack of disclosure makes it harder for outsiders to monitor what is going on in a specific business unit. By sharing less information, a silo can thus preserve more of its autonomy. The executive team has similar reasons for strategically controlling what information ultimately reaches the board of directors: preserving their ability to act with fewer constraints.

Sometimes the flow of information fails to happen because the business units fear the consequences of passing it on. Information that highlights risk in particular could make the unit 'look bad', or prompt requests from headquarters to undertake some proactive action they would prefer to avoid. Of course, in other cases information may not flow simply because headquarters did not ask for it or make it clear that it is considered important.

We can conclude that when silos are present there is likely to exist a structural lack of information about risk exposures centrally in the firm. One of the roles of ERM is therefore to make sure that the right information finds its way to the upper echelons of the firm. When this works well, managers and directors do not have to make decisions regarding the firm's risk-return profile based on a flawed or partial set of data. ERM seeks to remove the impediments to effective risk management due to data hoarding and lack of data aggregation capabilities within an organization.

THE AGENCY PROBLEM OF RISK MANAGEMENT

In the academic literature, the agency problem refers to a conflict of interest between the principal (shareholders) and the agents (managers). The agent is contracted by the principal to carry out a task, which in this case is running the firm. Managers control corporate policies but may primarily have their own interests in mind rather than shareholders'. As a result, they may enjoy excessive perks like corporate jets or hunting cabins; or build business empires for personal satisfaction. One corporate policy where interests can diverge is, not unsurprisingly, risk management. Managers are usually depicted as more risk-averse than well-diversified investors, because they have a much larger portion of their wealth tied to the survival and success of the firm. So, they keep risk lower than would be desired from the shareholders' point of view – for example, by over-diversifying or over-relying on safe but expensive equity.

In these models, the agency problem can be resolved by monitoring, by which is meant a fairly hands-on supervision of the firm's affairs, such as when a large shareholder, with enough at stake to intervene, takes a place on the firm's board of directors. The problem can also be addressed by aligning managers' interests with those of shareholders through compensation schemes – for example, by rewarding them with stock options rather than a cash salary. A manager holding stock options is thought to take a more positive view on risk-taking because of the potential windfall they stand to get from large increases in the stock price.

What these academic models tend to overlook is that many firms have decentralized business models (which implies silos). Even if the executive team and the directors are reasonably attuned to the desirability of maximizing firm value, the silos may first and foremost pursue goals that are more local in nature. That is, while all employees presumably share the desire for the company to do well, value is likely to be a less meaningful metric for decentralized units because it is an abstract concept far removed from their everyday course of business. It can be hard for a specific business unit to see how their actions drive the value of the company in a meaningful way. Instead, for motivation they are provided with a set of very tangible key performance indicators (KPIs) that determine how the unit's performance will be judged. KPIs are one of the core features of modern-day firms. They are essentially a list of all the areas of improvements and specific targets that the unit in question is expected to pursue in the next budget period. KPI achievement is usually a decisive factor when it comes to calculating performance-based bonuses.

With a system of KPIs in place, the question of diverging interests comes into sharper focus. For anyone handed a KPI, risk takes on a new meaning: the risk that the target level is not met, or what has been referred to as 'goal achievement risk' (recall our discussion in Chapter 2 that risk follows goals.) And with decentralized decision-making the business units can control the use of corporate resources in a way that affects the chance of achieving the target. Now why might this be a problem? Aven and Aven (2015) argue that there is sometimes a tension between locally framed goal achievement and the overarching objective of increasing the value of the firm. At the root of the problem is that KPIs are imperfect proxies for value creation. If the targets are achieved, we can hope and surmise that value has been created in the process. But there is no guarantee. After all, many KPIs are aspirational in nature, and often quite arbitrary. This is especially true for those that refer to financial performance, like revenue or operating profits. If the target is a 5% increase in operating profit, the step from 4% to 5% is very meaningful for the unit, because it implies goal achievement, but is not likely to be more valuable than the step from 5% to 6%.

The basic problem is that managing goal achievement risk can violate the principle of proportionality in the firm's response to the risk when looked at from the corporate perspective. To see how it can be counter-productive, let us say that a unit has defined as one of their objectives to complete a development project by a certain date and within a certain budget. Upon realizing that the project is likely to extend beyond the target date – that is, there is a high risk that the goal is not met – the unit managers may decide to accelerate the pace by engaging expensive service providers. The unit may be able to do so and still remain within budget, but the value-maximizing alternative for the firm could well be to accept a few weeks' delay rather than shelling out large sums on these providers. Managing the risk that targets are not met can be too costly for the firm's own good.

We can conclude at this point that, even if the conflict of interest between investors and the leadership of the firm has been addressed, there remains an agency problem *within* firms with a decentralized structure. There is a potential tension between pursuing goal achievement, on the one hand, and what would objectively be in the best interest of the firm, on the other. Aven and Aven (2015) state that:

> Current thinking on performance and risk management does not capture the above conflicts . . . in current practice, the KPIs often become goals themselves and the risk management is about increasing the probability for achieving the targeted KPI. The link to the principal objectives [of value creation] is often weak or missing

The agency problem of risk management implies situations where, seen from the corporate point of view, risk management efforts (and costs) are not proportional to the cost of risk. The problem of the **over-management of risk** refers to situations in which agents undertake risk management that is in fact undesirable from the viewpoint of the firm – that is, the silo spends too many resources on mitigating the risk. The problem of **undermanagement of risk** refers to a situation where the silos fail to undertake risk management when this would in fact be desirable for the firm as a whole. In both cases, the expected value of cash flow, and therefore long-run firm value, is lower than it needs to be. We will now take a closer look at these two phenomena.

OVER-MANAGEMENT OF RISK

Over-management of risk happens when managers prefer to spend money on risk management even when it is not justified on purely economic grounds. Following our discussion in this chapter so far, one way that over-management could happen is if a business unit has already reached its performance target for the year, and therefore wants to avoid any risk of falling back below the target level. The unit might then feel tempted to utilize risk management to reduce the probability of slipping back below the target. The resources spent on risk management primarily serve to secure that the objective is reached, but they may not be proportionate to any benefit the firm gets from a reduction in the cost of risk.

Generally, over-management tends to happen for risks that are salient and grab our attention. That is, they are comparatively easy to observe and appear imminent and important. When risks become salient, for whatever reason, our natural dislike of risk makes us liable to over-manage them. Most market risk exposures (commodities, exchange rates, and interest rates) fall into this category. They are often highly visible and connected to the firm's financial performance in a direct way. Once a currency exposure gets established, say by initiating exports, it is evident that the firm's margins will be exposed, making it a salient risk factor. Because the exposure threatens the unit's operating margins, some managers might prefer to hedge even when it may be a perfectly acceptable exposure for the firm as a whole. The desire to 'protect' margins against market risk is often observed in the business world and can arise as soon as a unit or project is measured on the basis of its financial performance.

Another example of how risks can become salient and start commanding our attention is a recent failure or accident. According to Lynch (2008), people typically overreact to crises. Once a negative event has occurred, it receives undue focus and attention. Even if the probability of it happening again is objectively small, it may not appear that way to managers caught up in the frenzy. When people are in reactive mode the result is often that too many resources are spent on managing the risk of a recurrence.

Risks can also be over-managed because people worry about their own reputation in relation to a reference group. Deviating from the crowd amounts to sticking one's neck out, and one could be called out on this bet if things go wrong. It is therefore often a safer approach for an individual to be wrong when everyone else is too, so they stick to similar strategies. This behaviour has been observed among fund managers but is also relevant in the context of managers' developing business strategies. Obviously, mimicking the strategies of the reference group will cap any upside potential too, and lead to any unique insights or skills not being capitalized on. Follow-the-herd is thus low risk from the agent's perspective, but may not be so interesting for the principal.

UNDERMANAGEMENT OF RISK

Despite our natural aversion to risk, we may also find ourselves managing too little risk compared to what would be optimal for the firm. Again, short-term incentives in the form of targets potentially play a role in distorting risk management decisions. Managers may be incentivized against taking action to manage risk if the cost associated with proactive risk management *reduces* the probability of target achievement. This is more likely to happen when the target has not yet been achieved, and the expenditure related to risk management brings the unit even further away from it. Just like being ahead of a target can lead to over-management of risk, being behind one can lead to undermanagement of risk.

This point is discussed at length by Lynch (2008) who argues that firms' incentive systems often do not support the additional costs (e.g. risk professionals and technology) required to address risk proactively. Business units indeed have a very strong focus on their operating margins, and proactive risk management creates expenses that immediately chip away at those margins. Consequently, many managers adopt the attitude that risk management is complicated and impacts the bottom line, and they are prepared to take the risk that disaster will not take place on their watch. Lynch (2008) quotes one manager as saying: 'All I really want is to make sure that the vendor that I hired to create this continuity plan charges me rock bottom for the project . . . whether it's a good plan or not . . . nothing bad is going to happen here anyway.'

In rare cases, targets can have another kind of unintended consequence that is equally, if not more, dangerous. It turns out that target-setting, if done too ambitiously, can in fact *generate* risk and set the firm on the path towards problems. How could this happen? The answer lies in psychology. The research of psychologists Kahneman and Tversky (1979) indicates that the psychology of risk-taking changes in important ways when we have already incurred a loss. Then, in contrast to our normal loss aversion, we may be inclined to take *more* risk in the hope of putting us back in winning territory. Once on a losing streak, we behave as if we were relatively less averse to additional losses, to the extent that we are sometimes willing to gamble for resurrection. The crucial point for our purposes is that not having achieved a target is, from a psychological point of view, effectively the same thing as being in the domain of losses. Therefore, the incentive to double down is potentially there, with excessive risk-taking as a possible consequence.

While incentive schemes are certainly important to consider, often powerful behavioural biases are the root causes of the undermanagement of risk problem. Shefrin (2008) has defined a bias as a predisposition to make a mistake in a decision situation. Often these biases originate in behaviours that had some evolutionary advantage in historical times but serve us poorly in today's complex and modern environment. A decision-maker may have the best of intentions, that is, no conflict of interest whatsoever, when it comes to running the firm in the interests of shareholders, but still end up doing suboptimal risk management. Three of these behavioural biases, which conjoin to produce the undermanagement of risk problem, are reviewed here: over-simplification, over-optimism, and overconfidence. Generally speaking, undermanagement of risk is more likely to occur for high-impact–low-probability risks, because this is the setting that enacts these biases.

Our inability to deal well with high-impact–low-probability risks is a famous theme in Nassim Taleb's book *The Black Swan*. According to Taleb (2007), the human mind copes poorly with randomness, and we are notoriously bad at predicting, or even granting the possibility of, those highly unlikely but highly consequential events that disproportionally affect the world around us. Since information is costly to obtain, store, and retrieve, humans search for simplifying rules that reduce the dimensions of the issue at hand. Because of this **over-simplification**, we leave ourselves vulnerable to Black Swans, events that lie outside the realm of regular expectations but can have a large, or even extreme, impact. Over-simplification means we have a preference for simplistic but coherent narratives, and convenient chunks of easily digestible 'truths', over rigorous analysis that challenges our assumptions.

Our tendency to over-simplify matters, and thus become blind to the potential impact of unlikely events, is joined by **over-optimism** in creating the problem of undermanagement of risk. The manager quoted by Lynch earlier illustrates well how the optimistic bias plays into risk management decisions ('nothing bad is going to happen here anyway'). According to Kahneman and Tversky (1979), we tend to view the world as more benign than it really is, so that people produce plans and forecasts that are unrealistically close to best-case scenario. This bias has major consequences for corporate risk-taking. Kahneman (2011) summarizes:

> The evidence suggests that an optimistic bias plays a role – sometimes the dominant role – whenever individuals or institutions voluntarily take on significant risks. More often than not, risk takers underestimate the odds they face, and do not invest sufficient effort to find out what they are.

The last part of this sentence is important, because it suggests that there is more that could be done by checking the statistics of similar cases in the past, but the optimistic bias makes us prone to skip this step.

Overconfidence is a third behavioural bias that bears on the problem of undermanagement of risk. In this case, humans are prone to overrate their own abilities and the level of control they have over a situation. Plous (1993) argues that a large number of catastrophic events, such as the Chernobyl nuclear accident and the Space Shuttle Challenger explosion, can be traced to overconfidence. He offers the following summary: 'No problem [. . .] in decision-making is more prevalent and more potentially catastrophic than overconfidence.' Overconfidence has been used to explain a wide range of observed phenomena, such as entrepreneurial market entry and trading in financial markets, despite available data suggesting high failure rates.

ERM AS A SOLUTION

While ERM is multifaceted, at its core it can be seen as a mechanism for addressing the effects of silos on optimal risk management reviewed in this chapter. When all business units and corporate functions across the enterprise engage in systematic risk management, in a joint and board-supervised process, the information gap at the corporate level is substantially reduced. By acknowledging the key principles of integrated risk management – utilizing natural hedges and correlations – the firm can design a better risk response and achieve substantial savings. And, at least from a risk management point of view, the units stop behaving as silos with separate agendas, occasionally prone to either over-management or undermanagement of risk. ERM thereby helps restore the principle that risk management should be proportionate to the cost of risk *as seen from the firm's perspective*. How can all of this happen? This is the question that the remaining chapters of the book deal with.

KEY CHAPTER TAKEAWAYS

- ERM can be construed as a board-supervised process for integrated risk management across the enterprise.
- Before ERM, risk management was done in a compartmentalized fashion by the so-called 'silos' (business units and corporate functions).
- Silos and decentralized decision-making are fundamentally desirable to achieve the benefits of specialization.
- However, the existence of silos can lead to risk management outcomes that are not optimal for the firm as a whole.
- A classic example is that silos lead to multiple overlapping risk management activities, which adds a layer of costs.
- A second example is that risk management activities are not coordinated in the silo approach, which may lead to an undesirable net exposure from the corporate point of view.

- A third example is that silos may prevent high-quality information on risk exposures from reaching headquarters, undermining attempts to manage the firm's risk-return profile.
- Finally, silos may manage risk with respect to local goals and ambitions rather than long-run firm value, leading to situations where risk management is not proportionate to the cost of the risk from the firm's perspective.
- The information problem of risk management refers to the difficulty in aggregating high-quality information about risk centrally in the organization.
- Business units may prefer not to report risk information because it will reduce their autonomy, prompt requests for costly action, or make them 'look bad'.
- The information problem is also caused by weak capabilities in collecting and aggregating the relevant data from the business unit level to headquarters.
- The agency problem of risk management refers to a conflict of interest between managers and shareholders with respect to risk preferences, and it can play out at multiple levels in the corporate hierarchy.
- Undermanagement of risk occurs when managers omit to undertake risk management even when it would be economically justified.
- Undermanagement of risk is often associated with high-impact–low-probability risks and created by various behavioural biases, such as overconfidence and over-optimism.
- Undermanagement of risk is also created by financial incentives, in that the cost of managing risk affects operating margins negatively in relation to targeted performance.
- Over-management of risk is driven by general risk aversion and is often associated with highly visible risks that are connected to compensation systems.
- Over-management of risk is liable to occur if a business unit is currently above its targeted performance and wants to ensure that this remains the case.
- In theory, ERM minimizes the impact of the information and agency problems on optimal risk management.
- ERM can be viewed as a set of mechanisms that counter the negative effects of silos on corporate risk management.
- In ERM, one takes a portfolio perspective on the firm's risks by utilizing natural hedges and correlations, which leads to an improved understanding of risk and often substantial savings.

CHAPTER 4

Risk Culture

O NE OF THE THINGS associated with enterprise risk management (ERM) is the creation of a risk-conscious culture, or a 'risk culture' for short. A risk culture is that vaunted state of affairs where risk management becomes 'a way of life'. If such a culture can be instilled, chances are that much of the rest will take care of itself. This happens because taking responsible action, and giving risk the proper consideration, becomes the default mode. A risk culture is therefore an important part of the solution to the general risk management problems facing an organization that we encountered in Chapter 3.

Risk culture defies easy definitions, however. It is perhaps easier to see what it does when it works well. A risk culture is one in which the evaluation of potential threats is a self-evident and important part of the decision-making process. Employees are encouraged to report information about vulnerabilities upward in the system for resolution, and horizontally for the sharing of best practices. In other words, information about risks that supports decision-making should flow without impediments through the organization, and managers should be willing to act on this information. Risk culture, when it works along these lines, becomes a firm's first line of defence: risks find their way onto the corporate radar and receive the appropriate attention without any fuss. When a strong risk culture is present, this sequence is automatic and frictionless. The organization is attuned to risks and takes them seriously.

In our view, a risk culture is a major factor in determining how risks get identified and assessed, and how that information travels through the organization and ultimately affects decision-making. For it to work along these lines, identifying vulnerabilities in the firm's value chain must be second nature to employees, meaning that they are good at both spotting risks on an ongoing basis and evaluating what consequences may be implied by changing circumstances. Employees must also be willing to freely share this information with managers higher up in the corporate hierarchy. That is, rather than hoarding data and hiding it from view, it gets passed on upward in the firm and is received with encouragement. Upon receiving it, managers promptly consider what the appropriate response might be. When these three elements work in harmony, the firm's response to risk gradually becomes proactive and longer term in outlook, and a natural part of the decision-making process. To sum up, we have the following three ingredients in a well-functioning risk culture:

▪ Heightened awareness to detect risks on an ongoing basis
▪ Willingness to share and report risk-related information
▪ Willingness to incorporate risk into decision-making

Our model for risk culture is summed up in Figure 4.1.

There are three cultural dimensions in Figure 4.1. Risk culture is predicated on a heightened **risk awareness** in the daily course of business to the potential impact of different threats. This awareness expands the organization's line of sight with respect to its risks. That is to say, the lens through which employees see the world has been expanded to cover the risk dimension

FIGURE 4.1   Risk culture

in a more explicit way. They are attuned to the dynamic nature of the world and the fact that there are many contingencies that can set things off in an unexpected direction.

Risk awareness can be contrasted with formal risk mapping exercises. It turns out that when called upon to do so, people are quite good at uncovering various risk exposures, and at assessing the potential harm they could inflict on the organization. While useful, such risk mapping exercises may be sporadic or few and far between. In business, however, the pace of change is high, and every change in corporate policies or external circumstances may call for a new evaluation of the firm's vulnerabilities. For an ongoing assessment to take place, the firm's employees need to have a certain 'sensitivity' to the risk dimension in decision-making situations.

Once risks are detected, what happens next depends on whether there are **open lines of communication**. This refers not just to established procedures for how to communicate but even more to the climate in which issues related to risk can be brought up. There may exist formal lines of communication, but that does not help much if there is a climate of fear holding back their use. For lines of communication to qualify as open, people should have no problem standing up to voice their concerns without any fear of negative reactions. Or, for that matter, fear of admitting mistakes.

Finally, a risk culture is characterized by **proactive decision-making**. The opposite of proactive is a reactive approach, where decision-makers do nothing of substance and instead just hope for the best. As discussed in Chapter 3, various behavioural biases and common financial incentives lead people away from proactiveness. With a risk culture, however, people rise above any inclinations to turn a blind eye to the problem at hand and instead assume responsibility for it. They also rise above letting themselves be influenced by any negative impact on short-term performance numbers from the additional costs that may be incurred. 'Doing the right thing' despite personal incentives to the contrary is about personal character, but it is also an aspect of the culture.

 ## THREATS TO RISK CULTURE

The chain depicted in Figure 4.1 is no stronger than its weakest link. If the firm is successful in one respect, but fails in another, the desired outcome is unlikely to materialize. It turns out that there are several factors that work against a sound risk culture. We will discuss three of them: generalized optimism, inertia, and – our main focus of attention in this chapter – short-termism.

Generalized optimism

Many workplaces seek to promote an attitude of 'can do' and optimism, and may therefore not take well to 'negativity'. If bringing up a possible problem comes across as negativity it could prompt a harsh response from the managers on the receiving end rather than an interest in resolving the issue. Lynch (2008) recounts examples of how employees hesitate to elevate potential risks out of a fear of being labelled a troublemaker, and for distracting from the firm's 'real' issues. This cultural phenomenon of generalized optimism comes over and above the individual optimistic bias that we met in Chapter 3. There we concluded that people are by nature predisposed to be optimistic, which shows up, for example, as a tendency to think that the best scenario is also the most likely to happen. Thinking about potentially very bad outcomes is inherently unpleasant to some people, who prefer to stick to a sunny vision of life. Sometimes that becomes part of the culture of an organization.

Inertia

In business, one often sees a practice that involves making certain base-case projections and then taking those numbers to be the truth, without considering alternative outcomes seriously. We are only too happy to create a set of forecasts in a spreadsheet and think that the rest is someone else's problem. In these cases, there is no conscious effort to explore possible consequences beyond, at best, changing some input parameters to see what happens to the forecast. In this mode, people are on autopilot, numb to the dynamic nature of the world around them. Over time, while repeating similar tasks, our senses tend to get dulled, especially in the shielded environments of large organizations. We are disinclined by nature to exert conscious mental effort on complex issues, instead preferring to rely on simple heuristics that have served us well in the past. The more we become creatures of habit and correspondingly bureaucratic in outlook, the more our risk thinking is likely to deteriorate.

Short-termism

Proactive risk management implies benefits in terms of reducing the cost of risk, which by definition lies somewhere in the future. The cost of risk management is often upfront, however, coming straight out of the pocket and thus affecting the bottom line in the current period. As described in Chapter 3, this concern about short-term results makes a proactive approach problematic, and even risks that have been clearly identified may not get the appropriate response. Risk assessment reports, instead of being acted on, sit indefinitely on the shelf collecting dust. Lynch (2008) labels this sort of behaviour the AADD-syndrome: Analyse, Assess, Debate, and Drop. In a telling passage, he writes: 'Most will do a good job identifying [risks]. However, subconsciously they will begin to prioritize which [risks] should be mitigated based on what will require the least effort, time, and capital.' The failure of the culture to support proactive risk management could not be clearer. Lynch concludes that, due to this short-term orientation, many firms operate with cultures that are too complacent about risks. Risk containment, in these cases, is simply not a priority among employees.

 ## SHORT-TERMISM: CAUSES AND CONSEQUENCES

In what follows, we will investigate short-termism from various perspectives and study some of its consequences for firms' risk culture. A sound risk culture is unlikely to develop, we posit, in firms characterized by an intense interest in meeting earnings expectations and other short-term targets. How much weight the firm places on short-term earnings versus long-run value in turn depends on the broader corporate culture. We will continue the thread from Chapter 3 and examine how high-powered compensation schemes can shape, and even corrupt, the so-called 'tone at the top'. At the other end of the spectrum stands a 'risk-prone' culture, the very opposite of a 'risk-conscious' culture.

Rappaport (2011) defines short-termism as 'choosing a course of action that is best in the short term, but that is sub-optimal, if not out-and-out destructive, over the long-term'. It has been described by Kunreuther and Useem (2018) as 'the most crippling of all biases' in terms of hindering proactive risk management. Studies in economics show that people indeed have a strong leaning towards near-term gratification, or in the jargon, that we make 'inter-temporal trade-offs using a hyperbolic discount rate'. What this tells us is that people demand far more compensation for delaying gratification than models of rational economic behaviour suggest.

Short-termism is human nature, but it is also a cultural phenomenon. The corporate version of it shows up as an exaggerated focus on short-term earnings and related targets. The astonishing extent of short-termism among executives was revealed in a study by Graham, Harvey, and Rajgopal (2005). They interviewed 401 executives, who said they were preoccupied more than anything else with meeting quarterly earnings expectations. What is more, 78% of them admitted to being prepared to sacrifice economic value (e.g. decrease spending on R&D, advertising, and hiring) if that helped them reach earnings targets.

Short-termism is, for natural reasons, particularly endemic in publicly listed firms. Partly this seems to be driven by an orientation on the part of analysts and certain categories of investors towards short-term earnings rather than long-term cash flows. According to Rappaport (2011), many managers, observing this, believe that the stock market will not reward them for actions that promote long-term value. Instead, they decide to play the game and focus their energies on the short-term earnings benchmarks that analysts provide them with. It is also inherently pleasant for managers to meet expectations and deliver a good result, something akin to an 'ego thing'. Not meeting the quarterly expectation, in contrast, is associated with a worry that it will reflect poorly on their skills.

Short-termism not only undermines the firm's long-term value creation but it can also be a source of potentially company wrecking risks. The mechanism is straightforward: the more aggressive the pursuit of profits and near-term targets, the more the firm is likely to compromise its ethical norms, which in turn builds up significant risks that can wreak havoc on a firm's reputation and value. Many of the infamous corporate disasters in recent decades can in fact be traced back to a flawed culture that created an atmosphere of profit chasing. Greed, in this analysis, is a root cause of risk, and one of its tell-tale signs is an exaggerated focus on the short-term payoffs. John Kay (2010) sums this point up nicely:

> A corporate culture that extols greed cannot, in the end, protect itself against its own employees . . . Lacking a corporate culture that valued the practice, as well as the profits, of banking, Lehman [Brothers] fell victim to the profit seeking it extolled.

Kay refers to Lehman Brothers, but the example of Valeant Pharmaceuticals in Chapter 2 is another case in point. Yet another is the US bank Wells Fargo, who experienced a downfall after its aggressive practice of 'cross-selling' led to a serious backlash from both customers and employees. Enron, the former energy company, of course remains perhaps the most spectacular example of how an increasingly desperate attempt to keep up the appearance of growing profits can lead to a firm's undoing. In this case, managers systematically engaged in criminal activities like fraud, bribery, and insider trading. It goes without saying that these behaviours are the antithesis of a risk culture.

The case of BP and its subcontractors also provides an illustration of how short-term target chasing can bring about behaviours that stretch the limits of decency and ultimately leads to disaster. BP suffered a high-profile accident when oil spilled out into the Mexican Gulf from its Deepwater Horizon platform in 2010. The episode caused a tragic loss of lives and environmental damage. The company sustained enormous direct costs from the clean-up efforts and the various litigations that ensued. Its brand and reputation obviously suffered in a big way too. The accident had complex technical causes, and many of the decisions in the lead-up fall under the business judgement rule. But the subsequent investigations did indicate that a strong contributing factor was that managers, in an attempt to prevent budget overruns and reach drilling targets, cut corners on safety procedures.

The takeaway is that when the financial incentives get the upper hand, the risk culture suffers. Consistent with this notion, the investigations showed that concerns repeatedly expressed by engineers regarding the safety of the cheaper alternatives were flouted, and that multiple warnings that arose hours before the explosion were ignored. A chronicler summed it up as follows:

> As one former BP manager told me recently, no one ever tells workers to cut corners but that winds up being the result because the emphasis from top executives is always on the financial . . . The issue is not whether BP's employees made a conscious trade-off between safety and dollars, but whether the company's culture made such a trade-off inevitable. (Economides, 2010)

CORPORATE CULTURES AND COMPENSATION PACKAGES

It follows from our discussions so far that the risk culture is an extension of the broader corporate culture. Corporate culture refers to the firm's collective values and beliefs and how those ultimately affect behaviours. It has been likened to an operating system that encapsulates the values that everyone in the organization lives by and directs people towards the decisions that support its mission. Importantly, the operating system is supposed to protect its own integrity by not allowing communication or decisions that could harm those values, fending off influences that could corrupt it. As long as the system functions well and is aligned with the organization's mission, it can be an important catalyst towards achieving that mission. Examples of corporate cultures that stand out are not hard to find. Amazon, to take one, is famous for its relentless focus on becoming the most customer-centric company in the world. This has entailed developing a distinct culture that encourages hard work and a competitive mindset to a degree that seems somewhat extreme to many outsiders. But most would agree that the culture is highly aligned with the company's mission, and therefore supports its achievement.

The fact that risk culture is part of a larger corporate culture is an important observation, because risk culture is usually envisioned as being imposed from the top, only to trickle down the hierarchy until it finally permeates the entire organization. The term 'tone at the top' is sometimes used to communicate this idea. The firm's managers supposedly lead the way for others to follow by setting high standards and then being seen to live up to them. The notion is that the culture can be managed and improved by leading by example. However, we have seen that it can go the other way too; how an excessive focus on profits and short-term targets can undermine the culture. To continue the analogy, short-termism is like a malware that threatens the integrity of the whole system. If the tone at the top is flawed, so will be the example they lead by.

This shifts the question to: How can the 'right' tone be set at the top? By right we mean one that places more emphasis on long-run firm value and good citizenship than meeting quarterly earnings targets. When it comes to high-level objectives like these, it becomes a matter for the firm's largest owners, or its representatives on the ground, the board of directors. They are the only ones who can exercise some form of control and influence the objectives of the executive team from the inside. There is obviously no guarantee that the directors are inclined to take the ethical high ground and instil values that are inherently 'good', nor that they are successful in their attempts to influence the way things are done (in Enron, some of the board members were every bit as implicated as the executive team). The firm's owners and directors do, however, control an important parameter that helps shape corporate culture, namely executive compensation. The nature of these compensation schemes can have a major impact on the balance between the desire for profits and other, 'softer', values.

Compensation schemes often contain stocks and stock options in addition to cash salary. The theory behind it is simple: they attract talented workers and motivate them. The right kind of compensation package, the thinking goes, can pull managers up by their bootstraps and encourage them to put in maximum effort to make the firm successful. Option-based compensation in particular encourages risk-taking. To see why, consider that the holder of an option benefits from the upside potential, but is protected on the downside. The very essence of an option contract is the ability to walk away in unfavourable scenarios. Because of this asymmetry, anyone holding an option clearly benefits from more risk-taking because it amplifies the upside potential but leaves the downside protected. So, the incentives are skewed towards more risk.

When they arrived on the scene in the 1990s, the promise of these schemes was that they would align the interests of managers and shareholders. Instead of timid and disinterested bureaucrats, we would get dynamic entrepreneurs who make the best use of societies' resources and – of course – increase shareholder value in the process. Deployed in the right way, executive compensation indeed offers the possibility of turning a complacent and lazy organization into a formidable competitor that excels in all the areas it needs to. Executives who hold shares and options capture some of the rewards that come from bringing risk-taking to the optimal level, inducing them to launch strategic bets that make full use of the firm's comparative advantages. This, most would agree, is a change for the better in terms of the culture: the company becomes a better version of its corporate self.

Compensation packages do not necessarily have the explicit purpose of changing a corporate culture beyond a sharper focus on improving performance. But they sometimes seem to have a profound effect, triggering exactly the kind of excessive focus on profits and near-term stock price improvements that we have discussed. Option-based compensation in particular creates very strong incentives to reach the thresholds, because the options will expire worthless if the targets are not met. Our point is that incentives of this sort have the power to cause people to breach values that the company otherwise professes to adhere to, which creates risk. Instead of creating a risk-conscious culture, it leads to the opposite, that is, a risk-prone culture.

And this is precisely what the evidence shows. Executive compensation packages are systematically associated with a set of shady, but not necessarily illegal, practices known as 'earnings management', by which is meant the opportunistic use of discretionary accruals and assumptions in reported earnings. Research has furthermore shown an association between executive compensation and the opportunistic release of news to the market. Sometimes these behaviours cross the line to outright fraud. James Kaplan (2010), in a *Forbes* article that summarizes the evidence, notes that in the large majority of cases, accounting fraud can be traced back to the chief executive officer (CEO) and/or chief financial officer (CFO). As for explaining this pattern, the article notes:

> The most commonly cited motives for fraud included the desire to: meet earnings expectations; conceal the company's deteriorating financial condition; bolster performance for pending equity or debt financing; or to increase management compensation.

Again, we reach the conclusion that not only can aggressive targets be detrimental to the development of a risk culture, they can also be *generators of risk*.

Our point is not to demonize target-setting or compensation schemes. Managerial incentives and targets remain an integral part of running a business, and the power of incentives must be harnessed. But it is important to consider high-powered compensation schemes in the context of risk culture and 'tone at the top'. Targets that are too aggressive and too short term are likely to create behaviours that lead to a certain amount of impatience with risk management that tries to take a longer perspective. Getting this balance right is therefore fundamental. One wants to create objectives that provide direction, clarity, and motivation, on the one hand, and on the other hand avoid that the pressure to perform in the short term rises to the point where people compromise the ethical principles that safeguard the long-term value. This is where the responsibility falls heavily on the board of directors, which we will return to in Chapter 5.

CREATING THE BEHAVIOURS THAT SUPPORT A RISK CULTURE

Assume now that the firm's culture is such that it does not promote an unhealthy appetite for short-term profits. Instead, its managers and directors are interested in the two overarching goals of creating long-term value while remaining a good corporate citizen. How can they achieve a risk culture like the one described in the first part of this chapter to support this endeavour? That is, a culture in which employees are attuned to risks, good at detecting them, and comfortable to report them up through the system; and where managers are willing to take proactive decisions on this information in a spirit of openness and transparency. Our answer to this question is that they need to make risk management a core value and communicate this clearly and consistently. There should be no doubt that the top managers believe in the necessity of risk management and its contribution to the organization, lest it ends up in the heap of discarded management fads that the executives could never really commit to. **The management buy-in** is the moment when the executive team and directors come to see the potential of ERM and get behind it. There is a change in perception from seeing it as something that merely helps them satisfy outside expectations to something that has real value for the firm. ERM is no longer just something that allows certain boxes to be ticked off, or some side-show for specialists. Instead, it becomes seen as something that makes the firm run better, an essential part of doing business.

The buy-in, in turn, is greatly facilitated if there is a high-quality vision for ERM. For executives, buying into something requires some evidence of concrete improvements that have a clear impact on the bottom line. Proposals that have a solid case of saving money on costs, or helping comply with laws and regulations, often have a good chance of approval. ERM initiatives rarely have the luxury of pointing to immediate cost savings. Nor is it really about compliance, for which there presumably already exist corporate functions. Instead, ERM promises relatively abstract and longer-term benefits like 'fewer surprises', 'improved decision-making', and 'higher expected performance', all of which are forward-looking concepts. This is why the quality of the ERM vision becomes essential.

In what may seem like an infinite regress, we now need to introduce the **ERM champions**: one or more individuals who understand the mechanisms through which ERM creates value and are able to communicate this in terms that others can relate to and get excited about. It is of course also perfectly possible, but less likely, that the executive team spontaneously arrives at a similar vision from hearing or reading about it, or that consultants provide the inspiration to get the executives interested. But since ERM requires a sustained effort over time to take effect, some sort of in-house team that champions its cause is often a necessity. These individuals are the ones who will formulate a vision for ERM that is grandiose enough to inspire yet concrete enough to be actionable.

The combination of a high-quality ERM vision and solid backing from the CEO is what ensures that the desired path is taken: the one that leads to knowledge and behaviours that make a real difference for decision-making. It is in this kind of setting that we are most likely to see a healthy risk culture develop, one that contributes to long-term company value but also the goal of acting as a good corporate citizen. Coming back to our earlier analogy, the firm's operating system then runs at a permanently higher level, deflecting threats and misbehaviours with greater ease.

Once a firm is committed to building a risk culture, a combination of training and communication is what brings about the change in attitude towards a higher risk awareness. Training, or at least some exposure to the principles of risk management, is a good start. A risk culture is unlikely to happen if the work force only has a dim idea of how to think about risk and how risk management makes sense. Useful examples can be provided and discussions held for that specific purpose in workshops and similar. While training certainly has an important role to play, we believe it is even more important that expectations are clarified and the desired behaviours defined. How, when the risk culture is fully formed, do you envision people behaving? Chances are you are more likely to get there if you define those behaviours at the outset and communicate that those behaviours are fully expected of all employees.

This view can be traced back to a philosophy that says a culture is best recognized by looking at the actual behaviours of the people in the organization. According to David J. Friedman (2018), an expert on organizational culture, the culture must be defined in very clear terms, and the way to do that is to define actual behaviours. Defining values and beliefs is less likely to achieve success, because people can interpret these things differently, and they may not generate the intended behaviours. Values too often end up being a list of generic and empty clichés that few ever pay attention to, such as 'We value integrity, respect, and positive customer experiences.' Better from an operational standpoint, then, to be very explicit about the behaviours that are expected of people. Behaviours are, according to Friedman, how a culture is operationalized, and it is easier to teach, coach, and guide behaviours than values. To trigger discussions about what those behaviours should be, he poses questions like:

What do you want people to actually *do*?
What does this look like *in action*?

We believe many of the behaviours associated with a sound risk culture can be successfully defined, and that this is preferable to listing values that one hopes should translate into a risk culture. But it is still true that risk management as such must be perceived by everyone involved as a core value. According to Friedman, a core value acts as a high-level operating principle that aims to answer the following question: *How* do we go about doing our business? Most certainly, we argue, a firm should go about its business by being diligent and skilful at managing its risks. That message should be consistently reinforced and repeated, along with a clear definition of the behaviours that the executive team believes to be supportive of that core principle.

A schematic overview of the elements conducive to the materialization of a full risk culture is summed up in Figure 4.2. With clear and unequivocal support from the executive team and board of directors the firm can create in-house ERM champions who supply the vision and know-how needed. These are the preconditions for establishing risk management as a core value. Once elevated to that status, the behaviours that are expected of employees are defined. When employees know what is expected of them, they are more likely

FIGURE 4.2   Risk culture

to conform, and a risk culture will gradually start to diffuse throughout the organization. Obviously, a host of other factors will play into the formation of a risk culture that are outside this simple model. Nor are we saying that a risk culture cannot happen unless all these components are in place. Some firms have what amounts to a sound risk culture by default, perhaps because it simply seemed like the best way to operate to the people involved.

Achieving a risk culture takes persistence. While certain routines may be changed in a relatively short amount of time, replacing old attitudes with new ones takes longer. But gradually a new 'way of life' will emerge. Risk management is now viewed as a self-evident and desirable part of the firm's pursuit of upside potential, in which the right kinds of risks are taken and others are managed. Experiencing surprises and not knowing one's risks is considered unprofessional and simply not acceptable. Risk management is thought of not just as something that stabilizes performance but that *improves* it. Risk management has become a core value when these attitudes are diffused throughout the organizations. The sequence of being aware of risks, detecting them with ease, and reporting them up without fear is then embedded in every aspect of the business. The firm deals with vulnerabilities and potential threats in a climate of openness and transparency – without any fuss or notion of negativity. It accepts the necessary cost of proactive risk management even when it conflicts with short-term targets: the goals of long-run value and good corporate citizenship come first.

KEY CHAPTER TAKEAWAYS

- A 'risk-conscious' culture, or risk culture, is one in which risk management becomes 'a way of life', practised by all employees.
- A risk culture is characterized by a risk awareness among employees, open lines of communication, and proactive decision-making with respect to risk.
- When a risk culture functions well, employees are good at detecting risks, do not hesitate to report them upward for resolution, and the information gets acted on by managers without any fuss.

- In a risk culture, employees do not feel afraid to voice concerns for fear that they be labelled 'negative' or distract from the 'real' business issues.
- A risk culture is undermined primarily by three things: generalized optimism, inertia, and short-termism.
- Short-termism is a general preference for short-term gratification, and in its corporate version translates into an exaggerated focus on short-term earnings expectations and related targets.
- Short-termism creates an environment that makes it difficult to bring attention to risks and take the upfront costs often associated with proactive risk management.
- A deficient risk culture and short-term target-chasing can be linked to several high-profile corporate disasters, meaning that short-term targets can be *generators* of risk.
- Short-termism is thus associated with a performance pressure that creates a risk-prone culture rather than a risk-conscious one.
- A risk culture is an outgrowth of a firm's broader corporate culture, which encapsulates its values and beliefs and how those shape behaviours.
- One determinant of corporate culture is the relative importance placed on short-term gains, as captured by its compensation systems, compared to upholding values consistent with being a good corporate citizen.
- Consistent with this, fraudulent behaviour has been linked to a desire by senior executives to meet earnings expectations and collect bonuses.
- Setting a 'tone at the top' starts with the firm's board of directors, who control executive compensation and therefore to some extent the degree of short-termism.
- A risk culture is facilitated by a buy-in from the executive team in which risk management is elevated to a core value.
- Risk management as a core value promotes the notion that proactive risk management is a self-evident part of achieving value creation and being a good corporate citizen.
- This commitment to risk management as a core value must be visible, and credibly and consistently communicated to support the ERM effort.
- Establishing a risk culture is greatly helped if employees throughout the firm understand the *expectations* with respect to risk management.
- The behaviours that support risk management as a core value can be successfully defined and communicated.
- Defining behaviours directly is a more effective way to establish a risk culture than touting values or beliefs that one hopes should translate into the desired behaviours.
- A risk culture is also facilitated by establishing 'ERM champions' who are capable of creating an appealing vision of ERM and promoting it internally.

CHAPTER 5

Risk Governance

THE BASIC PREMISE IN this book is that risk-taking is necessary and desirable to fulfil the overarching goal of creating long-term value, and that risks arise as a natural consequence of doing business. Risk-taking can become excessive, however, or there may be a negligence and lack of oversight with respect to important risks. Risk culture attempts to fix these problems by way of instilling values and behaviours that promote proactive risk management. Risk governance, in contrast, aspires to do so by formal processes and protocols. It sets out to establish who does what in the risk management process.

When practitioners speak of risk governance, they usually have in mind the clarification of roles and responsibilities as they relate to the risk management process. The general idea is that for a risk to be managed properly, somebody has to take responsibility for it. It has been observed that often accidents and failures happen simply due to lack of attention when managers do not feel personally responsible, or just assume somebody else is going to deal with it. Shared responsibility is no responsibility, as the adage goes.

On a theoretical level, risk governance can be viewed as a set of mechanisms that counteract the agency problem of risk management, which we met earlier in this book. To recap, it refers to the fact that the managers, at various levels in a decentralized organization, may have incentives and behavioural biases that cause risk management decisions to deviate from what is in the best interest of the firm as a whole. There may be *too little* risk management due to neglect, overconfidence, or an unwillingness to accept the expenses related to proactive risk management. There can also be *too much* risk management if a risk grabs our attention or threatens the achievement of a target, thus triggering our natural risk aversion. Risk governance encompasses, in theory, various mechanisms adopted by the board of directors to reduce the extent to which such conflicts of interests and biases influence risk management decisions. These mechanisms include, as we shall see, independent risk and internal control functions, risk reporting, and risk ownership. But first we need to explore the role of the board itself.

THE ROLE OF THE BOARD OF DIRECTORS

The basic function of a board of directors is to act as a check on management power and make sure that the executive team lives up to its fiduciary duties towards shareholders. One important role that the board plays as part of this task is to review the strategy proposed by the chief executive officer (CEO). At the end of their review, possibly after some iterations and modifications, the board endorses the company's strategy. Along with the strategy, the CEO informs the board about the risks involved and any actions taken to manage them. The board of directors, again after discussions and iterations, then signs off on the risks being taken as well. Every strategy comes with risks, and these need to be understood and scrutinized by the board.

This, as far as brief summaries go, is how the interaction between a board and the CEO is supposed to play out in principle. The inherent risks are usually not as well articulated as the strategy itself, however, and the risk management strategy is often much patchier and less coherent. This is where risk governance begins. Ensuring that the risks inherent in the firm's strategy are properly understood and managed counts among the tasks of the board of directors. As the representatives of the shareholders, they are in fact the ultimate 'owners' of the firm's risk profile. This sentiment was articulated in letters published by the investment company Vanguard in 2017, which stated that 'directors are shareholders' eyes and ears on risk' and 'shareholders rely on a strong board to oversee the strategy for realizing opportunities and mitigating risks' (Lipton, Niles, and Miller, 2018).

The directors are not involved in the day-to-day running of the firm, however. From a practical point of view, the board's responsibility is instead understood as relating primarily to **risk oversight**. Risk oversight involves ensuring that a process for risk management is in place and that it lives up to commonly accepted quality standards. As part of this work, the board should stay informed and up-to-date on the firm's major risks and what is currently being done to address them, and regularly check the progress and execution of previously agreed actions with respect to risk management. The quality of the process can be evaluated, for example, in terms of the qualifications and independence of the staff involved in risk management, or in terms of the presence of a well-functioning system for identifying and reporting risks.

One of the more important aspects of risk oversight is that the board challenges the executive team and asks them to justify their current actions (or lack of action). This means engaging with them in an ongoing dialogue as to whether the risk management strategy in place is the correct one given the firm's objectives. The board, or the subcommittee entrusted with risk oversight, needs to probe deeper into the issues than merely be satisfied that some sort of risk management seems to be going on. It comes down to challenging the core assumptions that motivated the selected or proposed risk management strategy. Generally, the CEO needs to be held accountable at a fairly detailed level – just taking somebody's word that risks are being managed does not count as risk oversight.

Surveys regularly confirm that boards of directors are taking risk oversight more and more seriously and that a wide range of risk topics find their way onto the board's agenda. Outside expectations on the company's directors to fulfil this role are also increasing. A failure on the part of the board of directors to challenge the executive team in response to 'red flags' has led to several public reprimands and even cases of legal action. For example, in 2018 the Federal Reserve characterized 'lack of inquiry and lack of demand for additional information' by the board members of Wells Fargo as a failure of board oversight after the scandal that involved creating millions of fraudulent savings and checking accounts (Lipton, Niles, and Miller, 2018).

A risk management strategy is fundamentally forward looking in that it deals with possible future events. However, the board needs to also be attentive to risks that have been taken in the past. What we have in mind here is the critical questioning of profits. Large and consistently growing profits can of course be a sign of a successful strategy where the risks are controlled and are appropriately taken. But it could also be that management is taking a lot of risk and that the higher profits merely reflect a lucky bet. Unfortunately, profits that are better than expected rarely get questioned because people are happy with the numbers they see and want it to continue. But this may be exactly the right time to ask critical questions. What risks did we take to achieve those results? Was it prudent to take those risks? How bad could it get if we are not as lucky next quarter? Mapping out the connection between the risks taken and the observed profits provides a good framework for the board to do its risk oversight well.

Gains that are due to financial instruments should be viewed with particular scepticism, not least in non-financial firms. If a firm posts a financial gain that is several times its operating profit alarm bells should ring. Gains of such magnitude can almost never happen without large risks being taken. When the firm's luck ends, the loss could be of an order of magnitude that it struggles to cope with. Before that happens, some serious questions need to be asked as to why that activity goes on and who has authorized it. It falls well within the scope of risk oversight to ask tough questions regarding the risks being taken when high and rising profits are reported.

For the board to fulfil its roles of risk oversight and providing a useful check on management's proposals it takes a fair amount of information about risk, and in many cases even some basic education in risk management principles. Board members are rarely risk experts and are at a significant information disadvantage compared to the executive team. For sound risk governance to take place the risk awareness of the board has to be at a sufficiently high level, and board members must have timely access to the relevant information on the firm's major risks (the lack of which is the information problem of risk management that we came across in Chapter 3). In fact, the hallmark of strong risk governance is that the board of directors at all times is kept well informed about the firm's most important risks and what is being done about them, as well as the nature and extent of the firm's risk-taking in terms of investments and new strategies.

Having somebody challenge the executive team and ask them to justify the risk management strategy is very important for raising the standards of conduct. It is about bringing multiple perspectives and a critical outlook to bear on risk management, which serves as a useful corrective to the misguided incentives and reckless behaviours that so often precede corporate misfortunes. While much progress has been made in this area, plenty remains. Lynch (2008) writes the following on the contribution of boards:

> The board's role in a comprehensive risk oversight program should be one of actual leadership. This should not be a revolutionary idea, but in many organizations, it is just that . . . With so much emphasis on bottom-line thinking and profits, risk-related matters are too often ignored, and this is where the board's role is so critical.

The awakening of boards with respect to risk oversight is underway, however, and will continue to escalate. To create the right expectations in this regard, Fraser (2010) proposes the following conversational example of how a chairman might introduce the board's role in overseeing and becoming involved in enterprise risk management (ERM):

> We will begin to have regular, more structured and explicit conversations with management on risks, that is: what risks we are taking, and how we are identifying, analyzing, evaluating, and treating these risks. Time will be set aside at each board meeting to hear what is uppermost on management's mind regarding the risks to achieving our strategic and tactical objectives, as well as issues that are evolving that could impact us in the future.

RISK OWNERSHIP

Because the board does not run the firm on a daily basis, significant decision-making authority must be delegated to the administration of the company. This brings us to the important topic of **risk ownership**, where being the owner of a risk means being responsible for its management. Responsibility means, first of all, that one is expected to assess a risk's status on an ongoing basis and report it to those concerned. But there is a deeper implication, which is that the risk owner gets to decide the risk response. That is, the risk owner is the one who decides *policy* with respect to the identified risk. Should something be done about it, and if so, how? Without this kind of decision-making authority, it is in fact impossible to own anything, and we are left with the tasks of identifying, monitoring, and reporting. Risk ownership is therefore of some importance as it deals with decision-making authority and the control over corporate resources in response to identified risks.

So, due to the conventional division of labour, the board of directors delegates the overall risk ownership to the CEO, who is entrusted to run the firm on their behalf. The CEO too, however, will find it impossible to take direct charge of all the risks faced by the firm. That kind of direct engagement is simply not possible from a practical standpoint, given time constraints and the complexity of the issues involved. Risk ownership in practice must therefore be delegated even further. We will initially frame this in terms of a choice between a centralized and decentralized approach to risk ownership, or one that mixes elements of both. We will come back to a more granular analysis of exactly who does what within these two approaches.

Centralize. Headquarters owns the risk management policy and decides directly which actions are taken. Business units, to the extent that they are involved, merely accommodate and execute these decisions.

Coordinate. The business units control the risk management activity, but headquarters directs or influences these efforts by issuing guidelines, policies, and other means of influence.

Decentralize. The business units own the risk management policy. Headquarters governs the risk by making sure that a reasonable process for managing the risk is in place, and that they receive information on its status on a regular basis.

Which of these gets implemented, we argue, ought to be determined by the size of coordination benefits relative to any comparative advantage that the business unit may have in monitoring and assessing risk. **Centralization benefits** exist when the firm has multiple instances of exposure to a risk factor that are located in different business units, and when the risk factor in question depends on (co-varies with) other risk factors. Through centralizing, the firm can achieve the desired net exposure at a lower cost. Without any sort of coordination, the right net exposure may fail to materialize, and the company is likely to overspend by duplicating risk management efforts in different parts of the organization. **Decentralization benefits** of risk management, in contrast, exist when business units have a comparative advantage in understanding the business activity and are updated on its status on a more frequent basis. This allows them to make a more well-informed assessment about the cost of risk (its severity and probability) and the appropriate form of risk management (given the cost of available alternatives). The choice is basically one between speed and synergies in risk management. With a decentralized approach one can act quickly and decisively without involving the full corporate process, which sometimes needs significant amounts of time to go full circle. However, this advantage of speed possibly comes at the price of sacrificing coordination benefits.

Centralizing the risk ownership tends to make sense when a risk is likely to crop up in more than one of the business units. A useful example is market risk. Here there are obvious centralization benefits. Exposure to foreign exchange rates in particular tends to be generated in many business activities that are separated along organizational lines. Letting each unit manage its own exposure independently would create the kind of inefficiencies we met in Chapter 3. The benefits of centralizing FX exposure management to headquarters are therefore substantial: netting of exposures, negotiating better rates with the banks, increased control, eliminating a layer of costs in business units, and so on (for an extended discussion of the benefits of centralization, refer to Jankensgård, Alvinussen, and Oxelheim, 2020). By first netting all the gross exposures into a single net number, the firm can proceed to hedge only the part of the exposure that is desirable from an enterprise point of view. Similar arguments in favour of centralization can be made for other market risks.

Coordination is the appropriate route when business savvy and speed are still of importance but there are also benefits from taking a broader corporate view. That is, where there are both centralization and decentralization benefits. Credit risk can serve as an example. The units have a natural interest in increasing sales, but they will eventually run into the question of whether a buyer is creditworthy enough to be granted the sale on credit. If the counterparty is financially weak, it may end up defaulting on its payable. The business unit, especially if it has been doing business with that firm for many years, may have superior knowledge regarding its character and intention to pay, as well as its importance as a customer over the longer haul. A case could therefore be made that the unit should decide whether it is worth accepting the credit risk given the cost of risk (the risk of default) and the cost of risk management (denying the customer an otherwise profitable transaction). This could be looked at as a pure business decision, best left to those carrying out the business. But headquarters also has an interest here. They need to worry about things like the financial position of the corporate group – for example, its liquidity – and from that perspective a default could carry consequences beyond the loss registered in the business unit. It is not unthinkable that the same customer is buying from more than one of the units, meaning there may be a concentration of credit risk that is not obvious to any of them individually.

As a result of possible risk concentrations, or a concern about the group's financial standing, headquarters may decide that the ownership of credit risk must be coordinated. Complete centralization is not ideal in this case because it would imply that corporate would need to interfere with the decision of whether or not to grant credit to a customer on an almost daily basis. Instead, headquarters can exercise its influence and achieve the desired coordination through other means. It can issue a formal policy that outlines how credit risk is to be assessed (the methodology) and establish what constitutes the minimum level of financial health for a customer to be extended credit. The policy may alternatively stipulate that sales above a certain size are conditional on evaluation and approval by headquarters. With coordination, the units can go ahead and operate as they see fit in the normal course of business, but in certain conditions, stipulated by the policy, the corporate view is triggered.

Decentralization benefits typically exist most clearly for operating risks that are specific to a certain line of business. The business unit in question has a comparative advantage in managing the risk because of its expertise in that area. In these cases, the exposure of the silo tends to coincide with the net exposure of the corporate group. There are therefore no obvious benefits to coordination, since the exposure is unique to that unit and the group does not have off-setting exposures elsewhere. Supply chain risks are often in this category. Supply chains are highly complex: an intricate web of suppliers, intermediaries, warehouses, and modes of transport. To understand points of vulnerability in these networks, and what could be done to mitigate these at acceptable cost, calls for the kind of knowledge that only the operating unit is likely to have.

When risk ownership is decentralized, however, headquarters must guard against the general risk management problems reviewed earlier related to over-management and undermanagement of risk, respectively. A case could in fact be made that there should be involvement by headquarters for *any* risk exposure above a certain magnitude. This is to ensure that ultimately it is the corporate view of costs and benefits of risk mitigation that carries the day. The corporate view encapsulates the basic goals of value creation and good citizenship, and takes into account the full range of pros and cons on a firm-wide basis. This includes not only the direct monetary costs resulting from the risk but also indirect ones such as any damage done to the company's reputation.

Decentralized risk management must therefore be accompanied by some form of monitoring by headquarters. The goal of this monitoring is to ensure that risk management efforts in business units meet acceptable standards. For this purpose, the firm puts in place a formalized process for **risk reporting**, the main output of which is an inventory of the business units' major risks (i.e. a risk register, to be covered in detail in Chapter 6). The ongoing dialogue that accompanies the risk reporting process also means that headquarters retains some degree of influence even though the risk is still primarily managed by the unit. Risk reporting furthermore fulfils the important role of closing the risk information gap that exists at the top of a decentralized organization. As we have seen, the information problem of risk management implies a structural lack, at the top of an organization, of high-quality assessments regarding the firm's major risk exposures. With a well-functioning risk reporting process that is updated on regular intervals, much of the relevant risk information starts permeating upwards in the organization in a timely and systematic manner.

 ## A MORE GRANULAR LOOK AT RISK OWNERSHIP

Up to this point, we have discussed centralized and decentralized risk ownership as if they had a fixed meaning. In reality many questions remain unanswered in terms of exactly how that ownership is structured on each level. Starting with decentralized risk ownership, we have so far assumed that the risk is owned at the business unit level (where a business unit can be a division, business area, or subsidiary, depending on how the firm is organized). The logic behind this assumption is that risk ownership should be broad in scope, which is to say that the unit's leadership should assume full responsibility for both the risk and the return of its activities. The principle in these cases is that risk ownership follows profit and loss (P&L) responsibility (i.e. a net income statement for a specific unit). Because risk management often requires upfront expenditures, incentives are better aligned if the risk owner internalizes the threat that the risk poses in terms of lower future revenues or higher future costs (the reduction of this threat is what constitutes the benefit of risk management). For these reasons, risk ownership for decentralized risks is often passed on to the head of each business unit.

While decentralized risk ownership should, in principle, follow P&L responsibility, risk ownership is often pushed further down the organization. In practice, risk owners can be found for a host of different activities, such as specific projects, product lines, or a specific part of a supply chain. As before, the purpose is to increase accountability and provide incentives to take proactive action. At this point, however, risk ownership becomes detached from the overall P&L responsibility. The teams and individuals that own risks at this level can control expenditures to a certain extent, but do not get evaluated on a P&L basis. This situation is likely to lead to a certain over-management of risk: the risk owners suspect that they will be held accountable for any negative events that might happen, yet do not have the same immediate concern about the P&L as do the heads of that unit. Logically, the preference of these individuals would therefore be to spend as much as they can on risk containment to cover their own backs. It is not difficult to see that this can sometimes lead to the cost of risk management being out of proportion to any benefits from reducing the cost of risk. The solution at hand is again monitoring, but this time by the heads of business units who have the P&L responsibility that relates to the activity in question. To keep the agency problem of risk management in check, each time risk ownership is decentralized one step further down in the organization this activity must be monitored through a combination of risk reporting and dialogue.

Centralized risk ownership also has many potential definitions. We have used the term 'headquarters' up to now, evading the question of exactly what that means. As noted already, the ultimate responsibility for risk oversight lies with the board of directors, who delegates the ownership of the risk management process to the CEO. The CEO, in turn, has at their disposal several functions to assist in carrying out various tasks, like accounting, tax, and treasury. Thanks to their expertise in carrying out a particular task, these departments may be seen as the most well-suited place to put responsibility for managing the risks related to that task as well. The treasury function, for example, has a comparative advantage in managing financial risks.

What is often overlooked is that placing risk ownership with corporate functions reintroduces the possibility of silos in risk management. For obvious reasons, these functions normally seek to optimize the outcome for the corporate group. It is what they are there to do, basically. The tax department, for example, has evolved to be highly adept at minimizing the overall tax burden of the group, working across borders and organizational units. But corporate functions are not beyond silo tendencies. By this we mean a distinct jargon and culture, and a narrow interest in subgoals, that stand in the way of a holistic view of the company and its performance. As a result, we arrive at the important conclusion that *risk management may be centralized but not integrated.*

We can use foreign exchange risk management (FXRM) to exemplify the principle that corporate functions can remain silos in their outlook. FXRM refers to managing the impact of exchange rates on corporate performance. Firms often pursue a centralized form of FXRM, in which the treasury department handles transactions and decides on policy. As noted, centralization yields a whole suite of benefits compared to having each business unit manage its own exposure. The question now becomes to what extent the treasury function operates as a silo, as opposed to a having a holistic outlook that is geared towards maximizing the long-term value of the firm. On the one hand, treasury typically does not have its own P&L, and it generally takes the broad corporate view on things like liquidity and financial ratios. On the other hand, treasurers are known to often adjust the usage of financial instruments solely from a view on how different market prices will develop. This is quite likely done out of a conviction that it is profitable for the firm, since they believe they can outwit the market. However, it certainly distracts from aligning FXRM with any efforts to manage the firm's risk-return profile in an integrated fashion. Another tendency that has been observed is that FXRM focuses on the hedging of near-term transactions (payables and receivables) rather than taking a strategic view on corporate performance. FXRM is most definitely a silo in the sense that its policy is, in a large majority of cases, decided in isolation from that of other risk factors. Even closely related risks like foreign exchange, interest rate, and commodity prices often end up being managed in different parts of the organization. In this sense, FXRM can be considered one of the classic silos. In fact, it may go even further than that. Jankensgård, Alviniussen, and Oxelheim (2020) write:

> In some firms, there are even silos within the FX silo. These are cases where Treasury's efforts to manage various facets of FXRM are fragmented rather than coordinated . . . There are numerous ways an FX exposure can be framed, and therefore many possibilities for different FX exposures to be managed in ways that are not integrated with one another.

 ## RISK GOVERNANCE TO SUPPORT INTEGRATED RISK MANAGEMENT

The case of FXRM, then, illustrates the point that centralization is not the same thing as integrated risk management. A truly holistic and integrated form of risk management, in our view, is based on the possible joint impact of many (correlated) risk factors on corporate performance. Corporate performance has several dimensions, but here we will emphasize financial performance in terms of measures like net income, cash flow, liquidity, and financial ratios. As we will argue extensively in the book, variability in performance can have negative consequences for the firm's ability to compete and create value. Since variability in performance is a function of many different risk factors, managing it calls for them to be looked at in the context of each other. This perspective is core to integrated risk management and provides the basic framework within which risk management policies should be set.

What happens to the concept of risk ownership as firms transition from centralized exposure management to integrated risk management? What needs to happen is that the various risk management policies are hammered out within a forum dedicated to integrated risk management. One possibility is to break the silos in a quite literal way and merge various corporate functions into a single unified support function. Mixing it up like that will strike many as unrealistic, however, and would also run counter to the core idea that specialization brings benefits. Instead, the most promising way of realizing the benefits of integrated risk management is the **ERM committee**.[1] The ERM committee is an advisory body without any operating responsibilities. For ERM to be impactful, it should be dedicated to the cause of integrated risk management and be as explicit about this as possible. Such a committee applies a holistic view on all proposed risk management policies, by posing questions such as the following:

- Is the cost of implementing the proposed policy proportionate to the cost of the risk being addressed, considered from a corporate point of view?
- Is the policy consistent with the twin goals of optimizing long-term value while remaining a good corporate citizen?
- In addressing the risk concerned, have we made sure to use a firm-wide perspective and considered any correlations and natural hedges that may exist?
- Does the proposed policy reduce variability in performance in a meaningful way, and how does that help in meeting important corporate objectives?

While not vested with any decision-making powers, ideally the ERM committee becomes the real arbiter on risk management policy in the firm. That is, any major proposal must be endorsed by the ERM committee before the executives go ahead and back it. To perform such an important task, the committee should consist of high-ranking members of the firm's main business units and corporate functions. When they are part of the ERM committee, however, they are not there to promote the interests of these units: their job as part of the committee is to arrive at a consensus regarding what is in the best interest of the firm.

The consequences of transferring this kind of soft power to the ERM committee are potentially far-reaching in some companies. The treasury department, for example, may not relish losing the ability to set FXRM policy

---

[1]The ERM committee is not to be confused with the risk committee that some boards put in place, and to which many aspects of risk oversight are entrusted for practical purposes. This is an extension of the board itself, whereas the ERM committee represents a pooling of company expertise from various backgrounds, aimed at supporting integrated risk management.

independently in the way it was previously able to do. While the board of directors was always supposed to formally sign off on the FX policy, this is often seen as merely rubberstamping the proposal that treasury puts in front of them. The perceived complexity of FXRM scares directors and many executives away from any deeper analysis that might end up questioning the policy. Treasury embodies the firm's expertise in financial matters and the rest of the organization usually defers to it when it comes to setting FXRM policy. This status quo is unlikely to hold as the firm transitions to an integrated framework for risk management in which policy recommendations for the firm's major risks are significantly vested in a risk committee.

The ERM committee can be an important catalyst in many ERM programmes, becoming effectively the ERM champion inside the firm and helping to secure a broader organizational buy-in. Its importance lies in the fact that this is the instance where the holistic perspective can materialize and be honed, thereby becoming a way to resolve many of the conflicts of interest that exist between short-term target fulfilment and the optimal decision from an enterprise perspective. In the early phases of an ERM programme, the champion is likely to be one person or a couple of individuals, but long-term success and impact is greatly facilitated if the committee takes it upon itself to pursue integrated risk management and champion its cause. That is when ERM is no longer tied to any one individual but embedded in the firm and somewhat more robust to the coming and going of different types of personalities.

Some firms may opt to create a new corporate function specifically devoted to supporting the ERM committee and, by extension, the executive team and the board of directors in matters related to risk. The **risk management function** accumulates expertise in risk management methodology, which allows it to provide decision support regarding various policy proposals. It seeks to raise the firm's analytical capabilities and to spread best practice in the firm. The risk management function also has an important role in the carrying out of risk identification and reporting, which encompasses processing the risk data provided by business units. The risk management function would normally also be given the task of operating and developing any quantitative risk models that the firm operates. As we shall see in Chapter 9, integrated risk management is greatly supported by a certain type of financial model that targets the firm's overall risk-return profile.

Who shall head the corporate risk function and the corporate risk committee? The answer to this question has in some organizations been the chief financial officer (CFO), or one of the more recent additions to the C-suite, namely the **chief risk officer** (CRO). Whoever chairs it would normally be responsible for setting its agenda, which implies having the overall responsibility for developing the firm's risk management capability. In firms with a quantitative orientation, the CRO is often entrusted with the task of supervising the work to improve the models used to measure and manage risk. In firms that are not large enough to justify establishing a full ERM committee, it falls on the CRO, or equivalent, to be the ERM champion who promotes an integrated perspective on risk management.

THE THREE LINES OF DEFENCE

In regulated financial institutions, a much-debated topic is the degree to which the CRO, ERM committee, and risk management function are to remain independent in their assessments vis-à-vis the executive team and the 'business side' of the firm. To preserve independence, it is argued, the most senior risk manager should have periodic access to the board of directors and meet personally with its chairman. This emphasis on independence implies that the function of risk management is primarily to check, or monitor, the level of risk-taking that goes on, and make sure that they are within pre-agreed limits. In performing this kind of task, the risk management function seems to fit well into the framework of internal control in its desire to keep behaviours and risks withing reasonable boundaries. This control aspect explains why risk management appears in the well-known **Three Lines of Defence** model (note the word defence).

In this model, the first line of defence consists of the business units, who are charged with managing risk as part of running their business. As we have seen, however, the units sometimes have misaligned incentives with respect to risks, or under-dimensioned capabilities for identifying, assessing, and managing them.

The firm's second line of defence is the risk management function, functions devoted to quality control and other business standards, and departments devoted to specific issues like security and environmental protection. The risk management function often leverages these other support functions to tap into their knowledge and networks, sometimes jointly coming up with a risk management approach that is aligned with other corporate policies in a particular area.

The third line of defence is the **internal audit** function. The internal audit is part of the firm's risk oversight in that it seeks to ensure that important processes are in place, are of sufficient quality, and do not stray or deteriorate over time. The primary task of internal audit is thus to preserve the integrity of important processes. The reach of internal audit extends to all aspects of the firms' management systems and governance mechanisms, and it operates with few constraints across all areas of the business. In this regard, it is essentially a monitoring function. It advises and informs but has no decision-making role. It is furthermore often entrusted with creating internal whistle-blowing arrangements, through which employees can report suspect behaviours and breaches of the law without fear of reprisals. If the board of directors are shareholders' eyes and ears on risk management, internal audit can be thought of as the board's eyes and ears in the daily course of business.

While risk oversight is central, internal audit is also about improving business practices in a proactive way. The mission of internal audit, according to the Institute of Internal Auditors (IIA), is to 'enhance and protect organizational value by providing risk-based and objective assurance, advice and insight' (IIA, 2017). In this view, internal audit is a repository of in-depth knowledge about the business and its various processes, which it can utilize to offer independent advice. Its main currency is its widely perceived integrity. Internal auditors, because they do not rely on fees and repeat business in the way external auditors do, can remain truly independent. An internal auditor, to come up with a benchmark for the audit, will typically bring a vision of what the ideal process should look like. Even when no serious deficiencies are detected during the audit, this 'ideal state' is a source of useful discussions on how practice can be improved. This represents a proactive stance whereby future errors can be eliminated, which is an important aspect of internal audits' role in today's organizations. In carrying out this role, internal audit faces a balancing act in that it must preserve its independence vis-à-vis the board while working with managers and remaining on good terms with them. Mutual trust and the recognition of roles are key factors in preserving this balance.

It is not possible to understand contemporary risk management without reference to internal audit and the **compliance** function. Though the emphasis is different, they work together with risk management to keep the firm safe from threats and to improve business practices. The relation between these three functions is interesting. In some organizations they have largely overlapped, whereas in others they have been split out, reflecting an increasing need for specialization and a desire to leverage specific expertise in the respective domains.[2] As noted, compliance has become a much more important issue due to the growing extent of regulations affecting firms, such as the

---

[2] Splitting them does not necessarily mean that they become new functions in their own right. Compliance, for example, comes under the legal department in many firms. Generally, practice is varied and many arrangements can be observed as firms accommodate them to their specific circumstances.

Sarbanes–Oxley Act (covering firms whose shares are listed in the US), and the fact that penalties for incorrect action have also gone up, not least in the financial industry in their dealings with customers. Risk management, for its part, has also been increasingly considered a separate discipline from internal audit, as discussed in Chapter 1.

Internal audit is best described as a generalist, specializing in protecting the integrity, and enhancing the quality of, important processes across the firm. The processes for risk management and compliance are no exceptions and can thus be subjected to an audit aimed at checking their effectiveness relative to some benchmark of perceived best practice. As for risk management, the challenge the auditors are presented with is that risk management is often not well defined, and it may be unclear what the 'ideal state' should look like given that it is a comparatively young discipline under constant development. Improving the 'auditability' of risk management was in fact a driving factor behind a project that was launched by the association of internal auditors in Norway (IIA Norway), resulting in a booklet published in 2017 called 'Guidelines for the Risk Management Function', which encapsulates a set of current best practices. Even strategy processes can be audited, in which case the auditors would first ensure that the company *has* a strategy. We are aware of at least one case in which the auditors concluded that the company in question lacked a strategy in the sense of having a clear idea of what it was trying to achieve, which was subsequently brought up to the board of directors.

 ## RISK MANAGEMENT INDEPENDENCE

As noted, risk management, in the Three Lines of Defence model, has a definite aspect of 'risk control' or 'risk containment'. This conflicts with another vision of risk management, in which the risk function works closely with the executive team to optimize the firm's risk-taking and performance. In this vision, risk management is expected to act more as an 'enabler' in matters related to finding the right balance between risk and return. As we shall see in Chapter 10, there are many proponents of a strategic role of risk management.

We share the view that a risk management function should always be able to form independent assessments of risk, and that these should be easily accessible by the board of directors. But we also believe that it can be engaged in the decision-making process and have an active role in finding the right balance between risk and return for various types of business decisions. Approached liked this, risk management is a decision-making support function, embedded in the business, albeit one whose outputs the board of directors should at all times have direct access to.

If one strips away the independence and direct channel to the board of directors, the risk management function is better characterized as an in-house specialized 'risk advisory' that supports the executive team in matters related to risk. Such a risk advisory can of course provide valuable decision support, but if the executive team can manipulate or suppress the conclusions of such an advisory unit the firm is going to be more vulnerable. There may be a point where such a risk advisory's estimates of risk suggest that risk is becoming exceedingly high, for example, in the evaluation of a large acquisition. The executives may by that time be committed to the deal and want to see it through. It would be all too easy for them to simply ignore the warnings of the risk advisory and selectively choose the pieces of information that are presented to the board of directors. The spike in risk that would result from the deal would be quite relevant to the board, however, as part of their risk oversight.

Although a rare occurrence, history has taught us that the executive team occasionally does get caught up in a frenzy of risk-taking based on questionable foundations. The job of a risk management function is, first and foremost, to keep the board well informed about the level of risk in the firm and provide an independent assessment on the consequences of various corporate policies. The risk management function is thus also called on to perform a balancing act: to enable the risk oversight of the board, but also to support the executive team and operating units as they pursue opportunities and try to find the value-maximizing solutions to business problems. We believe this is perfectly possible, but that there is a conundrum involved: to create this arrangement, it takes an executive team that actually wants to empower the board to perform risk oversight.

KEY CHAPTER TAKEAWAYS

- Risk governance is about clarifying roles and responsibilities in the risk management process.
- Risk governance is also about creating incentives that support proactive risk management.
- Risk governance begins with the board of directors, who provides oversight of the risk management process to ensure that it meets acceptable quality standards.

- Risk oversight also implies that the board of directors should challenge the executive team and ask tough questions regarding risk-taking.
- An important part of risk governance is to keep the board of directors well informed about major risks and risk-taking to enable them to carry out risk oversight.
- Risk ownership is the idea that for each risk there should be a specific individual or unit that has the responsibility for managing it.
- Risk ownership creates accountability in the risk management process and avoids the situation that failures or losses simply happen for lack of attention.
- A risk owner is responsible for assessing and reporting the risk, but importantly also has decision-making authority, that is, controls the firm's response to the risk in question.
- A risk can be owned, or managed, on a centralized or decentralized basis (headquarters versus business units).
- Advantages of centralized risk ownership include netting of exposures; utilization of correlations; and coordination of risk responses.
- Advantages of decentralized risk ownership include better access to relevant information and the ability to act quickly in response to changing circumstances.
- All risk exposures above a certain magnitude should involve some degree of centralization to make sure that the firm's risk response is based on the corporate perspective on costs and benefits.
- When risk ownership is decentralized, headquarters monitors the risk management process through risk reporting and dialogue.
- The corporate risk committee and risk function are part of risk governance at the corporate level, serving to elevate the firm's capabilities; spreading best practice; and supporting integrated risk management.
- The risk function ideally supports business decisions and works to optimize performance, yet maintains good lines of communication with the board of directors.
- Risk governance furthermore deals with establishing channels that allow employees to report behaviours that breach the law, or the firm's code of conduct, directly to the board of directors.
- Contemporary risk management cannot be understood without reference to internal audit, compliance, and other related function that also serve to keep risks in check.
- Internal audit is a more generalist function that, on behalf of the board of directors, provides assurance that the integrity of important processes is maintained over time.

CHAPTER 6

Risk Register

E VEN WHEN THEY HAVE every intention to do so, the executive team and board of directors may find it difficult to fully grasp the firm's risk profile. The sheer complexity involved in running a business is a big factor. But so is a certain lack of analytical capability, and the fact that much of the relevant information is found in the silos, that is, business units or corporate functions. An essential part of enterprise risk management (ERM) is closing this information gap by creating the necessary lines of communication and new analytics to describe risk.

Ensuring a continuous supply of high-quality information to support decision-making at all levels of the organization is what risk reporting is all about. However, there must be something useful to report in the first place. Even if the business units and functions have the relevant expertise about the risks in their line of business, they may not have the tool or techniques, or the language even, to express this knowledge in a way that executives and directors can comprehend and apply in decision-making. Before risks can be reported there has to be a systematic approach to identifying and assessing them, or what is commonly referred to as 'risk mapping'.

Risk mapping, and the reporting of the identified risks, fulfils several important functions. One is simply to reduce the frequency of surprises. Being caught unawares when things go wrong implies a lack of control and professionalism, the avoidance of which is an end to itself. Risk mapping also assists the executive team as well as business units in their work to craft an appropriate response to the firm's risks. Finding practical solutions that balance risk and return is greatly facilitated by having the right kind of information at one's disposal. But most importantly perhaps, risk mapping supports the risk oversight carried out by the board of directors. A board that is well informed about risk is much more likely to provide valuable oversight and to challenge the executive team when necessary. The process of generating the risk data often has significant benefits to the business units who provide it as well. Instead of an ad-hoc approach there is now a systematic and diligent effort to map out risks, supported by a common terminology, aided by the resources that the risk management function brings. Lastly, a major benefit of a risk mapping process is the very discussions it triggers. Simply by getting people in the same room and talking about risk, many organizations experience that risk awareness is greatly enhanced.

As part of the risk mapping process, firms can establish a so-called 'risk register' (alternatively called 'risk inventory' or, even more ambitiously, 'risk universe'). It seems fair to say that the risk register is the crowning achievement of many ERM programmes, or at least their most visible output. In essence, the register offers a snapshot of the firm's known risks. Drawing on the register, those concerned can get informed about the company's most pressing risk exposures, and these can be communicated to the board of directors for further resolution. This is when ERM has delivered on one of its major promises. The firm can, with reasonable assurance, answer the question: What are your top risks and what is being done about them?

WHAT SHOULD GO INTO A RISK REGISTER

The risk register is conceptually straightforward. Most would agree that the risk register is about providing an overview of the risks that the firm is exposed to and ranking them according to the level of threat that they represent to the organization. The register then forms the basis for further discussions so that the right priorities can be established. Given the limited time and resources at management's disposal, they should focus their efforts on the risks that really matter, and the risk register is supposed to help them do that. In what follows we discuss the principles behind creating a risk register and highlight how it connects with both risk governance and the firm's risk response, which will be the next step in our journey.

In practice, however, it is far from always obvious how the risk register should be implemented. We have observed great variety in terms of how the register is constructed and what kind of information goes into it. It is not rare to see risk registers that contain elements that, once you stop and think about it, seem fundamentally different from each other. And we do not mean that the risks appearing in the register are diverse, such as supply chain, credit, and reputation risk. That should only be expected. Bringing them all into a single view is in fact the point with a risk register. Rather, they sometimes appear to be different concepts altogether, suggesting that there is some confusion surrounding what exactly should go into the register. This undermines one of the key aspirations of the register, which is to put different risks on a comparable basis.

For a start, it is not always clear what is meant by 'risk' in the context of a risk register. It turns out that the brainstorming sessions that precede them often generate an astonishingly wide range of factors, events, and possible outcomes. They are usually united in the fact that they are all somehow 'bad' for the firm, but sometimes even that aspect is not obvious. One risk register we saw, for example, had 'debt' and 'equity' listed in it. In what sense of the word is debt a risk? Granted, if you have too much of it, there could be a problem. How is equity a risk? Equity is actually considered to be a good thing from a risk point of view, since it means that you are more financially robust. If you have too little of it, there could be a concern. Perhaps that is what the authors of this register had in mind. But having too much equity may be a problem too, as it decreases the return on shareholders' investment. It is, in other words, not clear in what sense of the word any of these two concepts can even be said to be a risk. On top of that, it seems like a case of two instances of the same thing, since having too little equity tends to translate into having too much debt.

A consistent risk register only contains elements that share a similar interpretation. Our suggestion is that only risk factors should go into the register, defined in this book as a stochastic (uncertain) variable that impacts corporate performance in a material way. A vast number of events and actions obviously influence performance in one way or other, but only some of them are worth considering. The goal is to get attention focused on the risks that matter. Finally, to be considered a risk factor at least some portion of the impact on performance must be negative, in the sense of creating losses or deviations on the downside from some forecast value. This does not preclude that the variable could also have a positive impact in other scenarios, in which case it is said to have upside potential.

We take the view that it is best to distinguish between the things that could affect performance (causes), on the one hand, and the things that could go wrong if performance falls sufficiently (consequences), on the other hand. As an example, performance can be affected negatively by things like unfavourable movements in exchange rates or customers defaulting on their payables, which create losses. Foreign exchange risk and credit risk are therefore risk factors according to our definition and should appear in the risk register. If the joint impact of such risk factors causes performance to go low enough this could trigger certain negative outcomes. This could refer to running out of cash; a downgrade of the firm's rating; failing to meet a bank covenant; or having insufficient funds to capitalize on a strategic opportunity. But these are *consequences* of variability in performance, rather than causes, and therefore should not be in the risk register. Analysing these potential consequences of variability in performance is a very important part of the ERM process, but it comes at a later stage (more on this in Chapter 7).

The typical risk register of a financial institution can serve to illustrate this point. Banks often break down their risk register according to three main categories of risk: credit risk, market risk, and operational risk. These are the three main areas where banks seek to control their risk. They also pay attention to 'liquidity risk', defined as the bank's ability to meet short-term cash flow needs. However, listing liquidity risk next to the other three creates the impression that they are essentially of the same nature, when in fact they are not. A more correct view is that credit, market, and operational risks can *lead to* liquidity problems. Let us assume that in a given quarter market movements cause a $50mn loss, whereas credit and operational losses amount to $20mn and $15mn, respectively. The combined loss is therefore $85mn, causing cash flow to go lower than expected. Depending on the firm's refinancing situation (the strength of its balance sheet and the conditions in the capital markets) this drop in liquidity could spell trouble and lead to all sorts of costly adjustments to deal with the situation.[1] So, credit, market, and operational risk are risk factors in that they drive performance (cash flow), whereas liquidity risk is a consequence of variability in performance (triggered by a fall in cash flow). A good analytical structure separates the causes and consequences of performance variability, but does not lose sight of either of them.

When creating a risk register, many firms prefer to sort their risk factors into various categories or boxes, such as 'strategic', 'operating', 'financial',

---

[1]Liquidity risk thus has two dimensions: experiencing a cash flow shortfall and refinancing risk, i.e. the circumstance that capital markets are unwilling to provide financing at acceptable rates, or at all. Refinancing conditions do change independently of the firm's status and definitely deserve managerial attention. We think refinancing risk is closely linked to the analysis of risk capacity and spare borrowing capacity, to be discussed in Chapter 9; but of course it can be included in the risk register if the firm wants to highlight it as a 'top risk'.

'external', and many others. Doing so can be appropriate in a given context to the extent that it fits with a certain way of viewing the world and making sense of it. Applying such categories may help generate additional discussions but is not a crucial aspect of the risk register. Language does matter, however, and the more precise we can be about the risk, the better. For example, 'credit risk' is more of a broad category. 'Customer default' is more precise in describing the actual risk factor. Customer default is a stochastic variable in that there is uncertainty about whether and how many customers will default in any given period. A bank, for example, routinely expects a certain loss due to defaults but the exact magnitude of losses is never certain. 'Customer ABC default' is even more precise. In this case, the worry is that a large and important customer may not honour its commitments. So, broad categories of risk can be broken down into successively smaller risk factors if there is a need for it (which obviously must be balanced against the need to avoid clutter and information overload). The main point is to bring attention to the risks that matter and generate good discussions, so the risk register should be adapted accordingly.

ESTIMATING PROBABILITY AND IMPACT

One of the main functions of the risk register is to put different types of risk on a comparable basis. Comparability is desired mainly in order to make the right trade-offs. With limited time, capital, and managerial attention, efforts must be focused. The only way to know which risks pose the largest threats and require the most attention is to make them as comparable as possible. This, we argue, happens when the risk factors are reported in terms of probability and impact. These two dimensions are what allow firms to achieve the desired level of comparability. The same is not true for two other approaches observed in practice: colour-coding and verbal descriptions. Just assigning a certain colour is too subjective and imprecise. What red ('risk of the highest order') signals to one person could be entirely different from how another person perceives it. Verbal descriptions, besides failing to achieve an acceptable level of comparability, tend to be long winded, clearly a problem in a world with short attention spans.

Unfortunately, probability and impact need to be quantified. A lot of people are fine up to this point but get queasy at the prospect of having to put numbers on these often vague and overwhelmingly complex possibilities. But any such reluctance needs to be overcome. It is true that one of the biggest benefits of a risk mapping process is the discussions it generates, but you can only get so far by talking about risks in broad terms. How much a firm can rationally spend on risk mitigation is, at the end of the day, a function of probability and impact (i.e. the cost of risk), so these have to be narrowed down. The benefit of a specific risk management action is that it reduces either the probability or the impact associated with a risk, so our estimates of those must be as precise as circumstances will allow. There should be reasonable assurance that we neither overspend nor underspend on risk management, and that managing it is actually worthwhile given the time and money it requires.

Careful thought needs to go into how probability and impact are defined. Even if we have agreed to focus on these two dimensions there is scope for misunderstanding. First, let us decide how the impact number should be understood. Contrary to the phrasing in some of the leading ERM frameworks, this part is not about failures to reach targets or objectives. Risk factors can certainly be threats to objectives. But as we have discussed throughout this book, targets are arbitrary and it is easy to show that spending resources to achieve short-run targets is not always economically justified. For decision-making aimed at value maximization, what counts is the impact the risk could have on long-run firm value. Here, impact should be understood as the present value of all the monetary losses that will incur if the risk materializes. This is what truly puts risks on an equal footing. Let us say that a risk, were it to happen, would cause a loss of $2mn in the next year and $1mn in the year after that. If the firm's discount rate is 8%, the present value of those losses is $2mn ÷ 1.08 + $1mn ÷ $1.08^2 = $2.7mn$. Another risk may only have a one-off effect estimated at $6mn in the next year, suggesting a present value of the impact of $6mn ÷ 1.08 = $5.6mn$. A third risk may imply losses that stretch out many years into the future. For example, if there is a four-year time horizon and the loss in each year is $1mn, the impact would be calculated as $1mn ÷ 1.08 + $1mn ÷ 1.08^2 + $1mn ÷ 1.08^3 + $1mn ÷ 1.08^4 = $3.3mn$. By discounting them back to their present values we can say something about which has the largest overall impact on the firm and therefore deserves the most attention. Out of these three, if they have similar probabilities of occurrence, the second risk should be prioritized by management.

We must also consider the role of expected outcomes when interpreting the impact figure. As we saw in Chapter 2, a fundamental point about impact estimates is that they are always relative to some forecast level of performance. When we plan for the future we usually have one outcome in mind that seems most likely to happen. This is our point estimate, representing what we believe will be the outcome if nothing unexpected occurs. Then a risk is introduced, that is, the possibility that something will happen that affects us negatively. Any stated monetary impact should be understood as creating a deviation from the forecast level. Let us say that we believe revenue will be $200mn next year. At the same time, we identify a risk that, if it materializes, will have a financial impact of $30mn. Then what we are saying is that if the risk comes to pass, revenue will be 200 − 30 = $170mn.

The baseline forecast is not always very explicit in risk mapping exercises, because it is taken for granted that the loss in question would simply cause performance to 'drop'. Where we might go wrong is when the risk is in fact quite likely to occur, say, when it has a 70% probability of happening. Then, because it is more likely than not to happen, it should in fact already be part of the forecast. It is not so much a risk anymore as something that should be anticipated and planned for. In this case, the 30% probability of it not taking place is actually a kind of upside relative to the forecast. That is, the forecast itself should be adjusted to $170mn, and instead we have some upside potential (the 30% chance that it will not happen, in which case revenue is $200mn). Due to this possibility, it is often a good idea to clarify what the baseline level of performance is, and *to what extent the impact of the risk being discussed is already incorporated into that forecast*. Otherwise, one could end up double counting when thinking about how low performance could go as a result of the risk.

If impact numbers are difficult to grasp, people seem to dread estimating probabilities even more. There is a clear reluctance to putting numbers on probabilities. Common reservations against quantification are: 'there is no way of knowing' and 'it is just too complex'. This unwillingness is perfectly understandable, though there are at least two good reasons for overcoming it. Firstly, not quantifying them is worse, because then the company is left with hunches and gut feelings. Lacking rigorous input, decisions could easily be driven by personal incentives and biases rather than a firm-wide perspective on costs and benefits. Secondly, once people have become accustomed to the idea of quantifying things, the reluctance is likely to wear off. It is a habit one can get into, especially as the benefits of comparability become more and more evident. Estimating probabilities so that they are neutral and reasonable – that is, cannot be improved in any obvious way – is a skill that can be honed just like any other, and over time the firm builds up a frame of reference and resources to support the activity.

As discussed in Chapter 2, subjective probabilities are what we have at our disposal in a world characterized by genuine uncertainty. It is a mistake to think that we need casino-like probabilities for the approach to work. Subjective probabilities function perfectly validly as decision support, given that three conditions are met. The first condition is that the estimate is based on **the available expertise** within the company (occasionally aided by consultants). The best minds in the company for the purpose should be queried. This could involve a team of engineers, or quantitative analysts, to give their expert opinion. Often, however, general managers need to be involved because they have the most thorough understanding of the business operations.

The second condition for using subjective probabilities is that the team involved has 'debiased' itself, a term proposed by Shefrin (2008). According to Shefrin, if a bias is a predisposition to make a mistake in a decision-making situation, **debiasing** is the act of consciously reducing the bias's impact. Known biases like over-optimism and overconfidence bear heavily on an activity like generating subjective probabilities and lead to inferior execution (though it should be said, for perspective, that the very act of focusing on probabilities and monetary impacts is already a form of debiasing as there is less reliance on emotions and gut instincts). Debiasing is generally about being aware of these tendencies and reflecting self-critically on how they might be influencing our thought processes. Debiasing can also be achieved by specific techniques, such as pooling independent estimates so that one person's low guess cancels out another person's high guess. The Delphi technique is a well-established method for capturing a group's expertise through a series of iterations and feedback that can be considered for this purpose. Another thing that can be done is to clarify the expectation that the goal of the exercise is to come up with neutral and honest estimates on a best effort basis, regardless of what those numbers actually are, so that minds are focused on precisely this as opposed to wanting to conform or second-guess the opinion of others.

The third condition for using subjective probabilities is that they are **fact-checked**. What do we know about similar cases from looking at the available data? Often it turns out we know quite a bit about this *type* of risk based on our collective experience, either within the firm or by consulting external sources. Where they exist, available track records should be investigated. This is basically how insurance companies operate: they amass large amounts of data on past accidents and failure rates, and then infer probabilities from that material. While the kind of data and resources at the disposal of insurance companies are rarely at hand for corporates, the approach of using data sources whenever possible is an important principle. In some cases, the estimate may be possible to base almost entirely on existing data. This occurs when there is a decent number of historical observations, and it is judged that these data points are representative for the risk in question in the future. Fact-checking of estimates like this goes a long way towards increasing their reliability.

Also, the time horizon for which the subjective probabilities apply needs to be clarified. For most processes, uncertainty grows with time. Give something more time and the likelihood of it coming to pass usually increases. Unless a cut-off is specified, we are talking about whether something might *ever* occur. Given enough time, a lot of probabilities edge towards 100%, which is hardly useful information.

When working with probabilities, it is also a good idea, as proposed by Gigerenzer (2015), to clarify the reference class, or base, relative to which the probability is measured. The background for this comment is that people can construe probabilities in different ways depending on the angle from which they choose to look ('A 30% chance of rain means that three out of ten meteorologists think it will rain' is one of Gigerenzer's examples of a confused way of thinking about probabilities). Subjective probabilities often do not have a well-defined base, or what statisticians call 'the sample space', so this issue is worthy of attention.

With a fair die, the probability mass is spread out over a set of defined outcomes according to a known function (a sixth of the mass is allocated to each outcome.) The world is not like a die, however, with a given set of predefined possible outcomes. As discussed in Chapter 2, its predicament is uncertainty, rather than known odds. It is rather like a black box, generating one observable outcome out of an infinite number of possibilities, through mechanisms and interactions that are beyond our grasp. So, for most risk factors, what we can discern are *possibilities* rather than well-defined probabilities. We may acknowledge that something could happen, in the sense that it cannot be ruled out. For example, we do not believe that we will lose our most important customer over the next twelve months, but realize that there is a possibility.

These possibilities are what we try to capture and quantify with subjective probabilities. Based on experience, observations, and reasoning, we grant certain outcomes as possible in the first place, and some of these possibilities we will also consider to be more likely than others. In the literature on the subject, this is referred to as 'degree of belief' or 'degree of certainty': a subjective estimate of the plausibility of an outcome *given what we know*.

To proceed in practice, then, we must first establish all the possible outcomes – the sample space – for the risk factor we are looking at. What is the range of outcomes that we are willing to entertain?[2] After that, we proceed

---

[2] Again, the reader is reminded of the Black Swan problem, or the fact that we are unable, due to shortcomings in our knowledge and imagination, to visualize or grant as possible certain scenarios, such that they are effectively assigned a probability of zero. See Chapter 2 for additional comments on this.

to allocate the probability mass to these possible outcomes.[3] This mass must always add up to 100%, which is as true for subjective probabilities as in the case of a die, and negative probabilities are ruled out. A subjective probability is essentially a relative frequency on a forward-looking basis: the number of outcomes in which the risk 'happens' divided by the total number of possible outcomes. As we shall see, this can be obtained through thought experiments where we repeat the same situation, or guided by observed frequencies when data is available.[4]

A simple example of a sample space is a binary variable where there are just two possibilities: either it happens or it does not. An example of a risk factor with a binary sample space could be engine failure. An easy way to think about it, and to generate a subjective estimate, would be to ask, if we were to operate a hundred machines just like the one we have over the next year (if years is our chosen time horizon), how many of them do you think would fail? If the answer is 'About three', the implied subjective probability is $3 \div 100 = 3\%$.[5] This is an approach for teasing out the most knowledgeable persons' best guess when there is no data. In fortunate cases where data is available, the estimate could well be based on an analysis of observed patterns: 'out of Y engines of this type, in use under similar circumstances as ours, X fail in an average year' ($X \div Y$ is then our estimate of the subjective probability). For other risk factors, such as losing a major customer, the estimate would be even more about subjective degrees of belief and less data driven, but it could still be helpful to think along these lines.

To this somebody might retort that it may not be an average year, after all, so we cannot take the historical average failure frequency to be a probability in the same well-defined sense as with a die. In fact, according to a common argument, the 3% failure rate is what we would *expect* based on historical patterns, and the real risk is that we experience a much higher percentage.

---

[3]This should perhaps be referred to as 'possibility mass' for uncertain variables that are subjectively estimated, but we will adhere to the convention and call it 'probability mass'.

[4]Recall that data availability does not make a sample space certain or known, as with a die. Think of the many ways one could build a model predicting the volatility in the US dollar–euro exchange rate. Depending on choice of data frequency, time period, and model used, one will get different answers. So, we subjectively choose to believe in one of them. And data-driven processes are obviously not beyond the Black Swan problem, which the negative oil price observed in 2020 clearly shows.

[5]Phrasing the question in terms of 'out of one hundred years, in how many do you think the machine would fail?' is potentially misleading because the person responding might think that we talk about the *next* hundred years, so that the machine gradually deteriorates with the passage of time. If the question is understood like this, we could expect an estimate close to 100% as the machine would obviously break down at some point given enough time.

This view corresponds well to how banks approach risk in their loan portfolios. If they have about a hundred loans outstanding at any given time, and observe three defaults in each year on average, that will become part of the budget – that is, it is an expectation not a risk. Then they would try to model the risk that losses *exceed* three defaults over the next year. However, in this case the bank's own loan portfolio is the 'universe' on which we base our historical estimate, and it is also what we try to forecast. This is different from the engine failure example. In this case, we only have one machine and would like to understand the risk that it fails over the next year. This remains a binary outcome, in the sense that the primary interest is in whether it happens or not, not whether there is an 'overshoot' of such cases relative to some baseline number. The negative impact of such a failure is not in the budget forecast already, so it is unaccounted for. It is just that, to get our estimate of the failure probability, we draw on data from a larger population of engines and not the in-house one (which is just one machine that may never have failed so far).

Of course, the overshoot argument has some merit. If you grant the possibility that the engine can fail again, within the same year, after being repaired or replaced following the first failure, there is indeed more risk involved. But at this point we deal with fairly advanced statistical processes involving failure rates. These are best dealt with as part of a quantitative modelling effort, whereas the risk register is probably best served by reporting the simpler subjective probability of experiencing at least one failure, which is what the forward-looking relative frequency really indicates.

Major inconsistencies and errors of thought can be made much less likely by thinking in a structured way about the sample space (the outcomes we grant as possible) and then allocating the probability mass to them. Another risk factor may be considered to have five possible outcomes (really bad, bad, expected, good, or really good), in which case a probability is assigned to each such that they add up to 100%. As we go from two to five possible outcomes in the sample space, we are still talking about discrete random variables. For some risk factors, notably market risks, there is no clear limit to the set of possible outcomes. Instead, there is an infinite number on a continuous scale. An exchange rate, let us say, can in principle be measured with any number of decimals. This is where probability impact estimates of the type 'either it happens or it does not' obviously are not reasonable approximations of a more complex situation. Market risks therefore do not fit easily into the typical risk register. The question 'What is the probability of an exchange rate risk?' does not have any real meaning. Instead, such risks are typically quantified in terms of sensitivities: the change in performance that is associated with a change in the exchange rate of a given size, say, 10%. These sensitivities are sometimes obtained by assembling forecasts in foreign currency, which are then converted into performance, measured in home currency, using a pro-forma statement. Alternatively, one quantifies an average relationship between market risks and performance with regression analysis based on historical data. It falls outside the scope of this book to go into these techniques for quantifying sensitivities, however. Refer Jankensgård, Alviniussen, and Oxelheim (2020) for further reading.

Many ERM teams, being well aware of peoples' reluctance to pick a specific number for probability and impact, opt to soften the blow by asking them to choose from a number of prespecified categories instead. For example, the impact scale can range from one to six, with one being a very moderate impact, and six being a massive one. Similarly, the probability categories can go from 'highly likely' to 'extremely unlikely'. In this case, the description of each category contains a reference to a range of probabilities that indicates the likelihood of it happening. This eases the burden on the individual to choose a single estimate, which strikes many as not humble enough given the complexity of the subject matter and the lack of historical data. As long as these predefined categories come with an indication of the range of values they represent, the risk team can, for analytical purposes, convert them into more precise estimates by choosing the mid-point of the range. But as the firm gains experience and becomes more comfortable with risk assessments, it should seek to shift to quantifying the probabilities and impacts more directly. When several categories exist, it is too easy to just pick one that seems initially plausible and be done with it, instead of thinking seriously about the subject.

A peculiar aspect of probability and impact estimates alike is that the data points in most risk maps are just a single representative estimate of the risk, whereas realistically, as already discussed, it can take on many different values, each with its own probability. We can be hit by a ten-year storm, but it could also be a hundred-year storm, where the latter has a bigger impact but lower probability. There is usually a whole range of possible outcomes. What goes into the risk register, however, is by necessity a kind of average effect, or the most plausible 'risky' outcome. Some firms tackle this by asking participants to specify more than one 'scenario' for the risk factor, each of which comes with its own probability impact estimates. Obviously, this is more realistic because it draws attention to the varying levels of severity involved, but it will also increase the information load and affect the ease with which risk can be communicated.

AN EXTENDED RISK REGISTER

The register, and the associated reporting, are part of risk governance. To emphasize this connection even further, the register should connect with the concept of risk ownership. Risk governance implies that risk ownership is assigned to all the risks in the register. All risks should be accounted for in this regard. The ownership dimension can be explicitly attached to the register, so that, once a risk is identified and put into the register, a discussion automatically ensues about who should take responsibility for it (if not already obvious). For the sake of avoiding any misunderstandings, a new column can be added to the risk register in which the owner of each risk is specified. At this point it is 'official' who is supposed to do what, and accountability is thereby increased.

The risk register should also be forward looking in that it connects with the risk response, which refers to the decision-making process that kicks in once a risk is identified and assessed (the subject of Chapter 7). Pinpointing the underlying mechanism that gives rise to the risk is an important step towards improved decision-making. To know how the risk could be managed, we may need to understand its drivers at a deeper level by carrying out a **root cause analysis**. A company might, for example, enter 'equipment failure' into its risk register. Any such failure would definitely cause accidents, damage, and financial losses. But why do we have this risk? When pondering such issues, it might surface that poorly trained engineers could lead to such an outcome. Or that inferior material is purchased in a drive to save costs. And so on. When the discussion is taken to this level, we obtain a much deeper understanding of the risk and why it is there.

As another example of 'deeper' levels of causality, we can use the example of a manufacturer of fertilizers and foliar products. Such a firm has many products that all serve the purpose of boosting agricultural output but differ in terms of their chemical structure. One such compound is urea, the industrial production of which is used primarily for fertilizing. Since this product price is immediately linked to the firm's performance, it is not unreasonable to list it as a risk factor. However, the price of urea has several determinants. An obvious one is demand for agricultural products. On the input side, there are also identifiable drivers. To manufacture urea one needs ammonia, which in turn is fabricated out of natural gas. The price of natural gas is largely determined by the price of oil, although in a lagged relationship.

This kind of drilldown to identify root causes can generate new perspectives and discussions about what the 'actual' risk is. For this purpose, a column can also be added to the register describing the underlying drivers in a few sentences. These descriptions of the cause of the risk often point the way towards the actions that would reduce it. In the case of equipment failures, adding relevant training sessions for the engineers would probably be helpful in mitigating the risk. Avoiding incentives for the procurement team to go for the materials that have rock-bottom prices is another possible action to the same effect.

As the name implies, the register is mainly about carrying out an inventory of the things that can threaten the firm's performance. A high-quality register by itself provides a solid contribution that helps close the information gap that exists at the top level of the firm. As far as supporting decision-making is concerned, however, it may become even more useful if the corresponding **upside potential** is also reported. After all, things could also turn out for the better. But why do we need to get this information into the register? Why not focus on the biggest threats, do something about them, and then simply enjoy whatever windfall happens if the more fortunate scenario plays out? The answer is that the upside potential could also be affected by the actions we take to manage a risk. A point we will develop later in the book is that a reduction in upside potential is a cost of risk management, just as upfront cash costs are, and must be part of the assessment of pros and cons. Moreover, having upside potential lined up next to the risk factor serves as a signal: that the real task at hand is balancing risk and return – trading costs and benefits – and not just controlling downside risk. To capture the potential upside, two more columns are added to the register, one containing an estimate of upside potential (impact) and another with the probability of this materializing.

A further extension for the risk register that can be considered is the addition of a new column that lists the ways in which the risk depends on, or interacts with, other risks in the register. The point of analysing **covariation** is to detect concentrations of risks, or risks that are more likely to be accompanied by other negative developments. Covariation among risks can amplify overall risk or, more rarely, dampen it. As folk wisdom has it, a misfortune never comes alone. In the financial markets, this insight is expressed by the credo that 'in a crisis, all correlations go to one'. By introducing this dimension in the register, one encourages this kind of thinking. When confronted by a register to be completed, people naturally do just enough to satisfy the expectation. If left out, there is a fair chance that this dynamic aspect of risk is not considered properly. Of course, such interactions between risks could surface as a topic in the ensuing discussions anyway, but by introducing it in the register it is less likely to get overlooked. Mapping out these relationships sets us on the path to one of the most important tools in the risk management toolbox, namely scenario analysis. Understanding risk has a great deal to do with understanding dynamics, interdependencies, and underlying mechanisms. While the risk register is by necessity a somewhat static device, adding a column for co-relationships tends to open up vistas that point to a more dynamic analysis of risk.

Table 6.1 illustrates a (highly simplified) extended risk register. Besides the standard descriptions, risk owners, and probability impact estimates, this register contains root causes, covariations, and upside potential estimates. The root cause of the risk 'production shutdown', for example, is considered to be a turbine failure. Pinpointing this causality is helpful in that the discussions presumably zoom in on the issue of turbines. Now one might argue that turbine failure is the actual risk factor and that production stoppage is just a result. That is a valid argument. The register could be designed that way too, absolutely. Our point here is rather that without considering the root cause, the firm might not get the right attention on the driver of the bad outcome, perhaps neglecting reasonable actions that could be undertaken. The upside potential column indicates that the product trial might also be a hit and exceed the expectations that are implicit in the forecast performance. Why is this information important? Well, any strategy the firm might go for in terms of reducing the probability of a trial failure could simultaneously reduce upside potential. For example, making the design more mainstream and similar to existing products could have this effect on both downside risk and upside potential. Having the upside potential explicit in the register makes it less likely that this dual impact is overlooked. Finally, the covariation column has identified that the risk of top engineers leaving the firm is closely tied to the outcome of the product trial in the sense that their departure is actually triggered if the trial is a flop and the project halted. This outcome would entail a high risk of them moving on to other firms where they can receive greater challenges sooner. The upshot is that the trial and talent risks are not independent. In fact, they are to a large extent one and the same, which means there is a concentration of risk, and that overall downside risk is larger than one might suspect from just looking at the risk factors individually.

Table 6.1 Extended risk register

Whichever level of ambition the firm settles for in terms of its risk register, in the end it must be looked at as a dynamic process with the purpose to generate discussions that find their way into actual decision-making. Too often firms seem to think that once the list is compiled, the job is done and that is that. When the risk register looks fairly similar the next time it is updated some will start questioning what the point is. Approached like a static device, the estimates in the register eventually become numbers that flicker past without conveying any meaning. To avoid this situation, we recommend so-called 'drilldowns', whereby each time the people responsible for a particular risk are invited to explain it in more detail to the executives and directors. These stories straight from the source about the nature of the risk, the work that has gone into understanding it, the reasons for the particular estimates reported, and so on, tend to make the subject come alive and deepen understanding very effectively, not just concerning that exposure but risk management in general. This sort of drilldown can be conducted for all the major risks in the register, one or two at a time. If there is a major change in the risk estimate for one of these risks, that should be paid due attention as well: What are the forces that have made us rethink this risk? Drilldowns into risk estimates, and material changes in them, serve to keep things more interesting and help build up knowledge that supports the risk management process.

KEY CHAPTER TAKEAWAYS

- Risk reporting is key to closing the information gap that exists between the board of directors and executive team, on the one hand, and the business units, on the other hand.
- Risk reporting must be preceded by an enterprise-wide effort to identify and assess risks ('risk mapping').
- The risk register is a compilation of the firm's most important risks, ranked according to probability and impact.
- A significant part of the value of the risk register is that the process itself generates good discussions about risk; challenges peoples' worldview; and raises risk awareness.
- With a risk register in place the firm is able to communicate to outside stakeholders with more confidence what the top risks are and what is being done about them.
- The probability impact estimates in the register should be quantified by the relevant expertise, fact-checked, and debiased to the extent possible.

(Continued)

- Probability impact estimates put risks on a comparable basis. Colour maps and verbal descriptions of risk factors do not achieve a sufficient degree of standardization.
- The risk register is about identifying causes of variability in corporate performance and should not contain things that could be considered consequences of that variability.
- A consistent risk register should therefore only contain risk factors, defined as stochastic (uncertain) variables that impact corporate performance in a material way.
- The risk register connects with risk governance by ensuring each identified risk is assigned to a risk owner.
- The risk register connects better with the risk response (the action taken in response to an identified risk) by specifying the root cause of each identified risk.
- The risk register connects better with the risk response if the impact estimates are given as present values of all future losses each risk would entail, as this indicates the scope of the spending on risk mitigation that could be economically justified.
- The register connects better with the risk response if the probability impact estimates of downside risk are coupled with the corresponding estimates of any potential upside that comes with each risk.
- The register connects better with the risk response if it indicates important covariations between different risk factors, which supports the identification of risk concentrations and gives input to scenario analysis.

CHAPTER SEVEN

Risk Response

T HE ULTIMATE GOAL OF a risk management process is to control downside risk at the lowest cost possible, while keeping as much upside potential as possible. The term 'risk response' refers to how the firm chooses to balance risk and return once a risk exposure has been identified and assessed as part of the risk register. The executive team must craft a response to each of the major risks that have been identified in the register. But then there is also that elusive concept of the risk of the firm as a whole. As we will emphasize in this chapter, the risk response also needs to reflect the firm's desire to safeguard various corporate-level objectives that are connected to the value creation process.

Risk response falls into three broad categories: risk mitigation, risk transfer, and risk retention.[1] Risk mitigation is any action taken by the firm to reduce the probability of a negative event, or its consequence should it happen, that does not involve outsourcing the risk to a third party. Risk transfer, in contrast, means writing a contract with another entity to effectively outsource the risk. To illustrate the difference, paying for a new surveillance system that deters theft is an example of risk mitigation, whereas paying for insurance that will compensate the firm if it suffers from theft is risk transfer. Risk retention means

---

[1] Of course, the firm could also choose to avoid the risk altogether by dropping or discontinuing the activity that would have exposed it to the risk.

accepting and keeping an exposure and any losses that could result from it. The overarching goal is to bring the risk that has been identified to an acceptable level in the most cost-efficient manner possible. Making the right decisions requires an understanding of how mitigation, transfer, and retention work and what their respective costs are. This is the subject of this chapter.

To start things off, we need a framework for evaluating how the different parts of the risk response relate to each other and where it fits into the broader risk management process. As noted, risk response traditionally comes after the steps of identifying and assessing the firm's risk exposures. Once you have done the diligence on the risk and mapped out its possible consequences, it is time to decide what action to take, if any. The ensuing risk response follows a natural sequence in that risk mitigation is considered first. In this step, a firm investigates if there are any actions it can take on its own behalf to deal with the risk. This means searching out ways to address it that involve changing the way things are done internally. The exposure that remains after all risk mitigation actions have been completed is called the 'residual risk'. The residual risk must then be 'financed', as it is called. Financing a risk is equivalent to establishing who will bear the losses and, if that is a party other than the firm itself, agreeing on the terms for assuming this responsibility (i.e. there is a risk transfer.) Risk retention, in contrast, means that the firm accepts any losses that would result from the residual risk. The relationship between risk mitigation, risk transfer, and risk retention is summed up in Figure 7.1.[2]

Risk financing

FIGURE 7.1   Risk response

---

[2]An alternative presentation is to define residual risk as the risk that is retained, i.e. after both mitigation and transfer (e.g. ISO 31000). Both ways of understanding the concept can be observed in practice.

RISK MITIGATION

Now that we have established how risk mitigation, transfer, and retention are related to each other, we will, starting with risk mitigation, proceed to analyse them in more detail, with a focus on how to think about their respective costs.

Risk mitigation is an action designed to reduce the probability or impact related to an identified risk. It refers to measures taken by the firm itself concerning its business activities and administrative procedures. Mitigation therefore has a decidedly operational aspect and is, in some ways, just business. It is often self-evident to managers that they need to have a plan B in case something goes wrong or take precautions to guard against undesired outcomes. People hardly think of those things as risk management. It is just common sense – reasonable measures that any businessperson would take knowing that things do not always turn out as planned.

The decision situation is more clearly defined as risk mitigation, and recognized as a separate decision, when the consequence of the risk is material and when the probability of occurrence is relatively low. Then it tends to fall outside the scope of 'general' management. It is still true, however, that we can approach risk mitigation not unlike how most people would approach any business decision: the benefits simply have to outweigh the costs. It just gets more problematic to execute because of the distinguishing features, namely that the risk carries potentially severe consequences, but is unlikely and may happen only in some distant future. Managers are trading actual resources here and now for a hypothetical future benefit.

Finding cases where risk mitigation actions can be implemented by simple measures and at a low cost is a source of value in risk management programmes. For example, a change in routines so that every transaction above a certain size is double-checked as opposed to being left to a single individual could greatly reduce the risk of erroneous or even fraudulent transactions. Such a measure can be taken with a very modest expenditure of money and effort yet save the company from potentially very costly and embarrassing outcomes. The expected value of cash flows therefore goes up, which in turn implies that value has been created. It is a win on two accounts. Not only is variance reduced, and negative consequences avoided, but we also increase the expected value of cash flow.

In other cases, the mitigation action may involve more substantial costs and there could be more of a trade-off involved. Generally speaking, risk mitigation actions create value, that is, raise the expected value of cash flow, whenever the money that has to be spent implementing it is lower than the benefits that come from reducing the risk. It is back to the principle that risk management must be proportional to the cost of risk. The cost of risk, given by probability times impact, is therefore an important piece of information because it informs us about the maximum amount of resources that one should be willing to spend on risk mitigation (absent any ethical aspects that suggest otherwise). The risk register, because it contains this information, gives an indication of the kind of resources that could rationally be spent on mitigation.

What does the cost of risk mitigation consist of? The most obvious component is upfront cash payments. These are out-of-pocket expenses needed to put the risk mitigation in place. But it could alternatively come in the form of structurally higher operating expenses going forward. The action may be such that it implies a recurring expense compared to the alternative of leaving things the way they are. Then again, just as with the cost of risk, discounting this stream of cash flow back to a present value is what makes decision alternatives comparable. A third way of paying for risk mitigation is by giving up the potential for gains. This refers to deviations on the upside from the forecast value. After all, the outcome can, for some of the risk factors described in the register, also turn out for the better and bring higher revenue (or lower costs). If the risk mitigation action implies that the potential for such gains is reduced, then this too counts as a cost in the economic sense. For example, by denying a customer credit to keep credit risk within limits we choose to sacrifice the positive operating margin that this deal would have brought. Capping potential windfalls decreases the expected value of cash flow, and therefore also firm value unless there is a large enough benefit from reducing the risk on the downside. Summing up, where PV stands for 'present value':

$$
\begin{aligned}
\text{Cost of risk mitigation} \quad &= \text{Upfront cash expenses} \\
&+ PV\left(\text{Future incremental cash expenses}\right) \\
&+ PV\left(\text{Lost upside potential}\right)
\end{aligned}
$$

It is no coincidence if this line of reasoning seems familiar to readers with a background in corporate finance or investment analysis. The risk mitigation decision is similar to any investment decision that involves trading off costs and benefits that occur at different points in time. In fact, one can think of the decision in terms of *investing* in risk mitigation, because often the benefits extend many years into the future, whereas the costs are more concentrated in the near term.

In the end, we are interested in comparing the cost of risk mitigation with the cost of risk. One possible way to achieve this is to attach two more columns to the risk register, one describing the current risk mitigation strategy and the other its estimated cost. Making the cost of risk mitigation explicit directly in the register directs the focus to whether the principle of proportionality is heeded. Lynch (2008) recounts an interesting episode in which managers were asked to list and rank major ongoing risk management initiatives in the firm. They were then asked to list and rank the major risks facing the firm. The overlap between the two lists was low, suggesting significant over-management of some of the firm's top risks, and undermanagement of others.

 ## RISK TRANSFER

Risk transfer is different from risk mitigation in that it involves a counterpart who agrees to assume the financial consequences of the risk. In return for a fee, an insurance company agrees to compensate the firm for any losses that might occur due to a specifically defined risk. The key difference between mitigation and transfer is that the former does not involve outsourcing a risk to another firm. The fact that risk transfer involves a counterpart is a significant step because it implies that risk has to be priced. We now enter the realm of markets for risk, and in a market everything has a price. The pricing of risk, as we shall see, is a key element in our quest to understand the cost of risk transfer, and therefore also the appropriate risk response.

An elementary example of risk transfer is insurance. Firms can insure against a broad range of adverse events. The common denominator is that the insurance company steps in and assumes the losses according to pre-agreed terms. For example, property insurance is a common form of insurance that protects the firm against damage to its facilities, for example, from fire or vandalism. Product liability insurance is also widely used. In this case, the insurance covers the legal and court costs resulting from claims that are filed against the company as the result of injury, property damage, or monetary losses caused by the firm's products. General Motors, for example, has experienced several product liability lawsuits over the years, related to faulty ignition switches, exploding gas tanks, and damaging chemicals. A third example of a type of insurance relevant to firms is business interruption insurance. With such an insurance the firm is reimbursed if it cannot carry on its business operations because its production is halted. Whereas property insurance relates to the physical damage, business interruption insurance extends the coverage to the income that is lost from the incident. Insurance, in short, is available for many types of risks and is widely used by corporations. But it should also be said that many of the most important corporate risks are not insurable. Figure 7.2 shows the twenty top corporate risks according to a survey from 2017. None of the top five risks stated by the executives is fully insurable, and only two out of the top ten risks are.

The second classic example of risk transfer is financial derivatives. Derivatives are financial contracts that derive their value from some price, or rate, called the 'underlying'. The underlying can be the price of oil, an exchange rate, or a share price, to mention just a few. In fact, the underlying can, thanks to advances in financial engineering, be just about anything these days. Hedging a risk means that the derivative is designed to yield a payoff in those scenarios in which the firm's operating performance falls. For example, take a gold producer that wants to hedge its price risk. It would enter a derivative contract that generates a payoff when the gold price decreases, thus offsetting the lower revenue and stabilizing performance.

1. Damage to reputation/brand
2. Economic slowdown/slow recovery
3. Increasing competition
4. Regulatory/legislative changes
5. Cybercrime/hacking/viruses
6. Failure to innovate/meet customer needs
7. Failure to attract or retain top talent
8. Business interruption
9. Political risk/uncertainties
10. Third-party liability (incl. E&O)
11. Commodity price risk
12. Cash flow/liquidity risk
13. Property damage
14. Directors' and officers' personal liability
15. Major project failure
16. Exchange rate fluctuations
17. CSR/sustainability
18. Technology failure/system failure
19. Distribution or supply chain failure
20. Disruptive technologies/innovation

Insurable
Partially insurable
Uninsurable

FIGURE 7.2　Insurable versus uninsurable risks

Source: Based on information in Aon Global Risk Management Survey 2017 (reformatted) https://www.aon.com/2017-global-risk-management-survey/index.html.

Derivatives can be grouped into two main categories: those in which the payoff is a linear function of the underlying (e.g. forward contracts) and those that are a nonlinear function (e.g. options). Forward contracts serve to lock in a price today for a transaction that will take place at some point in the future, thereby eliminating the price uncertainty. A firm stands to either gain or lose on the contract depending on whether the actual price at maturity is above or below the forward price that has been agreed. Option contracts have a favourable asymmetry, however. In the case of a call option, the purchaser stands to gain if the actual price turns out to be above the so-called strike price. With a put option, in contrast, the gain occurs when the price falls below the strike. In no way can the purchaser of the option suffer a negative payoff when the contract is cash settled at maturity. The payoff of an option is the larger of zero and the difference between the actual price and the strike price. This is in contrast to a forward contract, for which there is symmetry: you cannot walk away if the actual price ends up on the 'wrong' side of the forward price. Whereas a forward contract allows the user to lock in a certain price or rate, thus stabilizing performance, an option establishes a certain floor for revenue, or a cap on expenses, depending on the situation. For this privilege, the purchaser must pay a premium when the contract is initiated. This is the equivalent of an insurance premium: one pays upfront for the privilege of getting protection against a bad scenario. Figure 7.3 sums up the different kinds of risk transfer.

Risk transfer is an important tactic in the risk response toolbox. But what is the cost of transferring risk, and how does that compare to risk mitigation? We have to think differently about the cost of risk transfer. As mentioned, because it involves a counterpart in a formal transaction, risk is explicitly priced.

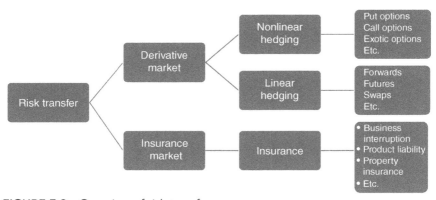

FIGURE 7.3　Overview of risk transfer

The most basic question to ask to understand the cost of risk transfer is whether the risk is fairly priced or not. Let us go back to the case of insurance. Then this question translates into: Does the premium paid correspond to the economic cost of the risk or not? It is important to see that a premium paid for a fairly priced risk transfer is not a cost in the economic sense because the firm obtains an asset whose value corresponds exactly to the premium. In that case, you get exactly what you pay for, so to speak. When you pay a premium related to an option contract of $4mn your liquidity decreases by that amount. Simultaneously, however, you recognize a financial asset of exactly the same amount in your balance sheet. This exchange of one asset for another leaves the firm's equity unaffected at initiation, so the premium is not viewed as a cost. Instead, the real cost of risk transfer lies in the extent to which the premium contains an implied (expected) profit margin for the counterparty.

Let us take a closer look at how insurance companies price risk. Being able to insure against a risk is usually predicated on there being sufficient data so that the insurance company can price it with some degree of confidence. For any given type of risk, it will analyse large sets of data and come up with a price for which they are willing to accept the risk. Car insurance fits this description well. Over the decades, insurance companies have amassed a great deal of knowledge about the frequency and severity of incidents, the two main elements that constitute the cost of risk. While random and idiosyncratic at the individual level, these statistics behave in a fairly predictable way in the aggregate. Thanks to the power of data and statistical analysis, the insurance companies can price the risk with reasonable precision. Because all of them have access to similar data, and offer similar products, the price of the risk tends to converge on its economic cost, as given by probability and impact. That is, competition ensures that risk is fairly priced. When this is the case, buying insurance is sometimes said to just amount to 'trading dollars', implying that the premium roughly corresponds to the present value of expected losses.

While large excess profits get competed away, the insurance premium is still set to ensure a certain level of profit. There is nothing strange or unethical about this. Insurance companies need to cover their costs and also ensure a fair return on investment for their owners. As individuals, we do not mind that what we pay for the home insurance is not 100% of its value in strictly economical terms. We want to sleep well at night, and that is worth paying for. Lottery tickets operate on the same principle, except that this time it plays on hopes and dreams rather than risk aversion. The price for a lottery ticket is never its economic value (probability of a win times the monetary value of the prize). The difference is a gain for the entity issuing the tickets, and we knowingly accept this. This gain for the insurance company is the real cost of using risk transfer for corporations, because we are not just trading dollars after all. Adding to this cost, one should keep in mind that the cost of risk from the insurance company's point of view includes an assessment of adverse selection and moral hazard, the traditional foes of this industry. People opportunistically use insurance when they expect to benefit from it; or change their behaviour after it has been signed. The premium therefore contains a component that compensates the insurance company for this, so that honest buyers of insurance end up paying for the misbehaviour of others.

We can therefore conclude that the real economic cost of risk transfer is related to the size of the counterparty's expected profit margin in the deal, because it means that the premium does not correspond exactly to the present value of expected losses. The principle we would like to bring attention to is that the more non-standard and exotic the product, the larger this component is likely to become. This is where firms need to approach risk transfer with more caution. Complex products hold the potential to be priced less fairly, as the lack of transparency affords the provider a chance to build in a higher profit margin. There is a partly offsetting benefit in that the insurance contract can be tailor-made to the firm's unique circumstances, but it remains the case that the economic cost of the risk transfer is likely to go up with complex contracts. This can partly be justified by the fact that the insurance provider has less data to build their estimates on and therefore has to absorb greater uncertainty. But there is definitely also room for sharp business practices. As a general rule, firms do well to stick, whenever they can, to simple products for which liquid and data-driven markets exist.

Another factor that adds to the cost of risk transfer is that the product may not end up providing the sort of protection that the buyer had anticipated. The insurance provider may dispute the claim, which could result in a multi-year and expensive legal process, where frequently the buyer ends up recovering much less from the contract than the nominal terms would indicate. This too is more liable to occur when the contracts are non-standard and customized, as there will be more contingencies and room for interpretation. Sometimes insurance products are packaged and marketed in general easy-to-understand terms, seemingly corresponding to the business need of the firm. But when a claim is filed, it all comes down to the exact terms in the legal part of the documents. The cost of using risk transfer goes up when the contract terms correspond poorly with the outcome the firm had in mind, or when the cost of enforcing claims is high.

While we have highlighted certain aspects that increase the cost of risk transfer and limit its applicability, there are also a couple of efficiency gains that point the other way. It could be argued that providers of risk transfer have a comparative advantage in dealing with the risk, and that some of the gains are shared with the buyer. An example could be credit insurance, in which the firm sells one of its receivables to the provider. The firm may be concerned with the ability of its customer to pay, and therefore prefer a fraction of the nominal value in ready cash rather than running the risk of non-payment. A possibility is that, due to superior expertise in the legal process and in recovering collateral from defaulting companies, the provider makes a different estimate of the cost of risk. Let us assume that the receivable has a nominal value of $50mn. The firm may think there is a 50% probability of a default and that they could recover $10mn in that scenario. The provider, in contrast, may make a similar assessment of the probability but expect to recover $40mn. The $30mn difference in post-default recovery means that the firm and the provider have different estimates of the cost of risk. This allows for a mutually beneficial contract to be written, and a cost of risk transfer that is lower than it would otherwise be. Other comparative advantages of insurance companies include effective administration of claims and the ability to reduce risk by pooling a large number of claims that are independent of each other. As stated by Ferguson and Smith (1993), corporate demand for insurance is related to 'the insurance companies' efficiencies in providing risk assessment, monitoring, and loss-settlement services'.

So far, we have investigated traditional insurance where the premium is usually paid upfront. Deferred insurance premiums can sometimes be negotiated, in which case a firm pays the premium according to a payment schedule that is divided on a monthly, quarterly, or semi-annual basis. Similar payment schemes exist for the premium paid for options bought in the derivative markets. For derivatives, however, firms have another choice when it comes to paying for risk transfer that is important to understand: they can transfer upside potential to the counterpart in the deal. Transferring upside essentially means writing, or selling, an option and collecting the resulting premium. The premium received is then used to buy options that reduce downside risk – that is, it finances the risk management strategy. When the premium on the options bought and sold exactly cancel out, the result is a 'cashless collar', a derivative strategy that is very common in practice. What has happened is that the firm has now transferred some of its upside potential to the counterparty at the same time that it has transferred some of its downside risk, and no cash has changed hands.

The general point is that upside potential represents another 'currency' with which to pay for risk management. An oil producer, for example, may decide to buy options at a strike price of $50 per barrel when the price is currently trading at $60. This guarantees that its cash flow will not go below a certain floor. However, rather than paying the associated premium in cash, it could decide to sell call options with a strike of $70 such that the two premiums exactly cancel each other. If the oil price goes up above $70, the producer benefits from being able to sell its output at a higher price. At the same time, it has to make good on the call options it has sold, so there is an offsetting loss on its derivative position. Its upside potential is effectively capped above this price. A forward contract can be viewed in the same light. In this case, the firm sells its output forward at the forward price of $60. It has transferred all its downside risk below this price to the counterpart, but also all its upside potential above it. Contrary to popular conception, forwards are not 'free', just cashless at inception.

Figure 7.4 shows the capacity of derivatives to modify a firm's risk profile with great flexibility. The figure compares three derivative strategies from a producer perspective (e.g. a commodity producer) that hedges 100% of its production over the next year. The put option establishes a floor for hedged revenue (defined as the sum of revenue and the payoff from the derivative). The forward strategy instead effectively locks in the forward rate price, leaving no exposure to the risk factor because the gain on the hedge perfectly offsets the loss on the revenue (and vice versa). The collar strategy occupies a place in between. It establishes a floor, which caps the downside, but its upside potential is also capped from selling call options to finance the bought puts. Any number of strategies, each of which comes with a distinct risk-return profile, is possible given the enormous flexibility afforded by derivatives.

When risk transfer is financed by transferring upside rather than paying with cash up front, there are a few additional things to consider when assessing the cost and suitability of the strategy. One is the creation of hidden risk in the form of so-called margin calls. In some derivative deals, both parties to the transaction put up collateral as a way to deal with credit risk, usually in the form of cash (e.g. 10% of the nominal contract). When the value of the derivative changes sufficiently, this could trigger margin calls, which are requirements to post *additional* collateral for the party on the losing side. In practice, this means that a firm can face sudden and potentially disruptive outflows of liquidity when it experiences unrealized losses on its derivative

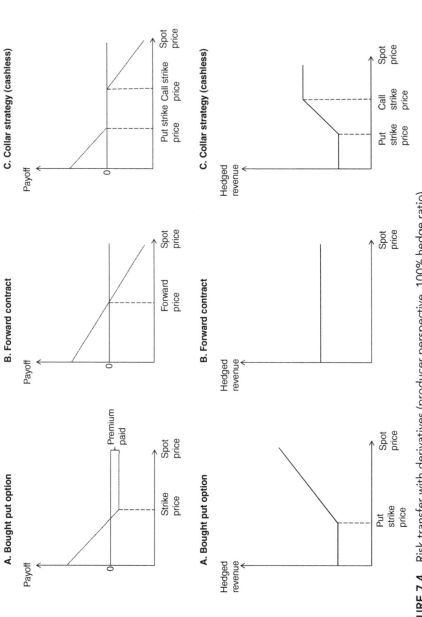

FIGURE 7.4 Risk transfer with derivatives (producer perspective, 100% hedge ratio)

portfolio. That unrealized losses on derivatives can become cash effective is a dimly understood principle that has caused many a surprise. Another inconvenience is that the changes in the value of the contract are required to be reported in the company's net income, creating more volatility there unless the cumbersome procedure of hedge accounting is applied.[3]

Risk transfers, on the whole, are also limited in that they can rarely be efficiently deployed beyond a time horizon of one year, and there are also limitations in terms of the size of the exposure that can be covered. As pointed out by Ferguson and Smith (1993), the scope for efficient risk transfer depends on the supply side of the market. Even in the insurance markets there is a limited capacity to absorb losses, and insurance providers want to maintain the ability to reset premiums if the facts change. In the derivatives markets, liquidity in the forward market rapidly thins out as maturities extend beyond one year. What happens is that the banks that are counterparties in the deals struggle to offset their positions at longer maturities. Normally they rely on their huge networks to find a sufficient number of companies that want to sell and buy forward, so that they effectively act as a market maker. If they have to keep the position on their books, they will demand a risk premium, which adds to the cost for the firm wishing to hedge. The lack of depth in the market also means that the pricing of risk will be less efficient for lack of competitive pressure and therefore be skewed in favour of the financial institutions providing them.

A final point to keep in mind is that the cost of risk transfer goes up the weaker the organization is financially. Recent theories in corporate finance have highlighted that whenever a firm wishes to pay for risk transfer by selling upside, credit risk becomes an issue (see, for example, Rampini, Sufi, and Viswanathan, 2014). The counterparty may harbour doubts as to whether the firm will be able to make good on any losses on the contract. As a result, they may ask for collateral, which is almost sure to be scarce in a weak firm. This reduces the amount of collateral available to support borrowing to invest in the business, such that risk management and investing become competing uses of scarce collateral. In these models, since investment in real assets tends to have a higher marginal return, risk management gets crowded out. This is one of the paradoxes of corporate risk management: the weaker you are,

---

[3]This happens because of an accounting mismatch: the derivative is fair value accounted, i.e. shown at its estimated value in the balance sheet with the changes in that value to be reported in net income, whereas the expected business transaction that the derivative was meant to hedge is not accounted at fair value. At maturity the derivative hedges, i.e. offsets, the price risk related to the business transaction effectively, but between inception and cash settlement the volatility from the fair value changes in the derivatives leads to larger fluctuations in net income.

and the more you need risk management, the harder and more costly it will be to obtain! Obviously, paying for risk transfer with existing cash is no easy solution, as that would crowd out real investment even more. Again, this suggests benefits from a proactive approach. The trick is to act when the firm is still relatively healthy and can avoid the problem of high credit risk affecting its ability to execute risk transfer at reasonable cost.

Complexity in itself is a liability in risk management, presenting us with still more arguments to keep it simple when it comes to risk transfer. Financial derivatives are in fact somewhat notorious for carrying hidden risks. If the contingencies are poorly understood, the instruments may end up creating losses that are beyond the imagination of the corporations who bought them. According to a standard narrative, derivatives that are more complex than necessary are often sold to people who lack the financial sophistication to evaluate all the possible consequences. The derivative disaster experienced by the US municipality Orange County in 1994 usually serves as an example of the dangers of complex derivatives that are not fully understood. Using simple instruments not only reduces transaction costs but also the risk of unpleasant surprises. And in any case, if corporate exposures to risk are straightforward and relatively simple, why should the instruments used to manage them be 'exotic' and complex?

 RISK RETENTION

The risk that remains after risk mitigation and transfer is said to be retained. Retaining means that we accept the possibility of certain losses. At some point it will be impractical or too costly to pursue further mitigation or transfer, so that we are better off keeping the exposure. But retaining the risk, naturally, comes with its own potential costs. For starters, it implies that performance can go lower than it would have been able to do with further mitigation or transfer. And a loss, if large enough, could wreak havoc on the firm depending on whether or not it has the financial resources to deal with it. With few such resources around, it may be poorly equipped to retain the risk. Risk retention is generally only a good idea if the firm can deal well with all, or nearly all, consequences stemming from the risk exposure.

The academic literature on corporate risk management has identified a number of possible negative consequences of risk retention. One is that if performance drops low enough, the firm may not be able to muster enough internally generated cash flow to support its investment programme (Froot, Scharfstein, and Stein, 1993). In this theory, the role of risk management is to coordinate investment and financing activities so as to avoid **underinvestment**. It has been observed that firms tend to curtail investment when they lack internal positive cash flow. External financing is not a perfect substitute for internal funds, as it is costly and complicated to obtain financing in the capital markets. Especially smaller and financially weaker firms are often capital constrained, meaning that they face a steep cost of funding from external sources. Others are positively capital rationed because they cannot get *any* new funding from the outside. These firms rely entirely on internal cash flow to maintain their capex programme, which makes them vulnerable to drops in performance. One consequence of retaining a risk therefore is that it could lead to a loss, which in turn means that the firm is unable to execute the value maximizing level of investment.

Another costly consequence of risk retention is financial distress. In its most extreme form, a loss leads to an inability to meet debt obligations and the firm goes into administration. **Bankruptcy proceedings** are costly due to legal fees, and because they distract managers from running the business in the best way possible. Shareholders may be wiped out in the process, such that they do not stand to share in the gain if the firm's fortunes rebound after reconstruction. But financial distress can lead to costs well before the point of actual bankruptcy. One consequence of financial distress is the possibility that various stakeholders will, at some point, become reluctant to engage with the firm if its risk is perceived as too high. When that happens, stakeholders like customers, suppliers, and creditors will demand a risk premium to deal with the company because they fear that it may not be a reliable long-term partner. This kind of **stakeholder risk premium** impairs a firm's ability to compete and create value (more on this in Chapter 10).

Financial distress also encompasses the possibility of **asset fire sales**. Once in distress, a firm might try to resolve a liquidity squeeze by selling some of its assets. Since it needs the money quickly, the firm may be prepared to accept a price below the fair value of the assets. This discount to fair value is especially large when the market for that kind of asset is illiquid, that is, few transactions being made due to a scarcity of active buyers. One can therefore expect an asset illiquidity discount, defined as the difference between the price in a rapid sale and the price under normal, unhurried circumstances. We know from academic research that this discount can be economically meaningful. In one study on the market for used aircraft, for example, it was estimated that financially distressed firms sold assets at a 30% discount to fair value (Pulvino, 1998).

To summarize, risk retention can lead to a costly disruption in the firm's operations and investment programme that hampers its ability to create value. The monetary losses that can occur when risks are retained may trigger indirect consequences that are detrimental to value creation: underinvestment, asset fire sales, stakeholder risk premium, bankruptcy proceedings, and so on. This is illustrated in Figure 7.5. The key observation is that all these outcomes reduce a firm's expected performance. If a firm's performance falls low enough to enact these negative consequences, they entail lower *future* expected cash flows. If a firm is forced to underinvest, for example, it will be in a weaker position going forward and perform less well than it otherwise would have. We have thus identified another way in which risk management not only stabilizes performance but also raises the expected mean of it, thus being a source of value.

The observations that there are costs to risk retention, and that these are moderated by financial resources, creates a natural connection between enterprise risk management (ERM) and capital management. Risk retention decisions should not be made without considering the firm's available financial resources. A strong balance sheet, which leaves ample room to retain risks, has two salient features: it has a high proportion of equity financing (as opposed to debt) on the liability side, and a high proportion of liquid assets (as opposed to long-term fixed assets) on the asset side. What 'high' means of course depends

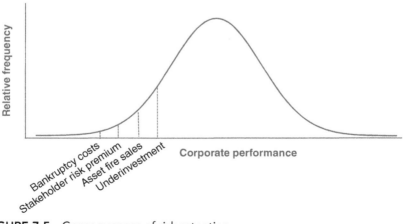

FIGURE 7.5 Consequences of risk retention

on the specifics of the situation, such as the nature of the industry, the competitive situation, and so on. But as a general rule, the more equity financing the firm relies on, and the more of its resources it keeps as liquid assets, the more robust it will be to withstand swings in operating performance. We will have more to say on this in Chapter 8.

THE INTEGRATED VIEW

The decisions to mitigate, transfer, and retain – together constituting the firm's risk response – are highly related, suggesting we take an integrated view on them. They all come with their own set of costs, so in a sense we are trying to determine what strategy for dealing with downside risk has the lowest cost and preserves the most upside potential.

As noted earlier, there is a clear sequence in that risk mitigation comes first. Many times, risk mitigation has a good business case, and these actions can be taken without regard to balance sheets or risk transfers – it simply makes good business sense. After all possibilities for value enhancing risk mitigation have been explored comes the issue of how to deal with, or 'finance', the remaining risk. The risk transfer and risk retention decisions are typically seen as two sides of the same coin. In fact, the academic literature stresses how the use of derivatives to reduce downside risk, that is, hedging, can be viewed as a substitute for equity capital. Hedging creates value specifically when the firm is undercapitalized. Under these conditions, hedging can be shown to reduce the expected costs of underinvestment and financial distress. The payoffs from derivatives generate cash inflows and profits that strengthen equity in the 'bad' scenario, so they can be said to represent *contingent* liquidity and equity.

To see how closely linked risk transfer and risk retention are, we can imagine a situation where the firm has ended up undercapitalized as a result of a string of debt-financed acquisitions. Retaining risks therefore becomes a less attractive strategy given the lack of a sufficient equity base. It would be a bad time to incur operating losses. After making sure it has exhausted its possibilities for cost-efficient mitigation, it may therefore look at risk transfer as a means to balance the overall risk-return profile. Since a derivative strategy makes disruptive shortfalls less likely, it could be considered value enhancing, and the various drawbacks of derivatives may be a price well worth paying in this case.

The point here is that the firm's status in terms of capitalization (i.e. its ability to retain risks) changes the assessment of costs and benefits related to risk transfer. The undercapitalized balance sheet tips the scale, so to say, in favour of risk transfer. Even risk mitigation actions that would not be initiated otherwise could be motivated when the firm is ill-equipped to retain risks. That is, a firm might conclude that mitigating a certain supply chain risk would be too expensive in relation to the cost of the risk, and therefore prefer to retain the risk. Mitigation, on its own, does not have a business case. But on finding its balance sheet currently weak, the managers may realize that losses stemming from this risk could actually imply difficulties in maintaining enough internal cash flows to support capital expenditures and execute the business plan. Then, the correct risk response might actually be to accept the cost of risk mitigation and go ahead with it despite its lack of a stand-alone business case.

On the flip side, when the firm has abundant capital it may choose not to transfer any risks at all, and exclusively mitigate risks for which there is a clear business case. For all these reasons, discussions about risk mitigation and transfer should take place in the context of a keen understanding of the company's risk retention abilities. Viewed in this light, many insurance strategies can be questioned. Unless the risk can be argued to wipe out a significant part of the firm's profits and cash balance it might be better off not paying for insurance. Insurance premiums contain a cost element, as we have seen, and running insurance programmes generates additional expenses. For 'business-as-usual' risks the variability in performance may be perfectly possible to finance out of existing cash. Unless the firm is convinced that the comparative advantage of the insurance company (as discussed earlier) brings the premium so low that it becomes advantageous, it would be better off self-insuring.

THE INTEGRATED RISK RESPONSE

There has been a profound shift in perspective throughout this chapter. We have moved from discussing the response to individual risk exposures to *the risk of the firm as a whole* – understood in terms of the ability to meet corporate-level objectives that are tied to the value creation process. These are essentially the negative potential consequences of risk retention discussed earlier: under-investment, bankruptcy, fire sales, and costs of financial distress generally. From this point on we will refer to this as **aggregate risk**. Coming up with a strategy against cyber risk is dealing with an individual risk exposure. The possibility that the firm's internal cash flow ends up being insufficient to fund the investment programme is an example of aggregate risk.

More specifically, we define aggregate risk in terms of a failure to reach critical threshold levels of performance that imply a costly disruption to the value creation process. This introduces the idea of 'risk as falling below critical thresholds of performance'. This is a novel way of conceptualizing risk, distinct from the others we have met so far in this book: risk as something negative in a very general sense; risk as a financial loss; and risk as failure to meet an objective or goal. Now, risk is a function of the critical thresholds that we have identified.

This way of framing risk is consistent with both our intuitive assessment of risk and theories for how risk management can create value in firms. This is where it differs from 'risk as not meeting objectives', because objectives can be highly subjective and aspirational. Critical thresholds, in contrast, are levels of performance where it is believed that the firm would start experiencing costly and negative consequences that make it more difficult to create value for shareholders. The firm's aggregate risk calls for an *integrated* risk response, in which various risk management strategies are determined on a joint basis with an eye to safeguarding the firm's ability to reach the crucial thresholds.

To facilitate an integrated risk response, it helps to establish a framework in which corporate performance is viewed in relation to critical threshold levels. This offers a way to practically get a grip on the firm's aggregate risk, and usually triggers good discussions as to whether the firm as a whole is safe. These threshold levels need to be understood in the specific context of each firm, so the analysis of aggregate risk thus requires the firm to carry out a **risk threshold review**. In Chapter 6 we argued that the risk register should only list risk factors that are causes of variability in corporate performance, and leave out those things that are better thought of as consequences of that variability because this should be a separate step in the risk management process. Well, the risk threshold review is this step. It is about making an inventory, just as with the risk register, except now we are looking out for consequences of variability rather than its sources.

While the circumstances are firm-specific, theory provides some guidance as to where to look. Generally, we seek to identify situations in which we believe the firm's investment programme would be threatened, or at which it starts experiencing costs of financial distress. As part of a risk threshold review, it is recommended to evaluate all loan agreements to see whether they contain financial covenants. If they do, the ratio they refer to and the specific value at which they would be considered breached can be noted. Such a covenant may stipulate, for example, that the debt-to-equity ratio must not exceed one, lest the firm be in violation of the agreement. This, then, becomes a reference point in the analysis of aggregate risk.

In a similar fashion, if the firm has a credit rating, one could establish which rating would be considered 'disastrous' and then investigate what sort of financial ratio values are likely to cause this downgrade. For example, the firm may suspect its credit rating will be downgraded if its funds-from-operations-to-debt ratio drops below 0.4. In other cases, where the firm is basically credit rationed, it may choose as a critical threshold the level of performance at which its operating cash flow is insufficient to cover its investment programme and other cash commitments. If the firm has some cash resources it can draw down on, the minimum acceptable level of cash to function normally on a day-to-day basis could be the threshold.

The risk threshold review in general also aims at uncovering hidden risks, an important part of reaching the overall goal of no surprises. There are many state-dependent events that remain hidden from view until, well, they happen and catch management by surprise. Generally, these are clauses or contingencies in different contracts to which the firm is legally bound. In some defined benefit plans, a firm may be requested to inject additional liquidity into the pension fund if its assets fall sufficiently below its liabilities. As noted, according to some derivative contracts, a firm is obliged to pay additional collateral if it experiences a large enough unrealized loss. If a firm has made a financial guarantee concerning the debt in some joint venture, this liability could be enacted in circumstances that could be reasonably well identified beforehand. In other words, there are often many contractual contingencies that need to be within the line of sight to prevent unpleasant surprises. Such contingencies occupy a place in between being a source of variability and a consequence of it. It takes some performance variability to trigger them, but once triggered they may lead to additional consequences that accelerate the breach of other, more serious threshold levels.

With a review of risk thresholds in place, managers can more easily detect instances where, absent any risk mitigation or transfer, the firm would be in danger of experiencing costly disruptions. It will therefore point towards the appropriate integrated risk response, which should aim at safeguarding the critical threshold levels. The evaluation of risk thresholds, and how close firms are to breaching them, calls for a more quantitative approach, to be covered in more detail later in Chapter 9. But before that, we need to address what happened to risk appetite. According to the buzz, risk appetite supposedly should dictate a firm's risk response, yet it has not been mentioned up to this point. Chapter 8 explains why.

KEY CHAPTER TAKEAWAYS

- Risk response refers to the actions undertaken in response to an identified risk exposure.
- Risk response comprises risk mitigation, risk transfer, and risk retention.
- Risk mitigation refers to actions taken aimed at reducing the probability or impact of a risk in the course of the firm's business operations.
- Risk transfer refers to outsourcing the risk by writing a formal contract whereby a counterparty accepts to take over the financial consequences of a risk.
- Risk retention refers to the act of accepting any potential losses that come from a risk exposure.
- All three types of risk response have costs that need to be understood and traded off against each other.
- The cost of risk mitigation involves a combination of upfront costs, higher future operating expenses, and reduced upside potential.
- The cost of risk transfer includes transaction costs, margin calls, reduced transparency, and inefficient pricing of risk.
- The cost of risk retention is that the firm might experience losses, business disruptions, or even financial distress.
- The firm's ability to retain risk is generally a function of the health of its balance sheet. A well-capitalized firm can retain more risk than a weaker firm.
- In addition to individual risk exposures, there should also be a well-considered response to the firm's aggregate risk ('total risk').
- Risk aggregation represents a profound shift in perspective: we move from discussing individual risk exposures to the risk of the firm as a whole.
- Managing aggregate risk calls for an *integrated* risk response, that is, determining the policy with respect to various risk factors on a joint basis.
- Aggregate risk is the risk of corporate performance falling below crucial thresholds that imply a disruption to the value creation process, such as meeting cash commitments and staying within bank covenants.
- In a risk threshold review, the firm maps out various threshold levels of performance that would trigger negative contingencies or other costly consequences.
- The goal of the integrated risk response is to manage variability in performance to safeguard the firm's ability to meet these critical thresholds.

CHAPTER 8

Risk Appetite

F IRMS TODAY ARE EXPECTED to be able to identify their core risks and provide evidence of good risk governance. Often, this expectation has been met through the implementation of enterprise risk management (ERM) programmes, which has meant an upswing in the amount of information available about risk. Many managers are struggling, however, when it comes to how this risk information should be incorporated into decision-making. Sooner or later, the question of how much risk is acceptable will be asked. Indeed, what is the right level of risk to take?

The rise of the concept of risk appetite can be viewed as an attempt to provide some guidance on this issue. Risk appetite is typically framed in terms of 'a firm's willingness and ability to bear risk in pursuit of upside potential'. Most people find relating risk to the pursuit of upside potential in this way a straightforward and reasonable concept. To explain how risk appetite is supposed to work, Power (2009) likens it to a thermostat:

> Firms seek to identify all material risks and to design controls for them, producing a residual risk consistent with a target risk appetite, akin to how a thermostat adjusts to changes in the environment subject to pre-given target temperature.

If risk deviates too much from what management thinks it should be, according to this model, actions are promptly taken to bring it in line with the firm's risk appetite.

Taken at face value, risk appetite has significant intuitive appeal. We can see two main benefits that it has brought. The first is simply in helping to draw attention to the question of how much risk is 'right' to take. To the extent that risk was previously a neglected dimension, any concept or idea that focuses peoples' minds on this question should be welcomed. Risk appetite has emerged in part as a by-word for getting executives and board directors to put issues related to the firm's risk profile on their agenda. The term seems to have a certain kind of appeal, which directs peoples' thoughts in a natural way towards the question of how much risk is appropriate to take. 'What appetite do we have for risk X?' is a pretty helpful question to get discussions started.

The second main benefit risk appetite has had since arriving on the scene is that it sharpens the focus around another very important question as well: Which risks are in fact good to take? In Chapter 2 we met the concept of comparative advantage in risk-taking. Depending on its skills, resources, and shareholder expectations, a firm *should* be exposing itself to certain kinds of risk. If one excels in an activity, there is a case to be made for maximizing one's exposure to it to gain the biggest return possible from that comparative advantage. For corporations this would typically be certain kinds of strategic risks needed to fulfil the corporate mission, such as exploring new markets with a certain product line or innovating through R&D to achieve the next big success. Conversely, some risks are decidedly unattractive because the firm has no real advantage in bearing them. Such risks usually arise solely as a by-product of being in business. For example, threats to physical safety can arise as an inevitable part of carrying out a task necessary to deliver a service or product. For such threats to safety, health, and environment, risk appetite is universally low. There may also be categories in between these two extremes, such as exposures to foreign exchange rates. These exposures are not driven by the corporate mission, nor do they come with any ethical dimensions that could prompt strict avoidance.

Just sorting out these priorities using the lens of comparative advantage in risk-taking makes for good conversations. This perspective may bring about more vigorous risk management in some areas (the 'bad' risks), but a willingness to increase exposure to others (the 'good' risks). These are useful questions to be asked and good discussions to be had, and risk appetite has helped to steer the dialogue in that direction.

WHY RISK APPETITE DOES NOT WORK

The evidence to date, however, suggests that risk appetite is struggling to make itself useful to firms when it wants to be more than an entry point for discussions. Many firms have interpreted the term to mean that they are expected to formulate a very precise 'risk appetite statement' that once and for all sums up its attitude to risk. But as pointed out in Quail (2012), there exists no standard, regulated, or widely accepted format of a risk appetite statement. The definition on offer by the instigator of the concept of risk appetite, COSO (2004), is in fact impressively vague: 'The degree of risk, on a broad-based level, that a company or other entity is willing to accept in pursuit of its goals.'

This vagueness has left the field open for various consulting firms as well as non-profit institutions to publish guidance papers on risk appetite. Surveying this rapidly growing field reveals a startling lack of consistency in the current thinking on the subject. It is hard to find common ground above the most basic idea that risk appetite somehow encapsulates a firm's willingness to accept risk exposures in pursuit of an objective. A look at the updated COSO (2017) document confirms this lack of precision. Risk appetite, according to this document, is any strategic, financial, or operating parameter, qualitative or quantitative, expressed in terms of a target, range, floor, or ceiling, and agreed on 'after management discussions and reviews of past performance'.

As it stands, risk appetite can be almost anything, quantitative or qualitative, as long as it somehow relates to risk. Quail (2012) writes:

> Different organizations' risk appetite statements take a variety of forms, from simple one-paragraph descriptions of high-level aversion to risk-taking, to detailed multi-page volumes outlining numerical limits for various exposures.

Viscelli, Hermanson, and Beasley (2017) offer the following summary of current practice with regard to risk appetite:

> Overall, it is apparent that most organizations are struggling to articulate their appetite for risk taking. Some organizations have attempted to define risk appetite, and they often find that process difficult and time consuming. Others have taken a more informal approach to describing their risk appetite, or they have made little, if any, effort to do so. They struggle to arrive at descriptions of an entity's willingness to take certain risks, while avoiding others, in the pursuit of strategic value.

It is when firms attempt to write formal risk appetite statements that it can become not just a distraction but a curse (Alviniussen and Jankensgård, 2018). A risk appetite statement is a kind of policy document that is supposed to encapsulate the firm's willingness to take risks and guide its decision-making. There is a danger that trying too hard to impose such written policy documents only serves to make firms more bureaucratic and over-governed.

Paradoxically, the danger is that they disconnect the assessment of risk from an active consideration of upside potential. This point can be illustrated by some examples in COSO (2017). According to the authors of this document, a floor-type risk appetite statement can be a 25% minimum in terms of how much of the operating budget is to be spent on (presumably risky) innovation. If the innovation-related part of the budget falls below this level the firm is taking too little risk according to its stated risk appetite. But what guarantees that this number is the value-maximizing level of spending on innovation? It seems arbitrary and disconnected from any analysis of business fundamentals. It replaces active assessment with a one-size-fits-all rule. A disservice has been done to the firm's shareholders if the arbitrary decision rules contained in risk appetite statements get in the way of strategic initiatives or other business opportunities that would have created value.

There is an even deeper criticism against risk appetite: in a sense, the firm is not even supposed to have one. It turns out that the whole concept of risk appetite does not have a natural place in a corporate risk management framework in which the objective is the creation of value on behalf of a principal (the shareholders). The concept of risk appetite has strong connotations to the preferences of the decision-makers as individuals. Clearly, people display different degrees of 'risk-loving' or 'risk-averse' behaviour. But these feelings and emotions are not supposed to matter. Instead, the fiduciary duty of directors towards the firm's shareholders would suggest that they deal with the risk-return trade-off in ways that are consistent with the goal of maximizing long-term firm value.

Also, recall that ERM-frameworks make plenty of references to the stakeholder model, according to which the firm exists to satisfy the needs of all its different stakeholders, such as employees, creditors, suppliers, and the state. Confusion about risk appetite is inevitably going to follow if ERM purports to cater to the interests of multiple stakeholders that have obviously different risk preferences. It is also worth recalling the elevated role of objectives and goals in the frameworks, which can sometimes be fairly arbitrary aspirations. What sense does it make to talk about our appetite for the risk of not meeting a stated aspiration in terms of increasing the operating margin, for example? It should not come as a surprise that an inherently vague concept like risk appetite creates confusion more than anything else when there is a profusion of arbitrary targets and different stakeholder perspectives.

The road to recovery therefore begins by reinstating long-run firm value creation as the ultimate objective of risk management. The upshot of a value orientation is that risk management decisions are viewed as essentially business decisions, and the way to make business decisions is to trade costs against benefits. Turning the concept of risk appetite completely on its head, this approach means that managers are actually supposed to act as if they are 'risk-neutral'. A risk-neutral individual is one who dispassionately seeks to raise the expected level of performance (and therefore value). Such a person is only interested in reducing the *variance* of performance (managing risk) if that can be shown to increase the *expected level* of performance – not in reducing variance for its own sake. As we have seen, there are actually many ways this can happen both on the level of individual risks (when the cost of risk mitigation is lower than the cost of risk) and on the level of aggregate risk (when risk management reduces the expected cost of underinvestment and financial distress).

 HOW TO MAKE PROGRESS

A takeaway from our discussion so far is that, for individual risk exposures, the real focus should be on understanding the cost of risk and cost of risk mitigation, respectively. It is better to be explicit about these elements, and quantify things to the extent possible, rather than shroud things in vague terms like risk appetite. Risk appetite does not fare any better when it comes to strategic risk-taking. It turns out that we cannot really have a fixed, or absolute, risk appetite if our goal is to maximize firm value: it is always conditional on the upside we have identified. As always, the name of the game is balancing risk and return.

Limits imposed on trading desks illustrate an absolute risk appetite statement in its purest form. They are quantitative and strictly defined limits framing how large exposures are allowed to get. Absolute limits may be relevant in certain specialized areas, such as trading, and for organizations whose fundamental objective is *value preservation*. In this category we include organizations that have a clear mandate to make good on future commitments to the ultimate claimants on its assets, such as pension funds and life insurance funds. Such organizations may not accept policies that imply even a slight risk of not meeting future commitments (i.e. they have basically zero 'appetite' for that risk).

Absolute limits on risk-taking prove harder to sustain, however, in organizations whose objective is *value maximization*. In this category we include the vast majority of operating firms. Again, in most jurisdictions around the world, managers and directors have a fiduciary duty towards the firm's owners to manage its affairs in the owner's best interest. It is difficult to find absolute limits on risk-taking that are always and everywhere consistent with this goal. An absolute risk appetite statement might say, for example, that the firm should never lose its current credit rating. But while certainly pleasing bond-holders, such a policy may be incompatible with shareholder wealth if it means passing up strategic initiatives that, though adding to risk, are still expected to create value.

In value-maximizing organizations, therefore, appetite for risk will always be relative. Think of the move by Netflix into producing content in-house. This is a fine example of risk-taking, involving large expenditures in return for an uncertain but potentially massive upside potential. Given its large debt, Net-flix's managers may have agreed to the desirability of maintaining various financial ratios and liquidity levels to keep risk in check. But they may none-theless have judged the upside potential of the strategy to be such that it was worth implementing. Some level of downside risk may always be acceptable given a big enough upside potential. This is a tension that makes absolute limits to risk-taking unsustainable in firms that are seeking to maximize value. These principles are summed up in Figure 8.1.

THE WAY FORWARD

Risk appetite, then, has merits in that it generates attention and conversations about important themes that may have been neglected in the past. 'Risk appetite', is too vague a term, however, to be practically useful in supporting decision-making. A key message in this chapter is that for a value-maximizing

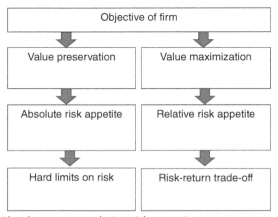

FIGURE 8.1 Absolute versus relative risk appetite

firm the approach to risk-taking should not be 'As per our statement, our risk appetite is such and such, so we will . . . '. This is the curse of risk appetite: a bureaucratic and static process where one attempts to define various arbitrary decision rules beforehand. As every businessperson knows, it all depends. It depends on how good the opportunities facing us are, and what exactly would happen to our risk profile if they were implemented. Consider a firm that has defined a limit to how large its exposure to the US dollar should be allowed to get. Then a business proposal appears, which seems to make good business sense. The catch is that it would increase the firm's exposure to the dollar and cause the limit to be exceeded. Should this firm automatically decide against the proposal simply because it makes the firm exceed its defined risk appetite for currency exposure? We think not, though possibly the increase in the dollar exposure may be a factor to consider and count as a negative in the overall assessment.

For practical purposes, risk appetite needs to be replaced by an analysis in which both downside risk and upside potential is made explicit. Rather than letting arbitrary targets and equally arbitrary risk limits dictate what decisions should be taken, managers need to evaluate the various pros and cons of the decision alternatives and reach a balanced assessment about which one offers the most attractive overall risk-return profile. *Pro-et-contra* is a classic mode of decision-making where advantages and disadvantages of various potential courses of action are identified and discussed. It is about pooling the firm's competence and experience in a meritocratic fashion to work out the risk-reward ratio of the available alternatives. At the end of the pro-et-contra, the team lands on a decision alternative where the magnitude of the pros in relation to the cons is particularly attractive, which is then recommended to the board of directors.

The term pro-et-contra, rather than costs and benefits, indicates that the scorecard ultimately will not be wholly done in quantifiable economic terms. There is also the restraint that comes from the goal of acting as a good corporate citizen. Here we can take cyber risk as an example. Let us say that it has been established that a cyber risk could cause a breach of customer's integrity that would most likely entail some level of personal suffering. This is a qualitatively different aspect of the risk, and one that does not lend itself to quantification. But it definitely should nudge up the amount of expenditure the firm is willing to spend. How much exactly is impossible to say, as it depends on so many factors. It seems safe to suggest, however, that a good way to arrive at a sound assessment of this is to entrust the evaluation to an empowered ERM committee that has internalized the twin goals of firm value and good corporate citizenship.

When it comes to strategic decision-making and aggregate risk, the scorecard looks a little different. Here, the pro-side recognizes the upside potential of the strategic initiatives, largely as they have been quantified through capital budgeting (the net present value [NPV] rule), and in exposure to windfalls that will happen in better-than-expected scenarios. However, any additional benefits from the perspective of the enterprise would also be given consideration, such as the creation of so-called real options, which are valuable but difficult to quantify.[1] The con side of the scorecard recognizes any increase in the firm's aggregate risk from implementing the initiatives. As explained in Chapter 7, by aggregate risk we mean breaches of critical thresholds of performance. A strategic initiative may bring the company closer to these thresholds, meaning that risk increases. The con side would also recognize increases in exposures to specific business risks – such as the potential impact on the firm's reputation risk – that tend to bypass the capital budgeting exercise of individual projects. Again, the estimate of pros and cons must, in the end, be from the corporate perspective, and this is the integrated risk response that ERM should strive to produce.

Power (2009) has suggested that because an organization has many stakeholders and levels of decision-making it cannot have a single risk appetite, and that it is therefore more relevant to talk about 'risk appetizing' as a process. In this process, the firm's risk appetite is worked out through a series of discussions and iterations. That is, risk appetite should be thought of as the outcome of a process. We agree that there is a need for a process rather than a fixed decision-rule, but we believe the term risk appetite is superfluous to describing this process. It is rather about establishing and understanding the upside potential in the decision-making situation, as well as the risk (and its various costs), to arrive at the correct business decision given the higher-level objectives of increasing firm value and being a good corporate citizen.

RISK CAPACITY

A concept that has attracted increasing attention in the literature on ERM is risk capacity. Whereas risk appetite emphasizes a firm's *willingness* to take risk,

---

[1]Real options represent possible courses of action in the future where the firm may act if circumstances turn out to be favourable but decline to do so if they are not. This asymmetry is valuable. It can, in principle, be quantified, but implementation difficulties usually mean that such attempts are rarely made. Our point is that such real options should be acknowledged and enter the pro-side of the decision.

risk capacity is geared towards its *ability* to take risk. At any given time, a company's willingness to take risk can be higher or lower than its actual capacity to do so. If a firm wants to take more risks but does not have the capacity to support it, it is constrained by its lack of risk capacity. If it nonetheless chooses to go ahead despite not having the capacity, it is engaging in excessive and possibly reckless risk-taking. If it has more capacity than it is willing to use, then it acts conservatively but could also be taking too little risk for its own good.

We envision risk capacity in terms of access to financial resources that helps to absorb potential losses and provide contingent financing in worse-than-expected scenarios. If there is enough risk capacity, a firm may continue to exist and to execute its business plan even in these scenarios. That is, risk capacity prevents costly business disruptions due to temporary drops in operating performance and/or spikes in short-term cash requirements. Financial resources are not just required to fund new initiatives here and now. Looking forward, any number of scenarios can happen, some of which would be decidedly bad. An enterprise must be able to withstand such poor outcomes and still execute its strategy, for which additional financial resources are necessary.

Risk capacity is related to the concept of **risk capital**, broadly defined as the amount of capital necessary to support the desired level of risk-taking. Doing business and investing are inherently risky activities, and some capital base is needed to protect against adverse outcomes. Risk capital is therefore essentially a buffer against risk. The financial industry has, in no small measures driven by regulatory demands, pioneered the practical application of this concept.

In a financial industry setting, risk capital is not referred to as risk capacity, however, but **economic capital**. Economic capital is a cushion of capital that allows a firm to endure losses without endangering its survival. The concept is used by banks and their regulators to manage the risk of insolvency, which is a key concern in this context given the systemic importance of banks. The meaning of the term 'capital' in this context is loss-absorbing equity. Some types of equity are considered high quality and therefore reliable in their ability to absorb losses (e.g. share capital and retained earnings). Other sources of equity are considered to be lower quality because they may evaporate quickly (e.g. revaluation and translation reserves) and therefore do not count towards economic capital.

The idea underpinning the economic capital approach is that a firm becomes insolvent when its equity is depleted, that is to say, when the value of its liabilities exceeds that of its assets. In practical terms, the bank needs to analyse the extent to which its main risk factors – market, credit, and operational – combine to produce losses that eat away at its equity. To put the concept into practice, the bank also has to decide on the level of confidence it wants to have that it can remain solvent. A confidence level of 99.5%, for example, amounts to saying that the capital is such that the bank only depletes its equity and becomes insolvent in one out of 200 years. Another way of framing it is to say that economic capital is the capital consistent with a 0.5% probability of insolvency.

The main distinction between economic capital and risk capacity is that the latter refers to liquidity rather than solvency. Economic capital absorbs losses whereas risk capacity absorbs cash flow shortfalls (Alviniussen and Jankensgård, 2009). Perhaps the most crucial difference, however, is that economic capital is concerned with survival, whereas risk capacity is concerned with survival *and* strategy. Strategy here specifically refers to the capital expenditure needed to implement value-creating investments implied by the strategy. In a sense, risk capacity requires more risk to be financed. If it is only survival that needs to be financed, the firm needs fewer financial resources. If strategy execution in worse-than-expected scenarios needs to be financed as well, a larger buffer is required. As we saw in Chapter 7, negative consequences of variability in performance start happening well before the firm reaches insolvency, and an additional buffer is therefore also needed to protect against those outcomes. The aim of risk capacity is for this broader set of strategy-related objectives to be protected rather than just survival.

Risk capacity is a buffer of cash resources, consisting of both existing and conditional sources of liquidity. Risk capacity is what determines the firm's ability to meet cash commitments on an ongoing basis in a worst-case scenario. More formally, risk capacity is the (conditional) cash consistent with an X% probability of falling short of cash commitments. **Cash commitments** comprises all payments related to existing liabilities in the firm's balance sheet, including interest payments and instalments on debt. But it also includes discretionary spending like capital expenditure. While not contractually committed like cash flows originating from liabilities, these are cash outflows deemed desirable as part of carrying out a firm's strategy and creating value. Not being able to meet cash commitments is therefore considered a negative and costly outcome that the firm wishes to avoid because it implies suboptimal strategy execution.

Cash commitments are, first and foremost, financed by internally generated cash flow. Whenever cash flow falls below cash commitments, a **cash flow shortfall** is said to occur. This is where cash resources, existing and conditional, come into play. A firm can obviously keep cash on hand in the form of cash deposits or its equivalents (highly liquid short-term credit instruments). But cash can also be conditional in that the firm accesses it only if a cash flow shortfall has already occurred. Conditional sources of cash include spare borrowing capacity and cash flows from insurance and derivative positions (i.e. risk that has been transferred and yields cash flows contingent on certain events materializing). Spare debt capacity is not a number that is directly available in the firm's accounting system. It has to be imputed by looking at the firm's current financial ratios in relation to threshold levels where further borrowing, at attractive rates, would no longer be feasible. Many firms may have some scope to meet cash flow shortfalls with new borrowing, especially if they are well below their debt capacity, but it is usually only prudent and practically feasible up to a point. Understanding this scope allows firms to determine the amount of conditional cash that can be obtained from external sources. Loan covenants, target ratings, and existing credit facilities may be used to infer the firm's balance sheet constraints, which is why risk capacity is intrinsically linked to the analysis of critical performance thresholds.

A key threshold in the analysis of corporate risk is the level at which internal cash flow falls below cash commitments, as strategy execution may hinge on this relationship. But the interpretation of such a shortfall, then, often depends on how the firm is doing in terms of its other critical thresholds related to the balance sheet, as they indicate the scope for external borrowing to cover up the difference. Some shortfalls may be viewed as business as normal because the firm can safely access funds, but others imply suboptimal strategy execution as the drop in internal cash flow cannot easily be replaced by other funds.

The broader point here is that any given level of risk capacity implies a certain probability that cash commitments will not be met, equivalent to how economic capital is associated with a certain probability of insolvency. Cash flow shortfalls can be met with existing cash and conditional sources of cash, but if the outcome is severe enough (i.e. performance goes low enough) its risk capacity may not carry it through. When this occurs, the firm will have to start cutting back its cash commitments. Since the first cash spending to be curtailed is typically capital expenditure, a situation of not meeting cash commitment may often be interpreted as underinvestment. This is illustrated in Figure 8.2, where the current risk capacity is such that there is a 4% probability of shortfalls that are large enough to imply underinvestment. If the firm had more risk capacity, the threshold at which the firm begins to underinvest is moved further to the left – that is, the probability decreases.

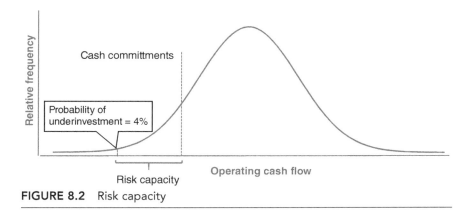

FIGURE 8.2   Risk capacity

Risk capacity is thus what determines a firm's ability to retain risk, one of the three possible risk responses discussed in Chapter 7. Low risk capacity essentially translates into a low ability to retain risk. When risk capacity is low, the firm lacks the resources to uphold its desired level of cash commitments, and therefore its strategy execution, in worse-than-expected scenarios.

QUANTITATIVE EXAMPLE OF RISK CAPACITY

To better understand the connection between risk capacity and risk retention, let us go back to a situation in which we have identified a risk exposure. Having done so calls for a risk response, which initially comes in the form of risk mitigation. The gross exposure net of risk mitigation leaves a residual risk. Due to the residual risk in question, performance could wind up lower than otherwise. If performance for Firm ABC is $100mn in the absence of any risk, and the residual risk has a range between zero and a maximum loss of $25mn, performance will be somewhere between $75mn and $100mn if fully retained. This risk must be financed somehow, either through risk transfer or risk retention. In the case of risk transfer, the loss is absorbed by the risk capacity of the counterparty in the deal, whereas if retained the loss needs to be absorbed by the firm's own risk capacity.

To analyse the consequences of risk retention, we need to introduce cash commitments. Let us say that Firm ABC expects $10mn in interest expenses and has an investment programme that requires capital expenditure of $40mn, resulting in total cash commitments at $50mn. It is also holding $20mn in cash. This configuration means that the firm is well capitalized. Even if performance were to hit its low point of $75mn the firm is safe. In this scenario it can still use its internal cash flow to fully finance its cash commitments and, on top of that, add $75mn − $50mn = $25mn to its cash balance (the positive difference between its internal cash flow and cash commitments).

Imagine now a different configuration. The performance and residual risk are the same, except that now the need for spending on capital expenditure is $90mn (and cash commitments therefore $100mn given the $10mn in interest expenses). Cash reserves are now assumed to be only $10mn. If the residual risk turns out to be the worst possible, performance is only $75mn and there is a $25mn shortfall relative to the need for liquidity as given by cash commitments. The cash balance, however, is not large enough to absorb this shortfall. Assuming that external financing is not available, the firm has to scale back investment by at least $25mn − $10mn = $15mn (the existing cash covers only a maximum of $10mn out of the cash flow shortfall of $25mn). In this case, Firm ABC has insufficient risk capacity and its ability to retain risk is correspondingly weak.

One way the firm could attempt to boost its capacity to carry risk is to arrange a risk transfer. Assume that it could spend $5mn of its cash to buy risk transfer (e.g. insurance or a put option) that yields a payoff conditional on performance falling below the critical threshold of $100mn given by its cash commitments. The contract could be designed to yield a cash flow that compensates the firm for any cash flow shortfall, but zero in all other scenarios. This risk transfer boosts the available cash precisely in those situations in which the firm has a need for it. By providing conditional liquidity in the scenarios in which the firm needs it for strategy execution, it therefore adds to risk capacity.

There are several takeaways at this point. First, we have identified an important threshold level of performance for the analysis of corporate risk: cash commitments. As we noted in Chapter 7, risk is a function of variability in performance relative crucial thresholds that entail some kind of negative consequence. Cash commitments constitute precisely such a crucial threshold. Second, risk capacity is what determines a firm's ability to meet its cash commitments across a range of scenarios. Existing or conditional sources of cash are what helps it do so even in worse-than-expected scenarios. The alternative is cutting back cash commitments, which often translates into underinvestment. Third, risk transfer is, in principle, a potentially more efficient way of financing risk than keeping cash buffers. This is because a risk transfer can be tailored to match the scenarios in which a cash flow shortfall occurs, whereas a cash buffer sits on the firm's balance sheet in all scenarios, including those where the firm generates sufficient internal cash flow.

Relying on spare borrowing capacity is the source of risk capacity with the poorest 'quality', since it assumes that attractively priced funding will be there as anticipated. In reality, capital markets are fickle and known to suffer breakdowns to the point where they almost come to a halt. At least once per decade there seems to be a severe credit squeeze that can quickly spell trouble for those who were counting on outside financing. So, spare borrowing capacity must be estimated with this kind of refinancing risk in mind, which supports a certain conservatism.

Risk capacity, the ability to ride out cash flow shortfalls, is of course 'nice'. But there is obviously going to be a catch. For it to work, the firm has to be well capitalized at all times, perhaps to the point where it starts to look excessively so to outsiders seeking a return on their investment. A strong balance sheet, which generates risk capacity, comes with its own set of costs. Large cash balances are also known to attract the interest of corporate raiders, who immediately upon getting control use the excess cash to pay a dividend or pay back loans. When the firm uses equity instead of debt it sacrifices the tax shield that debt offers (because interest payments are deductible in the tax income statement whereas dividends to shareholders are not). Using more equity also pushes down the return on equity, a number that many firms pay close attention to. With debt firms can leverage the operating performance and get the same overall return on a smaller equity base – the owners commit less capital and therefore enjoy a larger return on their investment. Cash, for its part, is generally unproductive when it sits idly in the balance sheet. The low return earned on bank deposits and short-term money market instruments pulls down the firm's overall return on assets. If instead returned to shareholders through a dividend, the money could be put to uses that earn higher returns. As always, then, there is a trade-off involved in that risk and return must be balanced.

KEY CHAPTER TAKEAWAYS

- Risk appetite is usually taken to mean a firm's willingness and ability to take risk in pursuit of upside potential.
- Risk appetite ultimately means imposing some kind of limit on risk-taking, that is, it provides an answer to the question of how much risk an organization is willing to tolerate.
- Risk appetite has proven helpful as an 'attention grabber' and bringing the question of risk onto the agendas of the executive team and board of directors.
- Risk appetite has also proven helpful in terms of generating discussions about which risks are good to take (i.e. value creating) and which are not.
- Firms are struggling, however, to embed the concept of risk appetite in management control processes, and there is a startling lack of consistency in how it is applied in practice.
- The concept of risk appetite is inherently vague, and confusion is bound to follow, especially when there is a profusion of aspirational performance targets and an emphasis on multiple stakeholders.
- When risk appetite statements are found, they tend to be arbitrary decision rules that can disconnect risk from any active consideration of upside potential.
- There are concerns that formal and written risk appetite statements in policy documents can make firms more bureaucratic, over-governed, and slower to respond to opportunities.
- For value-maximizing firms risk appetite is hardly ever absolute but relative, meaning that it is conditional on the upside potential of the different decision alternatives at hand.
- According to one view, firms are not even supposed to have a risk appetite, a term that appears to invite a discussion about managerial preferences and 'feelings'.
- Instead, managers should seek to maximize the expected value of performance, which implies a framework of trading costs against benefits without involving any subjective notion of 'appetite'.
- Accordingly, a more realistic approach to decision-making is to trade, in largely monetary terms, any cost of risk management against any reduction in the cost of risk.
- In the setting of strategic risk-taking, the trade-off between risk and reward is instead understood as comparing the increase in upside potential versus an increase in the cost of risk.
- Risk capital is related to the idea of having a buffer of financial resources to deal with potential losses.
- Generally, risk capital increases with the proportion of equity financing (liability side) and the proportion of highly liquid assets (asset side).

- Risk capital can be either economic capital, which targets survival, or risk capacity, which targets survival *and* strategy execution.
- Economic capital absorbs losses that deplete a firm's equity and therefore helps avoid a situation of insolvency.
- Formally, economic capital is the amount of capital (loss-absorbing equity) associated with a certain probability of insolvency.
- Risk capacity absorbs cash flow shortfalls relative to the company's need for liquidity and therefore helps avoid a situation of investing less than is optimal.
- Formally, risk capacity represents the existing and conditional sources of liquidity associated with a certain probability of underinvestment.
- Risk capacity consists of existing cash, spare borrowing capacity, and cash payoffs from risk transfer. These elements help the firm support its cash commitments and execute its business plan optimally.
- Risk capital, while providing a buffer against risk, also comes with costs in the form of lower return on assets and lower return on equity.

CHAPTER 9

Risk Budgeting

A N IMPORTANT SHIFT IN perspective is that of looking at the risk in aggregate performance as opposed to individual risk exposures. In the previous chapters we have taken the view that it is desirable to understand the risk that critical thresholds of performance are breached. This perspective means that we have to think about how the various risk exposures combine to create variability in the firm's performance, and how far we currently are from these thresholds. What is called for is a framework capable of showing the firm's performance in relation to the critical thresholds under a multitude of different scenarios. Once in place, management can use such a framework for a proactive risk assessment of various corporate policies.

It is at this conjuncture that most enterprise risk management (ERM) programmes fall short. The risk register, the key output of such programmes, actually has not been designed to produce answers regarding the firm's aggregate risk. Questions like 'What is the risk of the firm as a whole?' cannot be answered by the register. As we shall see, mending the risk register for this purpose is not realistic either. Despite bringing so many risks under the corporate umbrella, it remains primarily a tool for focusing attention on the firm's main risks, a centrepiece of its risk governance.

To make progress on aggregate risk, we need to change tack altogether. We need an approach that is specifically designed to deal with risk aggregation. Risk budgeting, the focus of this chapter, is such an approach. It takes a bigger-picture view on a firm's performance and risk, targeting not individual exposures but the risk of the firm as a whole. Crucially, it fits well into the decision-making processes of most firms because it builds on financial numbers long used by management to run the firm. Risk budgeting aims to generate a description of risk and return as it is under current policies and how that would look if a new policy were to be implemented. The ultimate goal is a proactive assessment of risk and return and the way it changes depending on which policy gets implemented. A wide range of corporate policies are covered within risk budgeting, including acquisitions, investments, capital structure, and hedging.

Risk budgeting analyses risk based on the firm's forecasted financial statements and any financial ratios derived from them. It is risk viewed through the lens of the firm's financial numbers: cash flow, net income, cash, debt-to-equity ratio, and so on (Alviniussen and Jankensgård, 2009). Most businesspeople accept the premise of expressing risk this way because the financial numbers are, at the end of the day, how the firm is judged. A company lives by the cash flows it is able to generate and keeps investors content by delivering a certain profitability and dividends. Its ability to fund the business depends on having a balance sheet that is in good shape. Because it corresponds well to the reality that most managers live with on a daily basis, it is not hard to find meaningful ways to frame a firm's risk in terms of its financial performance.

RISK BUDGETING AND QUANTITATIVE MODELS

Risk budgeting can only happen if there is a quantitative model to support the effort. The model must be able to correctly show the firm's financials across a large number of scenarios that might happen. Even in a stress test – that is, the worst-case scenario – the model must be able to indicate the firm's financial position realistically. Key to achieving this level of accuracy is that the model has considerable **accounting integrity**, that is, it is set up so that the various lines in the model hang together from an accounting point of view. Essentially, the model should, all the way through, be consistent with whatever generally accepted accounting principles that the firm adheres to (e.g. IFRS or US GAAP.)

But accounting integrity is not enough. The model must also be equipped with the right kind of **analytical integrity**. This refers to the relation between the different parts of the model, or how one part (e.g. operating expenses) is likely to respond to changes in another (e.g. revenue). Without correct dynamics, the model will be unable to represent the firm realistically and therefore not be a trustworthy companion in decision-making.

Risk budgeting uses performance thresholds as part of this analysis of financial performance. As noted, aggregate risk can be conceptualized as failures to meet critical thresholds. A firm can thus get a handle on its risk profile by analysing the **distance to thresholds**, and how severe a scenario would have to get before the threshold is breached. So, these thresholds are inserted into the model, thereby providing reference points for creating risk events, that is, indicators that flag up when a breach has occurred. Risk budgeting also puts into practice ideas related to risk capital. Because the analysis takes place in a financial setting, it is possible to quantify the elements that make up the firm's risk capacity. Since the goal is to describe the risk of the organization as a whole it is quite necessary to have a solid understanding of its risk capacity.

Then there is the performance itself. Clearly, looking forward there will be variability in performance because of exposure to various risks and contingencies. Performance uncertainty must somehow be incorporated into the analysis. Here two options are available, depending on the firm's level of ambition. The first is using **scenario analysis**. Many of the most important insights can indeed be teased out by a sensible application of various scenarios. Each scenario, such as a recession in the economy or a breakthrough in R&D, implies a different outcome for the firm's performance. **Stress-testing**, that is, the worst-case scenario, is an indispensable tool for understanding the financial robustness of the firm. The second option is to continue to do scenario analysis but, in addition, apply **Monte Carlo simulation**. This is an approach in which risk factors are modelled statistically and linked to corporate performance. As a result, it now becomes possible to simulate thousands of outcomes for the firm's performance. Effectively, the scenarios are automated and weighted by their respective probability of occurring. The forecasted performance thereby becomes risk adjusted, which means that we can obtain probability distributions for any output in the financial statements. It also becomes possible to derive quantitative measures of risk. For example, one can create measures that convey the probability of underinvestment or financial distress. Risk measures like these offer a concrete summary of the risk of the firm as a whole.

Many firms hesitate to take the step of addressing aggregate risk through any form of quantification. They are content with the lower-hanging fruits of risk awareness and risk governance. To these managers, the discussions that follow from mapping risks and having risk explicitly on the agenda are benefits enough. This is a totally respectable conclusion for firms that do not wish to spend resources in pursuit of something they perceive as being too complicated. In these firms, once the board has signed off on the list of identified risks and the actions in place to mitigate them, the job is done.

But the reluctance to pursue a more financial approach is also one of the reasons that the impact of ERM remains somewhat limited in some firms. There is a general failure to connect with the company's financial situation, expressed in terms of the numbers that appear in the financial statements (or ratios based on them). This happens to be the lens through which large parts of the organization view the world and communicate with it. The financial performance numbers attract huge amounts of attention from analysts, investors, and the business press. Naturally, they command the attention of managers as well, who are used to using budgets and financial forecasts as ways to gauge how the firm is doing. The planning, treasury, tax, and accounting departments all use these numbers to analyse and assess. When ERM fails to integrate into this world, the predictable result is a certain lack of impact. Financial performance is the language of the business world, but ERM does not speak it!

Our view is that the benefits of risk budgeting are considerable. It should, alongside the risk register, constitute the second of two visible outputs from an ERM effort. It will significantly enlarge the scope of risk analysis and the usefulness of ERM to the executive team and board of directors. We feel confident in predicting that almost any firm stands to benefit from the kind of decision support that risk budgeting can provide. Being able to execute scenario analysis well, and stress-testing in particular, is a crucial competence in risk management. And this activity, to be credible, must take place in a framework that has sufficient accounting and analytical integrity. A more financial approach furthermore brings rigour and discipline to the risk management process. The complexity of the subject matter is such that a financial model with enough integrity is the only realistic alternative. Few individuals, regardless of experience or skill level, can keep all these dynamics in his or her head to arrive at unbiased conclusions.

Risk budgeting generates a whole range of new discussions, which so often is the real benefit of a decision support tool. As we shall see, it brings attention to some very important determinants of corporate risk like operating leverage, flexibility, and natural hedges that otherwise tend to get ignored in many ERM programmes. It also leads the discussion towards the concept of a buffer against risk in a natural way: What is really our capacity to deal with downside risk, and should we do anything about it?

FINANCIAL MODELS WITH ACCOUNTING AND ANALYTICAL INTEGRITY

Of course, nearly all firms operate some sort of financial model already to help them navigate. What distinguishes risk budgeting from a traditional financial model is the degree of accounting and analytical integrity; how knowledge of risk gets incorporated; and the way it is capable of showing a firm's risk-return profile as a function of proposed changes in corporate policy. As noted, the goal of risk budgeting is to get a grip on the risk of the firm as a whole, and how that is affected by strategic decisions by the executive team and board of directors. A fully developed risk budgeting model effectively replaces the existing financial model and other decision support tools dealing with analyses related to the consolidated budget. It is a comprehensive, best-practice model for making financial forecasts, so it performs all the functions of a traditional model. However, it also adds a layer of features that considerably enhance the functionality and credibility of the model, especially with respect to risk analysis.

Starting with accounting integrity, this refers to the fact that the model, to a large extent, follows the same accounting principles that the firm applies in its actual financial reporting. If the firm follows IFRS, for instance, the financial statements in the model would be set up to mimic how different accounts are related to each other in these standards. For example, any change in an asset or liability that is accounted for using fair value through profit and loss would be shown in the net income statement as a gain or loss. Another important aspect is that the model self-balances. This essentially means that any forecasted cash flow, profit, or loss has the correct and logical impact on the balance sheet. That is, the balance sheet adjusts in the appropriate way to all the 'events' that take place in the forecast. For example, if an impairment of some asset in the PPE (plant, property, and equipment) category is predicted, then this amount is shown as a loss in the net income statement. The forecast of PPE is correspondingly reduced by the same amount. Since it is a non-cash event, the cash flow statement is instructed to show no impact from the event. By correctly reflecting actual accounting principles, the integrity of the model is preserved and it balances at all times. There is therefore no need for a so-called 'plug', an all too common mechanism in spreadsheet models around the world. The plug effectively forces the model to balance, thus absorbing all the errors or inconsistencies in the forecasts. In risk budgeting, the model balances by design, never leaving any unexplained residual. This accounting integrity enables a much higher confidence in the model's outputs, not least when used for stress-testing.

The first step in risk budgeting is therefore to make sure that the model has sufficient accounting integrity. The second step is to make sure that the analytical integrity is equally high. What is the difference between accounting and analytical integrity? Consider that from an accounting point of view, it is correct to obtain operating profits by deducting cost of sales and operating expenses from revenue. This relationship implies accounting integrity. Analytical integrity, in contrast, concerns the way cost of sales and operating expenses *respond* to a change in revenue. Let us say we assume an increase in revenue. How should the line cost of sales be instructed to respond to this change? One way is to set up a rule that cost of sales is always a certain percentage of revenue, for example, the historical average of that ratio. This will have a dampening effect on risk, as cost of sales is assumed to immediately and fully adjust to revenue. The opposite assumption would be to just hard-code the forecast of cost of sale, so that it does not respond at all to changes in revenue. This will have an amplifying effect on risk, as it indicates maximum **operating leverage**, that is to say, costs are fixed and do not vary with revenue.

From a risk point of view, it matters very much whether costs are fixed or variable. We have to choose our assumptions carefully if we want the model to depict performance in a realistic way across different scenarios. This kind of analytical integrity is essential for understanding the risk profile of the firm, but often gets much too little consideration in practice. Leaving cost of sales independent of revenue, for example, is likely to be a very poor assumption because most likely some of the revenue growth is driven by a higher volume of business (i.e. an increase in the number of units sold). When the number of units sold goes up, it would not be logical to leave cost of sales unchanged. In risk budgeting, these dynamics are given careful thought.

To implement risk budgeting, we proceed line by line to ensure analytical integrity throughout the model. After cost of sales one would typically ask how operating expenses behave with respect to changes in revenue. Sales, general, and administrative expenses (SGA) are of a different nature compared to cost of sales. They are normally not as sensitive to the volume of business, being instead fixed to a larger degree. Any firm has a certain infrastructure in place to support its business activities, and these costs tend to be allocated to one of its SGA lines. But of course, in the longer run, or in severe enough scenarios, few costs are truly fixed. Leaving potential cost efficiency improvements over time aside, we can note that if there is a change in the volume of business that looks to be permanent, the cost structure is likely to change as the firm adapts to a new reality. So, there will be links to revenue here as well, except that they may not be as automatic and quick to happen as with variable costs. It may be helpful to think in terms of trigger points where something happens that alters the level of SGA. From a risk perspective, a particularly interesting dynamic is the possibility of exiting certain costs if things get bad enough. This is related to the general risk management strategy of **flexibility**. Stated very plainly, the more flexible you are, and the more easily you can adjust to changing circumstances, the less risk you have. Flexibility means that you can make an exit from what has become an unattractive position. In risk budgeting, one therefore tries to identify sources of flexibility as well as the circumstances in which that flexibility would be exercised. For example, if revenue falls low enough, it may be warranted to make an exit from certain costs that can no longer be justified. The model could therefore contain a rule such that if revenue drops by more than 20%, SGA is reduced by 10%. This kind of decision rule, just like sensible assumptions about operating leverage, can greatly enhance the analytical integrity of the model.

Operating leverage and flexibility are important determinants of risk and are given full attention in risk budgeting. Another very general risk management strategy concerns **natural hedges**. These too would be mapped out and described to better understand the scope for variability in the firm's performance. A 'natural hedge', in our usage of the term, refers to an exposure on a cost item that fully or partially off-sets an exposure on revenue. Assume that we have concluded that revenue tends to fall when a certain risk factor goes up. But if the same increase in the risk factor simultaneously reduces the firm's costs, a natural hedge is at work. Obviously, natural hedges have a dampening effect on risk. One example of a natural hedge that we have already discussed is when a firm generates sales in foreign currency but at the same time has some costs in that currency, perhaps because it has a sales organization in that country or purchases some materials from it.

An often overlooked natural hedge is the way the firm's investment opportunities are driven by the same factors that cause changes in revenue. This idea was explored by Froot, Scharfstein, and Stein (1993). They argue that an oil firm has lower risk than one would be led to believe by looking at the highly volatile price of oil. The oil price fluctuates substantially, yes, but the key is to see that its investment opportunities also depend on that price. When the oil price is low, some investment projects will no longer be economical and can therefore be put on hold. Fewer projects that need funding effectively reduces the firm's need for liquidity, which means that scenarios with low revenue and low need for liquidity tend to coincide. Compare this to the car industry. They are in the midst of a very expensive long-term transformation into electric cars, which requires substantial capital expenditure. The need to fund this transformation is relatively unaffected by temporary swings in the business cycle. If the firm is to stay competitive, it cannot fall behind its competitors by underspending on investment. Therefore, low revenue states are not off-set by a matching decrease in the need for liquidity. Car manufacturers therefore have less of a natural hedge than oil firms (though they also have lower revenue volatility). To capture this dimension, the recommendation is to map out to what extent the company's investment opportunities depend on the same risk factors as do revenue. Equipped with some information about this relationship, simple rules of thumb can be incorporated into the model so that forecasted capital expenditures respond accordingly to changes in revenue. In this way the analytical integrity of the model is strengthened even further, and our assessment of downside risk becomes more accurate.

PERFORMANCE-aT-RISK

Risk budgeting thus proceeds by adding assumptions about operating leverage, flexibility, and natural hedges to the model, hence ensuring a high level of analytical integrity. Combined with the accounting integrity already installed, this adds up to a reliable tool for assessing, by means of scenario analysis, the risk of the firm as a whole. Regardless of which scenario is assumed, the model will, thanks to the dynamics in place, yield forecasts that are consistent and realistic.

Scenarios are highly useful for gaining insights about risk and return. Some of these are quite unlikely to happen, whereas others are more plausible. As we know from our earlier discussions, the probability of an event does matter – simply looking at the size of the impact alone can exaggerate its economic importance if the probability is low. This is true also for aggregate risk. So, is there any way we can summarize the firm's overall risk into a single measure that reflects each scenario's likelihood of happening? What we would like to have is a way to describe how the various risk factors the firm is exposed to affect it *on a joint basis*. We want to know to what extent they collectively put the firm's performance at risk, as opposed to looking at the individual impact of each risk factor.

Answering questions like these would appear to be a straightforward task given that we have so much information compiled about risk in the risk register. It might seem like the data points in it are the perfect building blocks for risk analytics of this kind. After all, they are reported in terms of probability and impact, which can be used for modelling purposes. There are several reasons why this approach is unlikely to work, however. One reason is that, as discussed in Chapter 6, the data points are, in nearly all cases, just a single representative estimate of the risk, whereas usually the risk factor can take on many different values, each with its own probability.

But the chief reason we cannot rely on the risk register for estimating aggregate risk is that the risks in it do not add up to 100% of the variability in performance. As noted, the goal of the register was never to build up something that explains *all* the variability in performance. Its real purpose is risk governance. It is basically a tool for compiling risks that need managerial attention. Quite often, the biggest explanatory factor for variability in revenue is not one of the risks in the register. Rather, variability is mostly driven by fluctuations in the demand for the firm's products and the average price achieved on those sales. Demand uncertainty, however, rarely features in risk registers as a risk factor in its own right. Many risks in the register are indirectly related to it, like reputation risk. One of the implications of an impaired reputation would be precisely that customers shy away from the company's products, leading to a drop in sales. Therefore, it contributes to revenue uncertainty, and so will other risk factors in the register. But nonetheless, these risk factors do not capture the overall magnitude of variability in revenue we can expect over a given time horizon, which is the reason why we recommend targeting revenue variability directly, focusing primarily on patterns in quantity and price over time.

The basic problem from an analytical standpoint is that the risk register is essentially only a snapshot of currently known risks. It falls short of telling us anything about the overall variability in performance we can expect. Being essentially a list, it does not contain the necessary information about how these risks could interact to produce a certain outcome. The key issue here is, as we have seen, that risks are inter-dependent and co-vary with each other in ways that are important. We have already used reputation risk as an example. This risk is typically triggered when one or more of the other risks in the register have already occurred, so it is not an independent risk. But many other types of covariations are possible. For example, oil firms in smaller countries typically find that their home currency exchange rate fluctuates substantially with the oil price, which is priced in US dollars. When the oil price goes down, the home currency tends to weaken against the dollar, which makes the home currency value of each dollar in oil sales go up. Because of this correlation between the oil price and the exchange rate, their revenue measured in home currency is less volatile than what the oil price measured in US dollars would suggest. Since they have most of their cost base in home currency, this fact matters. A risk analysis that ignores covariations is therefore incomplete.

As a complement to scenario analysis, in risk budgeting one has the option of modelling performance-at-risk using statistical methods. Doing so means taking the probability of each scenario into account, such that a probability distribution for performance is generated. This means going the extra mile and investing in capabilities to carry out simulations, which effectively automatizes the scenario analysis. One runs thousands of scenarios taking into account the correlations and co-dependencies between the risk factors included in the analysis. When simulations are performed, one obtains a probability distribution for any line in the forecast financial statements as well as for the financial ratios based on them. Based on such probability distributions one can create any number of quantitative risk measures. Cash-flow-at-risk and earnings-at-risk are two examples of such risk measures that have been used in practice. They indicate the maximum loss, relative to the forecast, that can be experienced with a certain probability. If cash-flow-at-risk with a 95% confidence interval is $200mn, for example, this tells us that we believe that there is a 5% probability that cash flow goes lower than its forecast level by an amount larger than $200mn.

The basic approach for estimating performance-at-risk is to infer volatility from historical data, complemented with managements' subjective assessments of probabilities where needed. It is beyond the scope of this book to go into details about how these methods work. However, to provide a stylized illustration, Figure 9.1 contains a traditional budget for a fictional ice cream vendor, complemented with information regarding two of the firm's main risk factors. Its revenue has been found to be a function of how much it rains during a summer. More rain means less revenue, so the amount of precipitation in the summer months can be viewed as a risk factor. Cost of sales, in contrast, is driven primarily by the price of milk. Based on the historical patterns of precipitation and the milk price, the ice cream vendor can anticipate the range of outcomes for its gross profit and the probability associated with each outcome in that range.

Using simulation methodology, this information can be incorporated into the forecasts. Figure 9.2 contains outcome distributions for the revenue, cost of sales, and gross profit, based on which a variety of risk measures can be created. Figure 9.3 compares a traditional corporate budget with the risk-adjusted one. The risk-adjusted budget is lower than the traditional one because there is more downside risk than upside potential in this ice cream vendor's performance – that is, the risks are skewed to the downside. This happens because the negative deviations from the budget are larger and/or have higher probability than the corresponding better-than-expected scenarios.

Revenue risk: Rainy summer

	Probability	Impact
Above average precipitation	15%	(40,000)
High precipitation	5%	(200,000)
Below average precipitation	5%	10,000
Low precipitation	2%	30,000
Base case	73%	0

Cost of sales risk: Milk price uncertainty

	Probability	Impact
Small increase	20%	(20,000)
Large increase	10%	(60,000)
Small decrease	10%	20,000
Large decrease	5%	40,000
Base case	55%	0

Ice Cream United

Traditional budget

	2010	2011	2012
Revenue	500,000	-	-
Cost of Sales	(400,000)	-	-
Depreciation	-	-	-
Selling & Adm	-	-	-
General exp	-	-	-
R&D	-	-	-
Other inc (exp)	-	-	-
Share P/L	-	-	-
EBIT	**100,000**	-	-

FIGURE 9.1 Traditional budget and risk factors

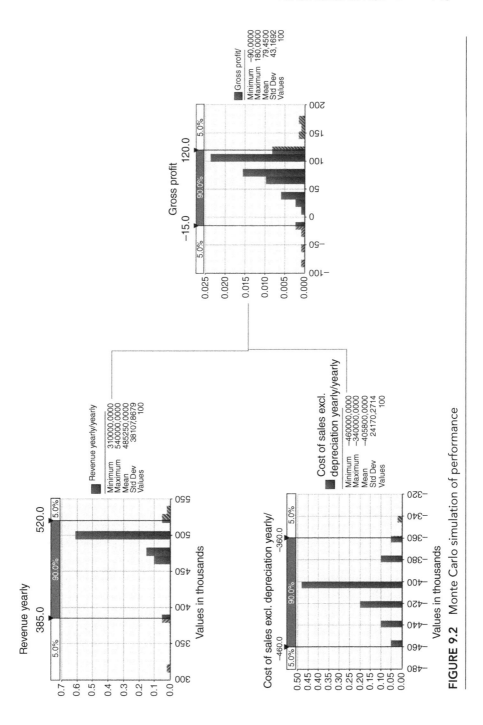

FIGURE 9.2 Monte Carlo simulation of performance

Traditional budget

	2010	2011	2012
Revenue	500,000	-	-
Cost of Sales	(400,000)	-	-
Depreciation	-	-	-
Selling & Adm	-	-	-
General exp	-	-	-
R&D	-	-	-
Other inc (exp)	-	-	-
Share P/L	-	-	-
EBIT	**100,000**	-	-

Risk-adjusted budget

	2010	2011	2012
Revenue	485,250	-	-
Cost of Sales	(405,800)	-	-
Depreciation	-	-	-
Selling & Adm	-	-	-
General exp	-	-	-
R&D	-	-	-
Other inc (exp)	-	-	-
Share P/L	-	-	-
EBIT	**79,450**	-	-

FIGURE 9.3   Traditional versus risk-adjusted budget

 INTRODUCING CRITICAL THRESHOLDS

The goal of risk budgeting is to gauge the risk of the firm as a whole and how that changes as a result of corporate policies. Risk can be assessed using either scenario analysis and/or simulation methods. But in order to better understand aggregate risk we need some kind of reference point that signals that a risky outcome has occurred. We have argued that these reference points are about identifying critical thresholds of performance where costly consequences start kicking in. Risk budgeting is the place where such thresholds can be monitored in practice. Supported as it is by a model with a high level of accounting and analytical integrity, it can keep track, in any scenario, of the distance to these thresholds and indicate whether one has been breached or not.

In risk budgeting the model would be programmed to treat shortfalls relative to the identified thresholds as a risky outcome, or a 'risk event'. That is, whenever the threshold is reached the model signals that a breach has occurred. When combined with scenario analysis, the firm can gauge its aggregate risk by a **distance-to-threshold analysis** (DTA). In the DTA it is first observed how far the firm is from breaching its thresholds given the base case forecast and the current set of policies. Then various scenarios are investigated to establish what kind of situation it would take for a breach to occur. How far would revenue have to fall or costs increase to put the firm in a problematic situation? Again, because of the accounting and analytical integrity of the model, this can be evaluated with a fair amount of precision. If it is found that the firm experiences a breach only in very severe stress-tests, its managers might conclude that aggregate risk is fairly moderate. If shortfalls occur for even relatively mild scenarios that are quite likely to happen the risk is obviously higher. The DTA can be performed again after a new corporate policy has been assumed, for example a large extra dividend. It might be found that, if the policy were to be implemented, the firm would suffer breaches of the critical thresholds much more easily and in scenarios that are not at all unlikely. A reasonable conclusion in this situation might be that the policy would bring the firm too close to its critical thresholds and that it is best to reject it.

The Monte Carlo approach opens up new possibilities for describing aggregate risk. It is now possible to construct risk measures that target the probability of breaching the critical thresholds. The model might report, for example, a 14% probability of falling below a key financial covenant. If 10,000 simulations have been run, this implies that the model registered a breach in 1,400 of them. Other risk statistics are possible too. Cash-flow-at-risk and earnings-at-risk have already been mentioned. Expected shortfall is another important risk measure because it takes the size of the shortfalls into account, which is not the case with a mere probability. It represents the probability-weighted shortfall relative the threshold conditional on a breach having occurred. So, there are many ways to construe aggregate risk within a simulation framework that builds on the firm's own assessment of at what levels of performance it would get into trouble.

Because risk budgeting takes place in a financial setting, all the elements of risk capacity can readily be incorporated into the analysis: cash, spare borrowing capacity, and risk transfer payoffs. The DTA analysis is in fact closely linked to an analysis of a firm's risk capacity. As previously discussed, the most subjective and hard to define of the three is spare borrowing capacity. However, some of the critical thresholds that have been identified are pretty good ways of putting this concept into practice. It might be assumed, for example, that the firm has some scope to use debt up to the point where a covenant is in danger of being breached, but not beyond that. In other cases, the unused portion of a credit facility might be how a firm's borrowing capacity is best understood. In others still, it might be assumed that the firm is effectively credit rationed and that there is no room whatsoever for adding debt. However spare borrowing capacity is construed, the chosen limit can be easily implemented in the model.

Risk capacity is primarily to be considered when one specific threshold is evaluated, namely that given by the firm's cash commitments. When internal cash flow falls below this threshold, the firm must have risk capacity to avoid cutting back on its cash outflows. Since capital expenditure is usually the first to be considered for cutbacks, we have argued that this situation can be characterized as underinvestment (investing less than the optimal level). This occurs when the firm's cash flow is below cash commitments *and* its risk capacity is exhausted. A simulation approach means that the probability of this scenario can be estimated. Such a measure can therefore be interpreted as the probability of underinvestment. Financial distress probabilities can be obtained as well if the firm defines a situation that can be assumed to trigger even more serious consequences. For example, this could refer to a situation in which the firm's cash flow is insufficient to cover interest payments *and* its risk capacity is depleted.

Bottom line: the firm can create a host of risk measures, each targeting a different aspect of downside risk. Taken together, they describe a firm's risk profile, or its downside risk, both as it currently stands and how it is liable to change as a result of corporate policies. The goal of risk budgeting – expressing the risk of the firm as a whole and connecting that to decision-making – has been achieved.

Risk budgeting is what practically bridges the risk analysis of the firm's operating performance with its capital management, that is, its balance sheet. It offers concrete decision support on the question of how to balance the company's business risk with an appropriate buffer for risk. As has been made clear in earlier chapters of the book, risk transfer and risk retention are closely related, and we have also seen that a firm's ability to retain risk is a function of its risk capacity. While managers are intuitively aware of these relationships, all too rarely are they implemented in a model framework with enough accounting and analytical integrity to be a trustworthy guide to decision-making.

One of the authors (Jankensgård) was involved with a firm that at one point wanted to increase its dividend. Another group within the organization was pushing for a large increase in capital expenditure. At the same time, the price of one of the firm's main products had been trending down recently. Through risk budgeting, it could be shown that the combined effect of these changes would have been a substantial increase in the firm's aggregate risk in the sense of reducing the distance to critical performance thresholds that could threaten the firm's strategy and survival. This was in no way obvious to the firm's decision-makers because of the complexity involved in understanding the joint impact of these events and policies. As a result of the before-and-after view of the firm's risk profile, the executives reconsidered their policies and chose one that implied a more moderate increase in the risk.

KEY CHAPTER TAKEAWAYS

▪ The goal of risk budgeting is to understand the risk of the firm as a whole – and how that is affected by corporate policies.

▪ Risk budgeting means looking at risk through the lens of the firm's financial statement forecasts and any financial ratios derived from them.

▪ Risk budgeting has the advantage of using the language of financial statements, which executives can relate to and care about.

▪ Risk budgeting sets out to describe the firm's performance-at-risk, that is, the overall variability in cash flow, net income, and other financial parameters.

▪ Risk budgeting allows managers to proactively assess a firm's risk-return profile under different combinations of scenarios and policies.

▪ In risk budgeting, risk is a function of the distance to threshold: the closer to critical thresholds, the higher the risk.

▪ The DTA framework indicates if a policy brings the firm closer to a threshold breach (risk increases) or further away from it (risk decreases).

▪ A model used to support risk budgeting is distinguished by accounting integrity, analytical integrity, critical thresholds of performance, and risk-adjusted financial forecasts.

▪ Accounting integrity means that the model correctly reflects the accounting standards that the firm follows, and that the model self-balances – that is, there is no need for an unexplained residual, the so-called 'plug'.

▪ Analytical integrity means that the cost structure in the model responds realistically to changes in revenue given what we know about operating leverage, flexibility, and natural hedges.

▪ Operating leverage is the fraction of variable costs to fixed costs and is an important determinant of corporate risk.

▪ Flexibility is a highly general risk management strategy: the easier one can adjust to changing circumstances, the lower the risk.

▪ The high level of consistency means that a risk budgeting model is ideally suited for scenario analysis and in particular stress-tests of the firm's performance.

▪ In risk budgeting, one can opt to use the knowledge available on risk to implement Monte Carlo simulation, in which case forecasts become risk-adjusted.

▪ Simulations allow the firm to quantify financial distress probabilities and other risk measures.

CHAPTER 10

Risk Strategy

ONE OF THE MOST talked about things in the risk management community is how enterprise risk management (ERM) can become more 'strategic'. There is a belief, desire even, among many of its proponents that ERM should take place in a strategic setting and contribute towards decision-making at the top level of the firm. Strategic risk management is in fact frequently touted as the next 'frontier' in ERM. To emphasize the message, it is often pointed out that most firms that suffer major declines in their market value do so due to strategic risks, as opposed to operational and financial ones. Despite this fact, the argument continues, it is the latter two that get the most attention by corporations.

Unfortunately, few ERM initiatives today have reached what anyone would call a strategic level. We can exemplify this point using acquisitions, events that are as strategic as they come. They are bold bets by the executive team that they can make money by taking control of an existing firm and doing things in a superior way. Most acquisitions promise a combination of cost-cutting and revenue synergies, for example, in terms of expanding internationally or broadening the product offering. It is not rare that a firm buys a direct competitor, thereby changing the competitive dynamics of the industry. Not only are acquisitions highly strategic, they are also very risky. Acquisitions are notorious for their high failure rates, often delivering poor results and destroying rather than creating value. This can happen for various reasons, such as overpaying, poor post-acquisition integration, or simply bad timing. To a fair degree, acquisitions are 'macro-plays' in the sense that their success depends more than anything on how the business cycle develops from that point on. Additionally, unless fully financed by stock, acquisitions mean using significant amounts of cash or debt, which increases risk. This point was illustrated by the collapse of the travel firm Thomas Cook in 2019, whose misfortunes were driven in part by unsustainable debt incurred through a series of acquisitions.

Despite the often very significant impact on aggregate risk from acquisitions, it is the exception rather than the rule that the ERM function is asked to do an assessment of the risks involved. In this chapter we reflect on this fact and its causes. We explore the various ways ERM could be more strategic and point to some ways to make progress. When an ERM programme starts out, the main goals are mapping risks and creating basic risk awareness. If it proves its worth in those initial stages, it gradually deepens its impact on governance and culture, permeating ever more aspects of the firm's decision-making process. If successfully embedded in a strategic context, ERM will have reached the final stage in the journey.

STRATEGY PERFORMANCE

A common way to conceptualize strategic risk is in terms of threats that lead to a strategy not being able to meet its goals. As if it was not enough that risk is an elusive and subjective term, strategy also can be understood in many ways. The exact definition of corporate strategy continues to generate controversy in a debate that may never be fully resolved. For our purposes, a strategy is simply an idea about how the firm intends to create value for its customers and shareholders. Strategy, in this perspective, is basically a value proposition: In the competitive landscape that we observe, how can we deliver value to customers and monetize some of that value for our shareholders? The answer to that question is with a firm's strategy.

Obviously, again we run into some thorny issues related to the fact that firms might have a broader mission that encompasses goals beyond shareholder value creation. Having multiple objectives and a broader scorecard is fine, and an overly direct pursuit of shareholder value can be counterproductive. But it remains true that an overarching goal remains creating value for shareholders, and we will take it for granted that this is what a strategy aims to do. Creating a café that is adored by customers and enhances the quality of life of the town's citizens may be a strategy for life fulfilment if money is no issue. Setting up such a café in a way that it also runs profitably is a corporate strategy.

Defining strategy is one thing, but to assess the potential for ERM to be strategic we also must have a clear picture of what it is that ERM brings to the table. Additionally, ERM can mean different things to different people, so we have to be precise. The impact of ERM on strategy is bound to be modest if it merely consists of an internal survey of risks that is compiled for the board of directors to look at. But as we hope to have illustrated in this book, ERM can be much more than that. It can be a comprehensive effort at identifying all material risks and devising optimal risk responses from the firm's point of view. In the process of doing so, ERM eliminates various forms of inefficiencies caused by a lack of relevant information and silo incentives. As a result, the firm can expect to become more resilient and less vulnerable. By eliminating cases of over-management and undermanagement of risk, ERM also raises the expected level of cash flow and creates value. If ERM reaches this level of impact it can justifiably be said to improve **strategy performance** and the resilience of the strategy. To clarify this point, a strategy is designed to perform. If ERM boosts this performance and makes it more stable, there is a sense in which it can already be said to be strategic.

The issue of ERM and strategy performance has another dimension, which goes back to the fact that many different scenarios can unfold from the point we are at today. A strategy must be able to perform well in all those possible states of the world, not just the one that we expect to happen. Some of those scenarios will involve decidedly negative outcomes, which will send the firm's aggregate risk higher. The observation that we will expand on here is that when aggregate risk gets too high it can cause a strategy to underperform, a point we mentioned briefly in Chapter 7. A stakeholder risk premium translates into difficulties in doing business, making it harder for the firm to execute its strategy. Airlines are a useful example of this. When the word gets around that the firm might be on the ropes, people will hesitate to book their tickets with that firm. The mere threat of the flight being cancelled because the firm might cease its operations can be enough to make them think twice. Such risk-averse behaviour on part of would-be travellers of course exacerbates the firm's plight, so its strategy performs even worse. In some cases, it gets to the point where the firm no longer has credibility even with suppliers and other business partners. In an extreme case of stakeholder risk premium, in 2020 it was reported that staff of Norwegian Air Shuttle, a troubled low-cost carrier, were even denied credit for a hotel room for fear that the firm might not be able to pay the bill.

Basically, the firm's future survival must not be in doubt for the strategy to work optimally. This is a logic that banks are all too familiar with. Doubts about survival can escalate to the point where a run on the bank is triggered, which is when panicked customers rush to collect their deposits to get them out of the bank before it collapses. Obviously, this becomes self-fulfilling and leaves the bank unable to function, that is to say, there is a complete breakdown of its strategy. Basically, any business model that in some way relies on the firm being around to honour its commitments and service its products will be sensitive to rumours of impending doom.

ERM can help bring attention to scenarios involving a dangerously high build-up of aggregate risk. If such scenarios are detected in plenty of time and placed on the agenda, pre-emptive actions can be taken to avoid aggregate risk growing to the point where it starts to affect the ability to do business. Again, in such a case it could be claimed that ERM improves the strategy's performance. In this case, however, it is not the strategy's *forecast* performance under business as usual that gets better. Rather, it is how the strategy performs in scenarios that are *worse-than-expected* that improves. But this too increases firm value. The better a strategy is expected to perform over a wide range of scenarios, the higher the price someone would be willing to pay for the firm.

One way that ERM can play this role is by exploiting the knowledge contained in the risk register for developing rich and credible scenarios. However, since the register has not been developed to describe aggregate risk in financial terms, there is a gap in its ability to identify scenarios that imply financial distress. The stakeholder risk premium starts materializing in scenarios where the firm's survival is questioned, which often is a question of a weak financial position. Risk budgeting, in contrast, is the ideal framework for investigating the financial consequences of scenarios, and for identifying threshold levels of performance associated with distress. That is, managers can think about what kind of circumstances would qualify as a financially distressed situation and implement those thresholds in the model. The model will then keep track of how different combinations of scenarios and policies move the firm either closer or further from the distress threshold where the stakeholder risk premium would rise to problematic levels.

STRATEGY FORMULATION AND SELECTION

Protecting and enhancing the performance of the strategy in place may not be enough for the more ambitious proponents of strategic ERM. An even bigger prize would be if ERM could be said to help decide which strategy is implemented. The process of deciding which strategy is to be undertaken out of the available alternatives is called **strategy selection**. At an even deeper level,

ERM would contribute to **strategy formulation** rather than coming in at a later stage and evaluating the consequences of fully baked strategies. Strategy formulation is when important elements of the strategy are decided and put together into a coherent whole.

New strategies are usually not formulated out of the blue, except perhaps for start-ups. They are often better thought of as extensions and modifications of the existing strategy. Essentially, a strategy frequently needs to change, as the world around the firm changes. Common examples are actions like extending the product line and entering new geographical markets. At any given time more than one plausible course of action is available, so management needs certain criteria for deciding which option is the best. Since it is assumed in this book that the overarching goal is value, the strategy that should be selected is the one that offers the best potential for value creation. Creating value, as we all know, has a lot to do with trading off risk against return, so risk must be part of the picture when different alternatives are compared. Looking at only the expected (hoped for) performance and ignoring the risk of a strategy would be perilous.

Since strategy formulation and selection involves assessing the risks inherent in each strategy, it would seem logical that this is where ERM can contribute. However, some will counter and say that strategy was always about risk and return. In fact, strategy could be viewed as risk and return in its purest form. Businesspeople have always searched for opportunities, well aware that there is risk involved.

Will demand for the product materialize?
Will we be able to deliver our products safely and on time?
Will there emerge tough competition?

These kinds of questions have always been at the forefront of decision-making in business. While the quality of the assessments can certainly vary, it is at least the kind of thing any businessperson worth their salt should be asking before launching the firm in a new direction.

If devising new strategies was always about trading risk against return, it is not immediately clear how ERM can play a constructive role. There are no obvious organizational frictions that ERM can be said to tear down, like in the case of silos leading to suboptimal risk management for the firm as a whole. Strategy, one might argue, is just the executive management doing what they have always been doing: trying to come up with smart ways to make money, which almost by definition is risky.

A possible response to such arguments could be to argue that the risk mapping that has taken place in ERM produces benefits in that it facilitates and improves the executives' work. That is, it helps them evaluate the risk and return associated with different strategies and do a better job of it. By closing the risk information gap, ERM makes it easier to make the trade-off between risk and return that goes on also in strategy selection. Some of the identified risks in the register may have a direct bearing on one or more proposed strategies. The work done on supply chain risk, for example, might lead to a better grasp of the mechanisms that trigger it and the damage that could be experienced. One of the strategies may, in light of this knowledge, be found to lead to a heightened risk of the firm's supply chain being adversely affected. This will of course count as a negative and change the perception of the value of the strategy, raising the bar for it to get chosen. So, it is not implausible that the knowledge gained in the ERM-process could be put to work when evaluating strategies.

Besides generating new information on risk and upside, it is clear that any contribution of ERM to strategy formulation and selection has to be about methodology. Even though an ERM function is expected to have a thorough knowledge of operations, its primary contribution cannot be business know-how. Some of the areas in which an ERM team can build up significant expertise that supports strategy include:

▨ Structured and systematic approach to risk identification
▨ Taking a portfolio perspective on risk
▨ Expressing risks and return in cash flow terms (quantification)
▨ Understanding the economic cost of different forms of risk management
▨ Identifying and assessing contingencies and hidden risks
▨ Identifying and assessing conditional investment opportunities
▨ Using scenario methodology
▨ Using simulation methodology

Possessing these skills makes for a comparative advantage of the ERM team in assessing risk and return. The fundamental difference is bringing a mindset highly attuned to the fact that there is a lot of uncertainty and interrelatedness. Many risks and opportunities are contingent on certain outcomes and therefore partly hidden from view. The ERM team should therefore excel at understanding such dynamics. It should be adept at finding cost-efficient strategies for protecting against downside risk, while also mapping out contingent opportunities that could present themselves in certain states of the world. For example, any time the firm accepts a clause as part of a contract that is beneficial to the customer, this creates a hidden liability and can represent large value transfers. Business managers, eager to close the deal or simply not trained to think about value and risk in those terms, may neglect that aspect of the deal.

Such a well-structured evaluation of risk and return will point towards the value-maximizing decision. It therefore counteracts any worry or tendency that the strategy process is primarily about evaluating the potential return and underplays the importance of risk, that is, that the risk-return balance is not calibrated enough. The argument here is that decision-makers are prone to have too rosy a view of the upside potential. All the biases afflicting risk management that were reviewed in Chapter 3 – notably over-optimism and overconfidence – are at work in a strategy setting as well. In fact, in may be even worse because on top of those biases you get the fact that managers tend to 'fall in love' with their projects. When people promote their pet projects internally, it is no wonder that they embellish the assumptions and emphasize the gains more than the risks. Pointing further to an optimistic bias in strategy making, corporate leaders are known to be overrepresented among people with a narcissistic streak, meaning that they have an exaggerated ego and crave glory and self-affirmation above most other things. So, in that case there *is* a bias in the strategy selection process, which amounts to an organizational inefficiency that lowers firm value.

If ERM can assist in reducing the impact of such biases, it creates value. But how could ERM find a place in the strategy process where it can counteract such tendencies and restore a balance between risk and return? The executives are hardly inclined to think that they suffer from any kind of bias, and unlikely to ask for a fix to a problem they do not see. What seems most promising in this regard is to have a fully informed and empowered board of directors performing risk oversight. A board thus informed can to a much greater extent engage with the executive team and ask the tough and critical questions that make sure no excessive risks are taken, or that the risks involved are not neglected. If ERM contributes to the board's being fully informed and ability to play this role more effectively, it has an effect on strategy, albeit an indirect one.

A more direct way to ensure that this calibration of risk and return actually happens is for the board of directors to propose a 'risk review' of each strategy, which is then carried out by the ERM function. In practical terms, it would mean that the ERM function, on the board's behalf, takes a look at a proposed change in a corporate policy to assess whether the consequences for risk have received due attention. This checkpoint is not necessarily about creating a new risk register for each proposed strategy from scratch, but about checking whether those responsible appear to have done a thorough enough job of analysing the risks and communicating them to the board of directors. Once the strategy proposal reaches the board it is understood that the ERM function has 'signed off' on the evaluation of the risks that come with the strategy.

 ## CORE STRATEGIC RISKS AND THE RISK RADAR

Some risks are intrinsic to corporate strategy, such as developments in product technology, changes in consumer tastes, or increased competition. Many more factors will affect the extent to which a strategy can ultimately deliver value, like supply chain issues, exchange rates, and geopolitical developments. But product technology, consumer tastes, and competition can be viewed as core strategic risks, in that almost any firm has to deal with them and they can completely pull the rug from under the company.

Some strategic risks call for a timely and resolute risk response, but in other instances in may actually be a case of realizing that the game is over and not wasting the firm's resources in the process. For example, with the arrival of the personal computers the days of typing machines were numbered and there was not much anyone could do about it. Often, however, something could and should have been done in response to an emerging industry trend. The failure of Thomas Cook mentioned earlier was not only due to overpaying for acquisitions and piling up too much debt in the process. They were also slow to respond to the rise of online and more flexible forms of travel booking, clinging to their time-honoured way of packaging deals. This is a different situation from the typewriter industry because it might have been possible to protect most of the value of the strategy if the firm had adapted in time.

What causes such flawed responses to emerging strategic risks? As with so many aspects of risk management, we have to be wary of our biases. In this case, the bias is that we tend to be committed to things that are in our possession and have worked well for us in the past. The endowment effect on the level of strategy can be thought of as a 'strategy endowment effect', except that it operates on the level of corporate strategy. The endowment effect means that managers are overly attached to a formula for making profits that has served the company well historically. The effect will be even stronger if this formula is closely related to the identity of the firm, a big part of how it defines itself.

Successful adaptation to emerging threats requires, besides a certain willingness to change, that the emerging strategic risks are detected and brought into the line of sight of the executive team and the board. One way to introduce a more systematic approach to strategic risks is to implement a **risk radar**. As we use the term, it is much like a risk register, except that it has a longer time horizon and focuses on strategic risks. Emerging trends in product technology, consumer taste, and competition are at the core of the risk radar, but it is not confined to that. Anything that could threaten the long-term viability of an industry or business model would be part of the exercise.[1] The focus is explicitly on detecting strategic risks in their infancy, and putting a spotlight on the question of whether the current response to these risks is the correct one.

With the full benefit of hindsight, we can speculate on how a risk radar could have worked for a firm in the typewriter industry at some point in the late 1970s. The PC would have entered the risk radar when it was still mostly a rumour and adopted by tech enthusiasts. Its entry on the radar would have triggered discussions that made sure it was within the organizational line of sight, all the way up to the board. As the possibility of a technology shift gradually loomed larger, these discussions would have prompted a risk response in the form of a change in policy. In the best of cases the response would have been to stop investing in mainstream typewriters, perhaps shifting some R&D to a niche that still might have a future in the new world, like a machine with a design that appeals to eccentric writers and other lovers of retro. Any capital remaining in the firm should have been returned to the shareholders and not spent on projects that were basically doomed. Compare this with the car industry. Here, the electric car would have appeared on the risk radar at the earliest stages when those discussions first surfaced, well before governments started implementing stricter laws and regulations on emissions. The conclusion might have been very different this time though, in favour of a forceful response towards initiating the transition as soon as possible. Not only is the strategic risk (falling behind competitors) managed, it might actually lead to an advantage (taking the lead). The boundary between risk and opportunity blurs at this point.

The difference between the two industries lies in the ability to redeploy core capabilities and available resources. According to certain schools of thought in academia, the source of a firm's superior performance is due to some unique combination of capabilities and resources (Prahalad and Hamel, 1990;

---

[1] In this respect the risk radar overlaps with managerial tools for evaluating strategies such as PESTEL or SWOT. If such tools are being regularly applied the risk radar may not add much information that could be considered novel. The less systematic and well-developed the firm's strategy process is in this regard, the more the chances that ERM can make a meaningful contribution.

Barney, 1991). When the world changes, such capabilities and resources can be rendered useless or successfully redeployed to continue to generate value. The typewriter industry had nothing to offer in the emerging new world of personal computers, and the logical response was therefore to ride quietly into the sunset. Carmakers, in contrast, are presumably the ones best suited to build electric cars. So, there is a transition that needs to be managed and the strategic risk failure lies in sleepwalking into this new reality. When core competencies are not redeployable, in contrast, the strategic risk failure lies in keeping investments up for too long, or even worse, making diversifying acquisitions into new lines of business.

The takeaway is that there are always emerging trends in technology, customer tastes, and competition, which give rise to strategic risk. As is so often the case, our biases work against us in that we easily develop blind spots and go into denial about things that are unpleasant to think about. Implementing the risk radar is one tool for avoiding the situation where such blind spots develop and simultaneously making sure that there is a timely response to these strategic risks.

STRATEGY EXECUTION

Another interface between strategy and risk has to do with the firm's ability to carry out its strategy once it has been decided on. We are now past the stage of selecting a strategy and instead shift our focus to **strategy execution**. Executing a strategy successfully requires managerial, organizational, physical, and financial resources. Presumably, the strategy selection phase took these input factors into account, so that the firm is capable of handling the implementation. One of these resources, finance, is external in the sense that different kinds of investors need to be willing to provide funding for the venture. External financing may be a non-issue if the firm generates abundant cash flows internally. But most firms are at some point or other dependent on the continued goodwill of the financial markets to finance them.

Now, why might this be a problem? If the strategy is a good one, getting someone to finance it should not be hard, one might reason. The problem is that the capital markets may not see it that way. To begin with, they do not have the same knowledge about the strategy's potential. Managers obviously have access to all the business plans and things that are going on inside the firm, but the markets do not. For understandable reasons, managers need to keep sensitive information away from competitors and others who might benefit from it at the firm's expense. These information asymmetries mean that it might be difficult to arrange financing even for strategies that objectively would be considered attractive.

As previously discussed, obtaining financing becomes even harder in challenging times. From a debt investor's perspective, lending even more to a firm that is already financially weak may not be prudent. Much of the available collateral may already be claimed at this point, in which case any loan would effectively be based on a hope that the firm can generate enough cash flow to service it. If the firm is financially weak, equity investors may also have reasons to hesitate. The equity that is injected in a weak firm will accomplish primarily one thing: making the existing (and highly risky) debt safer. Because it is now safer, the value of the debt goes up. Therefore, the equity issue represents an immediate wealth transfer from equity holders to debt holders. Knowing this, why would equity investors agree to it? This is why issuing equity is not a convenient path out of a troubled situation: it is a super-expensive source of financing. When Norwegian Air Shuttle issued equity in 2020 in a do-or-die fashion, it did so at an 80% discount to the price at which its shares were trading.

Arranging financing to execute a strategy is further complicated by the fact that financial markets have their own cycles of boom and bust. In good times, financing is plentiful and there is a widespread acceptance of risk. The search for yield and opportunities is the dominating logic among market participants, which makes it easy for firms to get financing. When the cycle turns, however, there is a sudden rush away from risky assets. A so-called 'flight to quality' occurs as the preference shifts to safe and stable assets. This phenomenon means that firms find it much harder to attract financing on decent terms, especially those at the risky end of the spectrum.

The upshot of these discussions is that strategy execution is conditional on financing, and that access to capital markets cannot be taken for granted. These observations form the basis for the influential theory of risk management in Froot, Scharfstein, and Stein (1993) discussed in Chapter 8. To recap, the theory posits that risk management can create value by making cash flows available when there otherwise would have been a shortfall due to lack of external financing. In this theory, the proxy for strategy is capital expenditure. Oftentimes investments are needed to implement a strategy, for example, in order to increase production capacity or run a marketing campaign to build up demand for a new product. The theory suggests that the risk of having insufficient financial resources to execute the strategy can and should be managed.

All in all, there is a decidedly financial aspect to the issue of how risk management relates to strategy. Aggregate risk, which is expressed using financial numbers, plays a key part. Being able to show the connection between the firm's overall risk and strategy is therefore a potential source of value for an ERM programme. While balancing risk and return from a pure business point of view may be something that managers generally do very well, they often have only a sketchy understanding of how a certain strategy affects aggregate risk, or how the aggregate risk feeds back into strategy performance and execution.

So, here were we have identified another shortcoming relating to strategy that ERM can help remedy. Yes, strategy is risk and return in its purest sense, but how aggregate risk feeds back into strategy performance and execution is often only dimly understood, as is how corporate policies drive aggregate risk. ERM can create much needed clarity on these issues. But it takes risk budgeting to get there, as the risk register has too many shortcomings with respect to analysing aggregate risk. Risk budgeting provides the tools needed to illustrate the extent to which strategy performance and execution is at risk. Crucially for proactive decision-making, the model provides feedback on how the risk-return profile is affected by various corporate policies and changing external circumstances.

STRATEGIC INTERACTION AND RISK MANAGEMENT

So far in this chapter we have taken a simplified view of strategy as essentially just an idea about how the firm can make money, leaving out any analysis of the competitive situation. But the competitive landscape is of course going to be one factor that shapes the strategy. There is a sense in which strategy refers to **strategic interaction**, that is, to outmanoeuvre the competitors and come out winning. The goal of a strategy is usually not just to 'make money' but to beat the competition and deliver superior returns. Because of the ongoing interaction, a strategy is rarely set in stone, but rather constantly modified and finetuned.

There are cases where firms that normally compete have a common interest in expanding the market segment in which they operate. All firms in an industry tend to benefit when the size of the pie grows. But within the segment, holding its size constant, there is a rivalry for market share and profits that is essentially zero-sum in character: what one gains is a loss to the other. It follows from this that a fledgling strategy of a competitor is a good thing, a principle that is abundantly clear from observations we make almost every day. For example, when Boeing experienced its setbacks with the 737 MAX model in 2018/19, this boosted the shares of rival Airbus significantly.

It is straightforward enough that failures on the part of a competitor can be advantageous for a firm. Sometimes a firm enjoys a windfall without any proactiveness, simply because a competitor has made a mistake. But in other cases, capitalizing on a competitor's misfortunes may take some preparation and, our point here, an increase in financial resources. The argument is similar in spirit to the one discussed in the section on strategy execution: executing a strategy optimally requires being able to find money for the capital expenditure that comes with it. Except that now the optimal level of investment is conditional on the financial weakness of a competitor.

The key point here is that the optimal strategy is generally 'state dependent'. Today we have an idea about how the world might develop – that is, a forecast – but things could turn out either better or worse. The optimal strategy is not necessarily constant across all scenarios. If a good scenario happens, this might lead to new opportunities presenting themselves, which the firm will want to act on. If a bad scenario happens, some opportunities for the future may no longer have a business case. This is the standard account of how investment opportunities co-vary with revenue. There are circumstances, however, in which investment opportunities are countercyclical, meaning that they appear *only* in what would normally be characterized as the *bad* scenario (thus adding to the capital expenditure that is needed for strategy execution).

In brief, the argument behind countercyclical strategies is closely linked to the argument that the risk of asset fire sales presents a reason to manage risk. What changes now is the observation that when the bad scenario occurs, some competitors become financially constrained or even distressed and start selling assets to generate liquidity quickly. Because they are in distress, they are prepared to accept a price that is below fair value. Capital markets provide no escape, as the risk premium goes up and there is a flight to safety. Asset fire sales, for some in the industry, become the only way to survive. This account is based on a theory by Shleifer and Vishny (1992). They call the phenomenon 'the general equilibrium aspect of asset sales', referring to the fact that in an industry slump, more or less all firms will be affected negatively and therefore financially weak. Because of widespread financial constraints, competitive bidding fails to materialize for the assets that are put up for sale.

The key observation for our purposes is that the asset illiquidity discount is a source of value for the buying firm. A financially healthy firm can create value by placing itself on the buying side of fire sales done by its liquidity-squeezed competitors. That is, a firm that manages to stay financially strong could enjoy buying opportunities that would not have been there in other scenarios. Quality assets that are a good strategic fit for the firm may suddenly be put up for sale. In 1998, for example, the financially mighty conglomerate Norsk Hydro was able to acquire the stricken oil exploration firm Saga Petroleum. Saga had gotten itself into distress through extensive use of debt in combination with a slump in the oil price, helped along by a disastrous derivative strategy. Various attempts at keeping it viable as a going concern failed, and it had to resign to being acquired. When oil prices started to rebound shortly after, this turned out to be one of the most value-creating acquisitions in Norsk Hydro's long history.

Capitalizing on countercyclical investment opportunities is the corporate strategy equivalent of the folk wisdom that the right time to buy is when 'blood is flowing in the streets', or when everyone else is panicking. But it takes overcoming financial constraints that might be formidable. The would-be countercyclical acquirer is likely hurting for the same reasons that other firms in the industry are forced to sell assets, and financial markets are most likely not forthcoming with funding. This requires a financial strategy to supplement the corporate strategy. One possibility is to stock up on cash. In hard times, having plentiful cash reserves can turn into a substantial advantage and may be a decisive factor in enabling countercyclical investments. This point is related to the notorious 'long purse' strategy, in which a firm with financial muscle uses its superior resources to get rid of its weaker peers. According to the long purse idea, a deep-pocketed firm rationally lowers product prices to below breakeven because it forces weaker firms out of business, allowing for the capture of additional market share. During a crisis, any such strategic benefits of cash are amplified.

Countercyclical investment opportunities are usually low-probability events, however. Having large amounts of cash on the balance sheet lowers the return on assets and does not go down well with investors and analysts who want their capital to be 'working'. A conditional strategy may therefore be best funded by a conditional source of financing. This brings us to the possibility of using risk transfer for the purpose of capitalizing on asset fire sales. A derivative contract could be designed to yield a payoff conditional on some event that would be judged to correlate with broad financial distress in the industry or target the financial health of a specific competitor. An oil producer, for example, may consider it likely that one or more competitors would become distressed at an oil price of, say, $30. It may furthermore consider it likely that these firms will attempt to sell some of their assets to solve immediate liquidity problems. If these assets are viable long term and fit well into the producer's portfolio, then being on the buying side of these transactions could be a good idea. Since it can often be assumed that outside financing is unavailable in worst-case scenarios, the payoff from a derivative may be the only way to ensure that the deal can be funded. The producer could therefore buy put options with a strike price of $30 so as to match its cash flows with the countercyclical investment opportunity. Because of this opportunity such a derivative position could be motivated even if the producer would cope well with a price of $30 and face neither distress nor underinvestment problems of its own. The usual preconditions for a derivative strategy to make sense identified in the literature are therefore not present, but the position is still expected to create value because it enables the (conditional) opportunity to be capitalized on. As so often happens, risk and opportunity fuse at the level of strategy.

What does it take for risk to translate into opportunity in the form of acquiring assets or capturing market share? Besides the ability to detect such countercyclical opportunities, and formulate proactive strategies to act on them, the answer is a difference in aggregate risk. The firm with the lower level of risk may be able to capitalize on the higher risk of its competitor. But this will play out only in some scenarios, namely those that would normally be considered 'bad'. Those are the scenarios in which financial distress will start weighing down on the strategy of the weaker firms, which in various ways can be taken advantage of by the stronger ones. So, the astute strategic risk manager would assess not only her own company's aggregate risk but also those of relevant peers. The optimal risk management strategy would be a function of the difference in those risk profiles, driven by a lack of risk capacity in the competitor. Good assets that have been burdened by too much debt are the most promising from the perspective of countercyclical investments. Observing a difference in aggregate risk, the strategic risk manager would then factor in the potential for asset fire sales and market share capture when devising their strategy. On top of any risk capacity to navigate through the bad scenarios, the risk manager would therefore make preparations by adding to the firm's 'opportunity capital' – that is, the conditional financial resources needed to profit from countercyclical opportunities.

While neat on paper, the strategy of capitalizing on countercyclical investments is of course a difficult and risky one to attempt in practice. It is usually only clear with hindsight when a crisis bottoms out. As events unfold, there is always the possibility that things get even worse. It is also possible that they stay bad for so long they start taxing even the stronger firm's ability to cope. So, it is definitely easier said than done. But a corporate strategy can nonetheless be informed by any excess risk among competitors. If risk transfer is used to make additional funds available in those scenarios, the stronger firm has the option, but not the obligation, to act on any opportunities that might present themselves. Whether or not it is prudent to do so can be determined once that particular scenario materializes. In any case, the firm will hardly regret having the extra buffers in those circumstances, whether they lead to countercyclical investments or not.

This chapter has demonstrated several interfaces between ERM and strategy. These are summed up in Figure 10.1. Ultimately it should be no surprise that ERM can contribute to the strategy process. But it cannot be just any ERM process. It has to truly have a comparative advantage in the methodology and mindset for trading risk against return, and to prove its worth in various situations until it gradually interlocks with questions of more strategic significance.

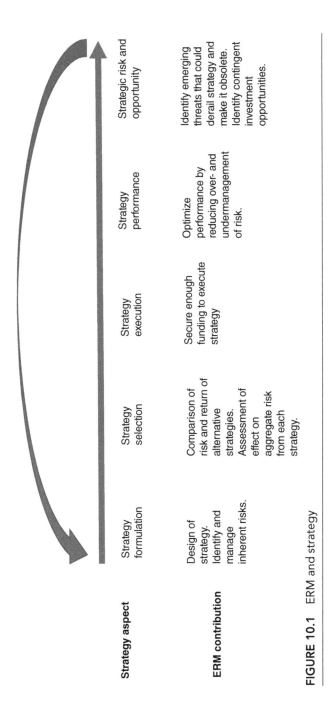

Strategy aspect	Strategy formulation	Strategy selection	Strategy execution	Strategy performance	Strategic risk and opportunity
ERM contribution	Design of strategy. Identify and manage inherent risks.	Comparison of risk and return of alternative strategies. Assessment of effect on aggregate risk from each strategy.	Secure enough funding to execute strategy	Optimize performance by reducing over- and undermanagement of risk.	Identify emerging threats that could derail strategy and make it obsolete. Identify contingent investment opportunities.

FIGURE 10.1 ERM and strategy

KEY CHAPTER TAKEAWAYS

- Strategic risk is often understood as the risk that a strategy performs less well than expected and does not meet its goals.
- It is often observed that major declines in market value are associated with strategic risks rather than the operating and financial ones that get the most attention by corporates.
- There has been a long-standing search for ways to make ERM more 'strategic' and integrate it with the decision-making processes at the top level of the firm.
- Currently, however, ERM often does not play a significant role in major corporate policies like acquisitions or investment programmes.
- There are many ways in which ERM, representing a higher risk awareness and improved methodology for trading risk against return, can interlock with the strategy process.
- ERM can enhance strategy performance by raising the level of expected cash flow and reduce its variability.
- ERM can enhance strategy formulation by providing the tools for detecting hidden risks and contingent investment opportunities.
- ERM can enhance strategy selection by providing the tools for assessing the risk-reward characteristics of each alternative on a comparable basis.
- ERM can enhance strategy execution by providing a framework for safeguarding the firm's ability to meet investment needs.
- ERM can enhance strategic interaction by providing the tools for detecting weaknesses in rivals that can translate into opportunities to expand market share or capitalize on asset fire sales.
- ERM can enhance strategic risk detection by providing the tools for detecting emerging threats that have to do with things like changes in customer tastes, production technology, and competitive forces.
- At the level of strategy, risk and opportunity tend to fuse – for example, when acting early on an emerging strategic risk translates into a head start and competitive advantage.
- Risk at the strategic level is often a function of aggregate risk, which the risk register is inherently limited in providing information on.
- To achieve a strategic role, ERM would in many cases benefit substantially from first becoming more oriented towards financial performance, as in risk budgeting.

CHAPTER 11

Risk in Practice: The Case of Equinor

ENTERPRISE RISK MANAGEMENT (ERM) in Equinor got under way in 1996, when Petter Kapstad, with a background in banking, was asked to systematize the management of risk in the finance department. The catalyst was the company executives' desire to better understand the exposure to financial risks, especially as they related to derivatives. At the time, derivatives had been implicated in several well-publicized scandals, and the executives wanted to increase their control over these risks. The result of Kapstad's work was that the risks managed by the finance department were measured and managed as a portfolio of risks with central oversight. It led to the establishment of four key principles that were to have an enduring impact on the company's risk philosophy:

- Risk and upside are two sides of the same coin
- Risk must be assessed holistically from a portfolio perspective
- Risk should be quantified to the extent possible
- The purpose of managing risk is to contribute to value creation

The then chief executive officer (CEO) of Equinor, Harald Norvik, realized that the same principles could be applied to the whole company. The integrated perspective essentially meant looking at Equinor as a portfolio of businesses with risks that were correlated with each other. The idea was that there would be benefits from coordinating their management across the enterprise. Thus, the enterprise perspective on risk management was born in Equinor, and again Kapstad was entrusted with the task of leading the company in this direction.

One thing that resonated with executives was the emphasis Kapstad put on using risk management to engage with the businesses and enhance value. This phrasing of terms helped shift their perspective on risk management, as it implied a more constructive role that would support the executives and business units alike. To generate the necessary backing for ERM, it was helpful to avoid the image of another cost-generating corporate function doing mostly some kind of controlling. The emphasis on risk and opportunity viewed together also went down well with the executives (and later the business units of the company.) The leadership of Equinor was composed of industrialists, who are attuned to the idea of accepting risks to pursue business opportunities, which is certainly true for the company's entrepreneurial-minded business units as well.

While Equinor's executives were generally positive to the idea behind ERM, they still wanted to know what was in it for them. An important part of the answer to this question came from a project group that investigated the costs and benefits to Equinor from various financial transactions, mostly hedging and foreign exchange transactions going on in the company. Kapstad and his group were able to show that there was an excessive number of such transactions, and that they made little or no sense from the corporate perspective. The overall conclusion was that the company was in fact paying a lot of money to *increase* risk and generally make things more complicated than they had to be. This struck the executive team as unacceptable. ERM had gotten the economic justification it needed, and a clear mandate was given.

Early on in the project, Kapstad met and started working with Eyvind Aven, who shared the same vision of an enterprise-wide approach to risk management. Importantly, Aven had a background in economic analysis, which complemented Kapstad's experience from trading units. This made them bilingual in the sense that they knew the specific terminology and ways of doing things that were prevalent both in the company's high-profile trading units and its headquarters. The ability to speak 'complementary languages' and not be viewed as outsiders was to prove very useful, as many tough decisions lay ahead with people who had an interest in preserving the status quo.

THE ERM VISION

Already in the early stages of the project it was decided that Equinor would not simply implement one of the existing blueprints for ERM. Kapstad and Aven did not want it to be, or to be seen as, yet another control function.[1] They had something else in mind. They wanted a framework that made sense to Equinor, and that centred on the two basic goals of the company: to create value and avoid accidents. Keeping people and the environment safe is the number one priority and supersedes any other objective.[2] Beyond those basic objectives, however, risks are to be managed in a way that maximizes the value of the company.

Consistent with the principle that value creation is one of the basic guiding principles for ERM in Equinor, Kapstad and Aven undertook the analysis of risk from a value chain perspective. Today, it is even written in the corporate directives that the company's approach is to 'identify, evaluate, and *manage risk related to the value chain* to support achievement of our corporate objectives' (original emphasis). Equinor's value chain is outlined in Figure 11.1 showing how its main activities progress from upstream (oil exploration and development) to downstream (petroleum refinement) to market (selling its products into various global markets).

What difference does the value chain perspective make? First, it serves as a clear signal to everybody involved (i.e. Equinor's employees and other stakeholders) that value creation is the metric being pursued through ERM, and it is the impact on Equinor's performance that ultimately counts. Another important benefit of the value chain perspective is that by sorting the risks into a value chain, one can more easily see the bigger picture and, through the lens of the company's business model, see how different categories of risk fit in and how they interrelate to form a coherent whole.

According to another of the four basic principles, risk encompasses not only downside risk but also upside potential. On this dimension existing off-the-shelf ERM frameworks were considered too oriented towards risk avoidance. The Equinor philosophy instead recognizes that risk-taking is unavoidable, even necessary, to create value for shareholders. The company's internal communication puts it in the following way: 'We live by taking risks'. What

---

[1]This is not to suggest that internal audit has been excluded from the ERM process. On the contrary, internal audit has been strongly supportive of ERM and contributed valuable resources to it.
[2]This is underscored by the fact that the risks related to health, safety, and environment are the responsibility of a separate corporate function (Corporate Safety).

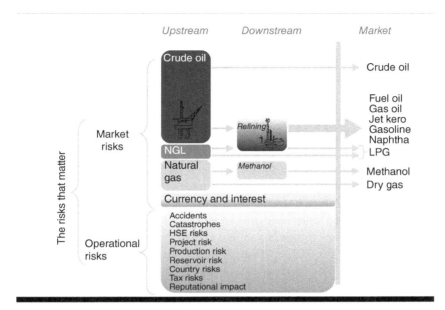

FIGURE 11.1   Equinor's value chain

matters is instead that the risks are well enough understood and found accept-able. The principle of viewing risk in the context of upside has been widely communicated internally right from the beginning, and found its way into the corporate directives of the company as well, where it is stated that 'both poten-tial upside and downside shall be considered when relevant'.

Despite being one of the basic guiding principles for risk management, value creation has not gone unchallenged as the main purpose of ERM. It is often the case that people tend to reach different conclusions as to what ERM should be about depending on their professional backgrounds. There have been alternative visions for ERM within the company. One was more in line with the established ERM frameworks, which speak at length about the need to protect various targets and objectives. The vision of ERM as promoting value creation prevailed, however. The thinking on this issue is that if ERM is centred around targets, the result will be that the business units pursue 'goal achievement risk' rather than value maximization.

A vision of ERM that is attractive to the executive team and business units alike has been an important success factor. Spending significant amounts of time *beforehand* thinking about what ERM should ultimately look like, and why, has proven to be very helpful in seeing it through its initial phases. Kapstad and Aven call this 'doing one's homework'. Having a coherent set of arguments ready to defend why it is a good idea to do something in a certain way has made it much easier to stand firm when people resist change.

 ## EARLY DEVELOPMENTS IN ERM

In the early phase of ERM a lot of the work revolved around applying the portfolio perspective to the firm's market risks. This priority was a natural consequence of the fact that the sale of oil and natural gas makes up a very large proportion of the firm's revenue, thus being the single biggest risk exposure in the company. Working in collaboration with investment bank Goldman Sachs, Equinor developed a model for quantifying the impact of market risk on the firm's performance.[3] It contained a sophisticated methodology for estimating the amount of variability caused by market risks, based on historical time series, as well as estimates of the tendency of these risks to co-vary. The market risk model allowed Equinor to sum up the firm's aggregate risk profile using metrics like earnings-at-risk. What is more, the user was able to observe how these risk measures would change under alternative courses of action. For example, the model allowed the user to overlay the probability distribution for earnings with a second distribution that takes into account a certain risk management strategy (e.g. buying put options covering a certain fraction of the company's net exposure to the oil price). Such an overlay is illustrated in Figure 11.2. The dark line is the outcome distribution for earnings under no hedging, whereas the light one shows how tail risk is reduced with hedging.

With a consolidated view of the firm's performance-at-risk from market risk, the company felt that because the amounts at stake were so enormous, no single executive, not even the CEO, should be solely responsible for any decision to hedge a significant fraction of the exposure using derivatives. This led to the creation of a committee whose function would be to support decision-making with respect to market risk. The market risk committee, established in 1999, consisted of representatives of finance, trading, and accounting.

---

[3]At the time of writing, Equinor is in the process of replacing this model with a new model framework.

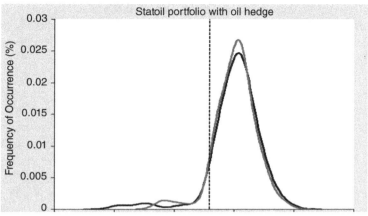

FIGURE 11.2 Performance-at-risk under alternative hedging policies

As Equinor gained experience in applying the enterprise perspective to risk management, the scope gradually expanded to cover other types of risks. One that was of central importance to the company was country risk. From the early 1990s international expansion had been a core part of Equinor's strategy, as it was deemed necessary to replace the gradually declining assets on the Norwegian shelf over time. To this end, Equinor formed an alliance with British Petroleum, which gave the company access to opportunities and ventures across the world. But there was a catch: oil is generally found in some of the politically most unstable societies in the world. The upside potential from investing in these countries was seen to be very attractive, however, so there was a willingness to accept many of these risks. But they had to be understood first. Getting the balance between risk and return right called for more information than the company currently had at its disposal. For these reasons, Equinor launched a project on country risk jointly with the consultancy firm IHS Global Insight. This effort has resulted in a large internal knowledge base on country risk, as well as a standardized methodology for evaluating country risk as part of new investment proposals.

In response to the broader scope of risks being covered, the market risk committee was renamed the ERM committee in 2002. The ERM committee was expanded to become a truly cross-disciplinary advisory body on risk, with participants from more units and functions than before. Ever since, it has consisted of a broad range of professionals with different backgrounds, such as the head of strategy, the heads of the main trading units, the chief controllers of different business units, and the head of internal audit. From the very beginning, the committee has been chaired by the chief financial officer (CFO). Its main task is to advise the executive team on risk issues, and it does not have any formal decision-making authority.

In 2000 a risk function was formally set up, headed by Kapstad, to support the ERM committee and build up the firm's technical expertise in risk management. Its main tasks consisted of developing a common methodology on risk, as well as overseeing the work on the company's market risk model. It has also been responsible for the process description for risk management in Equinor, which has been integrated into the governing documents of the company. The risk function (henceforth referred to as the ERM function) also participated as Equinor's representatives in the project on country risk methodology. Over the years, it has come to represent an unbiased view in decision-making situations, free of any agenda other than the best outcome for the company.

With the corporate risk committee, the risk function, and the risk model in place, the foundations for ERM had been laid. Significant steps had been taken to understand market and country risk, two of the most important risks facing the company. All of this is consistent with the ideas behind ERM, but Equinor was not yet truly enterprise-wide in its approach to risk management. The 'across the enterprise' part of the definition of ERM does not just refer to a set of corporate functions applying a portfolio perspective. It also means that all units and functions strive together to identify and assess risks according to a common methodology.

Around 2005, the time was ripe for expanding the scope once again and go truly enterprise-wide. As interest in risk management continued to grow, there was an increasing demand for an overview of the most important risks that could be communicated to the executives and the board of directors. The ERM function, for its part, had concluded that significant operational risks went underreported, and that catastrophe risks were poorly understood. Adding further momentum, some of the business units had taken an interest in the methodology on risk evaluation being developed by the ERM function. They could see that it was in line with their own thinking, and they were open to the possibility that it could help them find solutions that would have a positive effect on profitability. Another advantage in their view was that a common methodology reduced the burden of having to motivate and explain ad-hoc initiatives to deal with risk. Their interest in ERM was also helped along by the fact that the executive team and directors were clearly behind it. It was not just some exercise conducted by a few enthusiasts in the ERM function – the leadership of the firm was interested and intended to use the outputs. This fact has also helped reduced any appearance of control, which a risk management function otherwise easily obtains. Since the leadership's interest in risk management was beyond any doubt, the ERM function has been able to present itself in terms of 'we are here to help you deal with these expectations', creating a more collaborative relationship.

The overall positive reception by the business units is not meant to suggest that there has not, at times, been a healthy dose of scepticism. After all, every corporate initiative lays a claim on resources in those units. There may not be personnel available to deal with the initiative, meaning that resources must sometimes be redirected from other uses (or costs increased). What the Equinor experience suggests is that good arguments are crucial to win the sceptics over, and as well as being able to point to ways in which the outputs of the risk management process are helpful also to the units. Patience and pragmatism have been equally crucial. Being pragmatic has in fact been something of a mantra in the ERM function. The view taken has been that some progress is better than none, and that things cannot be expected to happen overnight. It has not been about imposing a corporate ideology in a top down fashion. Instead, one must be willing to listen and meet half-way, while trying to see things from the units' point of view. Better decisions and better dialogue have always remained the guiding principles in this interface with business units.

RISK MAPPING IN EQUINOR

As risk management went truly enterprise-wide, the next phase in the process was to be about systematically mapping out risks in the different business units. The goal was to compile a risk register for the company as a whole. Here, it is worth noting that a separate initiative to systematically detect risks across the business units was actually already under way in Equinor. In 2001, the internal audit function started conducting risk workshops aimed at raising the risk awareness among managers in the company's operating units. These managers were challenged to think about risk and what could go wrong in their operations, and how accidents and losses could be prevented. A lot of the interest in this project revolved around the managers' perceived and actual ability to control these risks. The internal audit function's ability to assume a leading role in the ERM project was limited, however, because of external requirements to preserve its independence. Internal audit lacks the mandate to get involved in a process that aims to support decision-making on multiple levels in the firm, the goal of which is to optimize risk and return.

When rolling out the risk mapping across the enterprise, the key principle within ERM of quantifying risks to the extent possible has been heeded. The voting techniques that had been used by the internal audit department were considered too imprecise. Instead, estimates of probability and impact were targeted, where impact is understood as the net present value (after tax) of the effect that the risk factor in question would have on the firm. To obtain the probability-impact estimates it was necessary to engage with the business units. But this could not be done by asking them to supply headquarters with their own numbers in any way they saw fit. The procedure had to be streamlined in order for the information to be comparable across units. A standardized tool for constructing risk maps was therefore developed in-house, downloadable through Equinor's intranet.

A common attitude in business units when faced with the task of quantifying probability and impact is to declare that quantification is not possible due to all the complexities involved (not infrequently claimed to be uniquely high in that unit). What has proven useful in these cases is to engage in a sort of provocation whereby the ERM function proposes an initial ballpark estimate of probability and impact. This triggers a response aimed at explaining why those estimates are not really the best. The discussion that follows then leads to estimates that the unit managers are willing to endorse, and they have often expressed that they have found these discussions, and the input from the ERM function, useful for looking at their own decision-making situations. The message from the ERM function is always that the estimates are not about millimetre exactness, and that the most important aspects of the exercise are to raise risk awareness and generate useful dialogues. The purpose of this is partly to mitigate a certain fear felt by some in the operating units that if something does happen later, it will reflect badly on those who provided the prior estimates and that they somehow will be held accountable for them.

The business units are expected to provide discussions and justifications for their assumptions, and risk is included on the agenda of their meetings with senior executives. These two facts – providing written justifications and meeting with representatives of top management and the ERM function – go a long way towards ensuring the quality of the outputs of this process. Since the business units know this lies ahead, they have every reason to do a good job preparing and thinking through their estimates of risks.

Using the joint methodology for risk assessment is required down to the business area levels – the largest operating units Equinor is divided into. These business areas in turn consist of smaller operating segments. At this lower level of the organization, the units are free to use whatever kind of risk map they want. The reasoning behind this was that they should be able to tailor the system used to their own specific needs. While the corporate methodology was available to them, some of these smaller units opted to develop their own risk maps. They felt that the corporate format was not well suited to their specific context and preferred something that was more attuned to their circumstances. These estimates still had to be converted to fit the corporate framework, however, and increasingly few business units have found it worthwhile to operate two parallel systems. Over time the usage of unit-specific risk maps has therefore declined.

The risk maps in use in Equinor has evolved over time. One important step was to graphically illustrate both downside risk and upside potential concerning the firm's top risks (early on there was just a compilation of risks in a spreadsheet). A continuous monetary scale was then introduced to measure impact. Later, it was decided that monetary values should not be attached to risks that related to health, safety, and the environment, introducing a separate scale for those categories of risk. The use of the colour red has been discontinued as it could be interpreted as 'stop' in some contexts, especially in the US (where the Equinor's shares are listed). The use of quantitative estimates of probability and impact has been constant, though, true to Equinor's philosophy of quantifying risks to make them comparable. Figure 11.3 illustrates a representative risk map in Equinor with a monetary scale and both upside potential and downside risk represented.

In the first couple of years of risk mapping, the ERM function met with the leadership of each business unit on an annual basis. Today, the risk-mapping process in Equinor follows a biannual cycle, which is the frequency at which the business units are required to update their risk maps. It is the role of the ERM function to consolidate this vast amount of information into a risk map that contains only Equinor's top risks. The risk register is the complete set of risks that is identified in the process, whereas the risk map is a visual summary of the most important ones.

Recently, in 2018, the original risk mapping–tool was replaced by a new management information system (MIS). The new system draws on the insight that taking risk is essential for generating profits, and that since taking risk precedes any profits it should come first. This means that the first view anyone logging onto the system sees is an overview of the strategic objectives, risks, actions, and indicators. The idea is to remind the user that certain risks are being taken in order to generate the performance, and to counteract any tendency to just take profits at face value without thinking about what kind of risks were needed to get there. This should be contrasted with the system that it replaced, which only contained data on key performance indicators (KPIs) and performance – but nothing on risk!

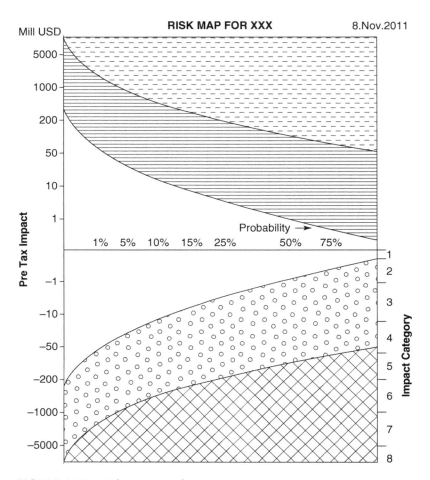

FIGURE 11.3   Risk maps' evolution over time

 RISK GOVERNANCE IN EQUINOR

Today, risk is firmly on the agenda of the Equinor board of directors. Whereas prior to ERM the directors were mostly involved in the most obvious price risk exposures, in the last two decades they have been involved in detailed discussions about major risks, including anything from catastrophic risk to cyber risk. Risk maps are a standing item on the agenda, along with any specific risks that may need attention as and when they arise. Over this time period there has been a noticeable increase in terms of the board's interest in risk management and the risk oversight it carries out.

The ERM committee in Equinor was set up as an advisory body to assist the company's executives and directors. It has indeed emerged as a guardian of Equinor's best interest in matters related to risk, and the holistic perspective is well established. Things only find their way onto its agenda if there is a clear corporate interest involved. Risk management policies that were earlier set by different departments independently now have to pass through the committee, who will assess whether the policy makes sense for Equinor as a whole. Major policies like strategic hedging are also evaluated from this perspective, and the recommendations are communicated to the executive team as well as the board of directors when relevant.

From a risk governance perspective, this is an important aspect of the decision-making process. While the CEO has significant decision-making authority, the policy is first evaluated in a professional forum dedicated to integrated risk management, and thereafter discussed and approved by the board of directors. This arrangement implies a very different balance of power with respect to the firm's major risks compared to a setting where hedging strategies change from quarter to quarter based on the CEO's ad-hoc view, or some other part of the organization that has been given the licence so to decide.

The Equinor experience illustrates the importance of getting the ERM committee right. If not established in the right way, such a committee will continue with old ways and look at risks in a silo fashion. Attendance will be low and the committee's utterances will carry little weight. If done right, however, it will develop into an effective ERM champion whose recommendations are widely respected and translated into action. As for how that outcome can be achieved, the importance of having the unwavering support of key individuals in the executive team cannot be overstated. Moreover, setting up an interesting agenda with a certain element of education (especially in the early days of the programme) seems to have been a key success factor for the ERM committee in Equinor. Ultimately, the risk committee needs to remain an advisory body, not an executive one, though it must carry enough standing to be seen as the real arbiter on risk-related issues in the company.

The ERM function has developed a considerable expertise in risk management that supports decision-making in various ways. They have maintained an independence in that they have direct access to information that will provide the board of directors with an expert opinion. One example of this is that the risk function writes a brief in response to the business units' risk assessment, which is sent to the executive team and board of directors along with the map itself. These comments may reveal disagreements, or simply a different perspective, regarding the estimates of risk provided by the business units. Another example of the independent role of the ERM function comes from the fact that it is asked to evaluate investment proposals, including acquisitions, that exceed a certain size. Because they potentially have a material impact on the company's risk profile, it is of some concern to the board that the risks are well understood, and the ERM function is available to provide unbiased assessments of this.

The business units in Equinor are responsible for managing the majority of the risks that arise in their line of business. However, when risks are material enough, they are discussed by the ERM committee to ensure that the risk mitigation is in line with the broader corporate philosophy. The business units have also used the ERM committee to obtain feedback when dealing with complicated issues related to risk. The management of some core risks, like oil price, has indeed been centralized, however, as the benefits from doing so are substantial. The concept of 'core risks' is an important one in Equinor and further underlines the central role of value creation as a guiding principle for ERM. To understand this concept, we need to go back to 2001, when the company's shares were listed on the Oslo stock exchange as well as the New York stock exchange. During the listing process, there were investors looking for arguments as to why they should invest in Equinor. Recognizing that investors were entitled to information about what exposures they were getting when they invested in the Equinor share, the company formulated the idea of core risks, understood as the risk exposures that an investor would expect, and even desire, to have from buying the Equinor share (the most important of which were exposure to oil and gas prices).

As core risks are centralized, there could arise some frictions in that the performance of the business units are still affected by them. If a unit is responsible for their own result, say in terms of earnings before interests and taxes, it seems only reasonable that they should have the freedom to manage the risk exposures related to it. However, this perspective conflicts with the legitimate goal of the headquarters to centralize risk management, given the substantial benefits of a centralized approach. Hence, we have a conflict between the desire to centralize risk management and the way the company measures the performance of its business units. To deal with this problem,

Equinor has ensured that the KPIs the company uses to evaluate its business units remain, as far as possible, unaffected by the centrally managed core risks. This is a very important principle because it resolves many of the conflicts of interest that could arise from centralizing risk management. This means that the company achieves centralization, but largely avoids the discontent that could result from business units having to live with large risk exposures they cannot affect.

RISK CULTURE IN EQUINOR

Because ERM involves organizational change, the impact it has depends on the ERM function's ability to shape attitudes. If the culture is such that the company gets behind the ERM effort, results are likely to be very different compared to a culture marked by indifference or even resistance. This has made ERM in Equinor as much a culture project as one about new knowledge and techniques. Today, however, ERM is thoroughly embedded in the business units' way of doing things, and firmly on the agenda of Equinor's executive team and board of directors. It can legitimately be said that understanding and managing risk is today a core value in Equinor.

The buy-in from the CEO in the late 1990s is the trigger that set Equinor on the path towards making risk management a core value. The signal was sent that the executive team sees risk management as something important and value creating. Several changes over the years have reinforced this impression. For example, in 2009 it was decided that the risk maps were to be a recurring item on the agenda in the meetings between the units and the CEO and CFO.[4] This was a symbol as clear as any of the commitment of the executive team to ERM. Another such signal came in 2013, when the board of directors asked to receive a risk map three times per year, rather than just twice as was previously the practice.

Being elevated to a core value means it is clear to anyone that the leadership is committed to risk management. When this gets noticed around the organization it changes how people view risk management and their predisposition

---

[4]The review meetings are occasions when top management meets with other business areas to discuss the unit's performance vis-à-vis previously agreed targets. This refers to the unit's overall financial performance as well as specific KPIs. Risk is therefore one of several issues on the agenda at these reviews.

to change their own behaviour in regard to it. But these behaviours can be influenced in a more direct way if they are clearly defined and communicated to the rest of the enterprise. In order for people to behave in a certain way, they have to understand first of all what is expected of them. In Equinor, two visible reminders have been helpful in this regard. One is a booklet handed out to all employees ('The Equinor book'), which describes core values, corporate governance, the operating model, corporate policies, and so on. This outlines the company's attitude towards risk and its expectations towards its employees. New Equinor recruits are required to read it, and many employees keep it close to hand on their desks as a source of guidance. The second visual reminder is the screensaver, which is shown in Figure 11.4. This is what greets all of Equinor's 20,000 employees every time they turn on their computers.

The motto on the screensaver defines two concrete behaviours that are consistent with risk management as a core value. To 'understand risk' creates an expectation that before taking actions one must take the time to think about the risks involved. This counteracts any tendency to skip investing time and effort to find out more about the relevant facts. To 'manage risk' creates an expectation that one must be proactive and make a conscious decision with respect to risk. Just spending time analysing the impact of risk

FIGURE 11.4 Equinor screensaver
Source: Used with permission from Microsoft.

on past performance, as risk controllers so often do, is not the desired behaviour in Equinor. Rather, taking responsibility for a risk means having a clear forward-looking strategy for it.

The ERM team has also sought to instil another important behaviour, which is to make it part of everyone's job description to think in terms of Equinor's best interest in given decision-making situations. This attitude actually antedates the ERM initiative and goes back to a programme called Arena, through which engineers and operating managers from various parts of Equinor join up and take a fresh look at projects that are waiting for decision. The philosophy behind this is to have a second pair of eyes looking at every major activity, and to provide the benefit of a critical but constructive look from competent people outside the specific team involved. The expectation to pursue what is best for the company fostered in Arena has carried over into ERM. This general attitude embedded in the broader corporate culture works against any short-term incentives that might distract from choosing what would be the best long-term solution.

Apart from shaping behaviours through expectations, the culture is influenced by other signals concerning the status of risk management. One such signal is that risk management's aim is not to physically separate the risk unit from the rest of the organization. The message is that risk management should not be viewed as something distinct from the business itself, but rather embedded in it. The risk managers of Equinor's asset-backed trading unit, for example, are situated in the same location as the line managers and naturally intermingle with them to discuss optimal solutions. Emphasis is also placed on risk managers building up a solid understanding of the value chain, which is seen as a prerequisite for them to be able to contribute constructively to the decision-making process (the 'enabling' role discussed in previous chapters). Yet, as we have seen, this has not come at the expense of its independence or ability to communicate with the board of directors. ERM in Equinor supports risk oversight *and* business decision-making.

Another culture-impacting effort has been to raise the status of risk management as a profession. The problem here is that people have been unsure about what this new occupation is about. The ERM function has sought to establish that risk management is indeed a profession in its own right that is held to certain standards and is here to stay. One initiative to change perception in this regard has been to create a 'career ladder', the point of which is to show that being a risk manager does not have to be a temporary position after which one returns to a more familiar role within the traditional functions or units (Figure 11.5). In part, the ladder was developed to instruct the human

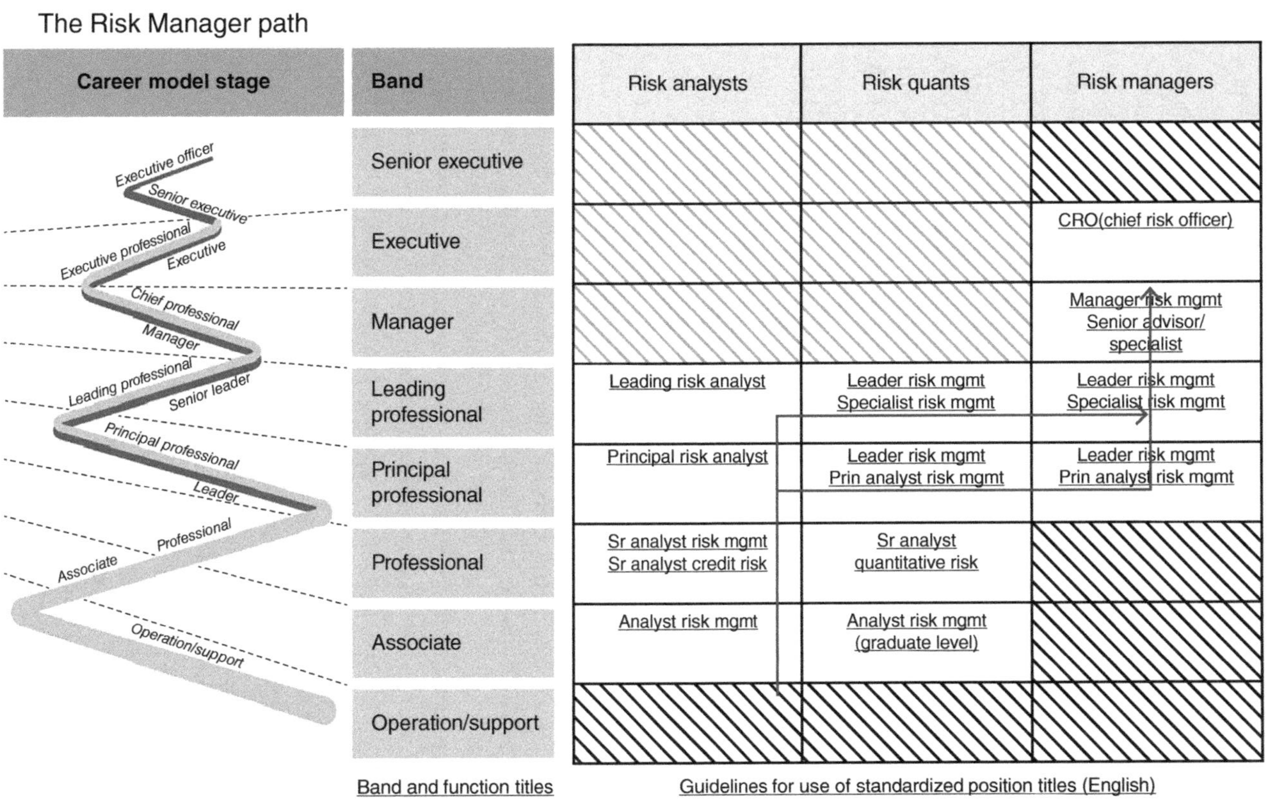

The Risk Manager path

Band	Risk analysts	Risk quants	Risk managers
Senior executive			
Executive			CRO (chief risk officer)
Manager			Manager risk mgmt / Senior advisor/ specialist
Leading professional	Leading risk analyst	Leader risk mgmt / Specialist risk mgmt	Leader risk mgmt / Specialist risk mgmt
Principal professional	Principal risk analyst	Leader risk mgmt / Prin analyst risk mgmt	Leader risk mgmt / Prin analyst risk mgmt
Professional	Sr analyst risk mgmt / Sr analyst credit risk	Sr analyst quantitative risk	
Associate	Analyst risk mgmt	Analyst risk mgmt (graduate level)	
Operation/support			

Guidelines for use of standardized position titles (English)

Band and function titles

Career model stage: Executive officer, Senior executive, Executive professional, Executive, Chief professional, Manager, Leading professional, Senior leader, Principal professional, Leader, Professional, Associate, Operation/support

FIGURE 11.5 Risk manager career ladder

resources department on what qualifications were sought after for risk managers, which to them was a new and poorly understood job title. The ladder outlines various steps that somebody starting out in risk management can follow and in their pursuit of an attractive and rewarding career within that field. The 'risk analyst' track is closest to the operating side of the business, which gives a good foundation for understanding the economics of the value chain. The 'risk quant' track develops specific insights about the models used to quantify risk, which is more of a specialized and technical field. The optimal path is to have some exposure to both of these environments before passing into the 'risk manager' track, which is more related to the ERM/corporate risk environment, where the highest step on the ladder is the position of chief risk officer (CRO).

 ## RISK OPTIMIZATION

Integrated risk management sounds simple in principle. Indeed, it is one of the supposed cornerstones of ERM. ERM texts routinely contain phrases like 'avoid duplicating costly risk management activities' or 'utilize correlations' – and emphasize this as one of the main benefits of ERM (as opposed to a silo, or decentralized, approach to risk management). For many firms, however, these benefits have turned out to be elusive. In this section, we will examine some of the paths followed by ERM to what could be considered a more optimal risk-return profile for Equinor. In Equinor, avoiding suboptimal decisions is known as 'optimizing total risk'. Optimization of total risk has been unyieldingly pursued by the ERM team, with several tangible benefits for the company.

One important example of optimization concerns the hedging of oil and gas exposures, which are two of the core risks mentioned earlier. As these risks were centralized, trading mandates throughout the company were substantially restricted and placed under central scrutiny. Likewise, the ability of business units to hedge their exposures was reigned in. This has led to a much more consistent hedging policy that is not driven by views on short-term development in oil price, nor by a desire to lock in prices that are attractive in relation to the unit's budgeted performance. If the business plan had assumed an oil price of $50 and it later climbed to $60, the business units could be tempted to use a derivative contract to lock that price in.

Today, Equinor's strategic hedging policy is guided by a clear and consistent philosophy with regard to the need to balance risk management with upside preservation. The process involves looking at Equinor's current balance sheet, cash flow levels, and investment needs to detect whether there is any weakness that could indicate that a hedge is needed to manage the risk of underinvestment. If it is found that the balance sheet is strong enough to deal with much lower levels of cash flow the preference is to leave the exposures unhedged. Primarily this is done based on the thinking that hedging reduces upside potential, and that anyone investing in Equinor does so believing (and wanting) to be exposed to the oil and gas markets. So, unless the level of downside risk calls for concrete action, Equinor prefers to remain unhedged. If the company does decide to hedge, it normally would use a strategy of buying put options rather than forward contracts. The goal is again to preserve as much upside as possible.

The sparing use of risk transfer (hedging) effectively means that Equinor largely retains its market risk. This presumes risk capacity in the form of a strong balance sheet. While maintaining a strong balance sheet also comes with certain costs, those must be compared with the efficiency of using transfer, or hedging of market risk in this case. For a large company like Equinor, it is exceedingly difficult to hedge a large fraction of its exposures due to limitations on the supply side in the market. Only a handful of global investment banks are able to act as a counterparty in these deals. Modest-sized transactions with shorter maturities can be divided up and used in offsetting deals with other companies, or with hedge funds seeking oil plays, leaving the bank able to earn money on the spread. But the market rapidly thins out for maturities longer than a year, especially for large companies like Equinor, and the cost of risk transfer sharply increases for the same reasons. Unable to find offsetting deals and earning on the spread, the bank must keep the position on its own book, which it will only do if there is a substantial premium for bearing that market risk. This explains why risk transfer is considered expensive for a company like Equinor for the kind of maturities that would have a meaningful effect on its aggregate risk. It also explains why keeping a strong balance sheet is considered a more reliable and economically sound strategy.

The policy with respect to FX risk has also been aligned with the principles of integrated risk management, which represents a considerable change compared to pre-ERM days. In fact, the treasury function in Equinor at the time illustrates well the point that risk management can be centralized but not integrated. Equinor is a company with a tradition of centralized management, and therefore all transactions related to FX and the loan portfolio were handled by the treasury, consistent with centralization. The treasury department, however, had by the late 1990s become a silo with a distinct culture and jargon of its own. The discussions were frequently geared towards technical issues that often did not make a lot of sense to general managers. For example, the then CEO was once asked 'Should the duration on the bond portfolio be 3 or 4?' This is a perspective quite far removed from the idea of deciding risk management policy to protect important corporate objectives, and a good illustration of the kind of narrow worldview that can arise in a specialized silo. Today, the ERM committee assesses the FX policy based on a view of what makes most sense for the company taken as a whole.

Equinor's approach to insurance offers another example of how something can be centralized yet not integrated. For many years, insurance policy was executed through a so-called captive (in-house) insurance company. A captive offers insurance to the operating units in the company, while reinsuring some of those risks in the external market for insurance. The idea is to pool the firm's competence and resources in insurance in one place, and then capitalize on that expertise. Operating in the insurance market requires highly specialized knowledge to detect mispricing, and the less knowledgeable business areas are likely to systematically overpay for insurance. The captive only reinsures when it judges that the going rate for that risk is attractive. This is a form of centralization of risk management, not unlike how the treasury function obtains more bargaining power vis-à-vis the banks and therefore better rates than the units could achieve individually. The problem was that the captive sought to justify its existence as a stand-alone unit by showing robust profits, which led to decisions that were actually not optimal for Equinor as a whole. This is not the right path from the perspective of ERM where the captive should rather be a tool for Equinor to optimize total risk. This is the situation today after carrying out a redesign of its incentives to maximize profits.

ERM has led to a more efficient use of natural hedges and correlations. We have already mentioned how the number of small and uncoordinated hedging transactions has decreased. This saved substantially on transaction costs and removed a layer of administration and accounting. In addition, many of Equinor's main products are strongly correlated. The correlation between oil and natural gas is well known, but there are also different varieties of hydrocarbon products that are less-than-perfectly correlated with the oil price. This creates a diversification effect and by extension a difference between risk on a gross and net basis. For a time, prior to its divestment, Equinor's business portfolio also included a risk-dampening effect from a negative correlation between the petrochemicals business and Equinor's main products.

In an effort to understand the effect of correlations, Equinor has observed that many of them are not particularly stable, especially at lower frequencies, such as days or weeks. In this timeframe, correlations often break down or even change sign. For many of the most significant correlations, Equinor's general conclusion has been that they stabilize only when using yearly data. On an annual frequency, the correlations behave in a more robust way and are therefore trustworthy companions when devising risk management strategies. Equinor has not, however, made any attempt to adjust the risk map to somehow incorporate correlation effects. Thus, the risk map contains gross exposures under the assumption that the other risk factors in it are held constant. Instead, a separate correlation analysis is performed, the purpose of which is to transition from working with many different gross exposures to the net effect of various correlated risk factors.

A natural hedge (of sorts) that is of utmost importance to Equinor when analysing risk on a net basis is taxation. On top of the regular statutory tax rate (22% in 2020), Equinor pays a 56% special tax on its offshore profits, that is, those from sale of oil and gas. Due to this heavy taxation of offshore profits, the post-tax numbers need to be used to understand the company's overall risk position. Hedging strategies, which are taxed onshore at the statutory rate, must account for the difference between these two tax regimes. There have been examples in the history of the Norwegian oil industry where this difference has been neglected, with severe and dangerous over-hedging as a result.

The risk mapping process covered earlier is not just a number's exercise, or about delivering a risk map to the board of directors. Some of the more qualitative aspects of this process also contribute towards risk optimization by directly connecting with the decision-making process. The explicit attention placed on risk and the need to think through the estimates of probability and impact serve to counteract the problem of the undermanagement of risk, and generate a more proactive approach. As noted, ERM in Equinor is not about just controlling or putting a lid on risk: it is about generating better decisions that create increased value for the company. The perspective is one of looking for better ways of doing things that increase the ratio of reward to risk, and thereby improve profitability. Consistent with this, risk mitigation actions are viewed in light of the estimates of probability and impact, which together constitute the cost of risk. When these items are quantified it becomes possible to say something about whether the mitigation actions are proportionate to the cost of risk. In explaining the nature of this decision-making problem, the ERM function has used insurance as an analogy. Just as it is self-evident to relate the insurance premium paid to any perceived benefit in terms of a lower exposure to losses, the company should try to see risk mitigation actions in the same way and compare expenditures with the reduced cost of risk.

Risk can also be optimized by avoiding cases of risk over-management. By applying the same methodology to every risk, these cases are more easily detected. One example of this comes from around the time Equinor was in the process of achieving compliance with Sarbanes–Oxley regulations, a requirement that followed the listing on the New York stock exchange. Failure to comply with these regulations was perceived by some in the company as a massive and all-important risk, worthy of almost any effort and cost to contain. Upon closer inspection by the ERM function, however, it turned out that the direct and indirect costs, in terms of fines, reputation effects, and so on, were in fact not that significant. The lesson learnt is that one should not only insist on quantification but do so specifically with respect to the firm's bottom line performance (which is to say cash flow or earnings). Many risks that feel like overwhelming threats may not be so after all, and the sentiment may be more driven by our gut instinct than anything else. The takeaway from this is that it pays to invest time in checking what the facts are because it counteracts such biases.

Risk optimization has also consisted of reshaping some of the flawed incentives that impacted risk management. Calibrating the use of KPIs to optimize risk-taking has been an important theme in the ERM journey. One of the roles of the ERM committee is resolving, *from an enterprise point of view*, issues that arise in the process of setting KPIs for business units. Wrongly formulated targets are seen as a threat to risk optimization because they may encourage a behaviour that runs counter to this goal. The ERM committee counteracts such tendencies by checking whether a particular target makes sense and is compatible with Equinor's overall best interest, a loop that in Equinor is referred to as 'pressure testing' the targets. Since the merger of ERM and the business performance unit the work to calibrate incentives for risk and return has proceeded even further.

ERM AND STRATEGY

Both strategy and ERM can mean different things to different people, so there is no clear-cut answer to exactly when ERM can be said to be 'strategic'. Pretty much regardless of one's definitions, however, there cannot be any doubt that ERM in Equinor interlocks with strategy in more than one way.

Country risk offers an example of how the ERM function has assisted in developing a methodology that facilitates strategy design. If a company is to make an entry into a high-risk country such as Nigeria, it can be done in many ways. It takes a lot of information to navigate these steps, but with the right kind of data it is possible to find a mode of entry that allows the achievement of the strategy's goal at lower risk than the alternatives. It should be clear that a systematic approach to risk and return can be helpful in this setting where risk is so palpable, and therefore in the design of the best strategy for any given country. This is an instance where Equinor's database and methodology for risk assessment has provided a major input to strategy formulation.

When a strategy for expansion into a particular country has been devised it may come up against an alternative, which is to invest in another country, say Angola this time. Again, the downside risk may be massive, but the venture offers significant upside potential as well. Maybe entering both countries would be an overstretch, so one has to be selected. How do you even begin to compare these two alternatives to decide where you believe you will get the biggest return per unit of risk? In Equinor's case, the answer has been to design the methodology such that all countries are compared with a neutral base case (Norway). Then different aspects of country risk, all quantified in the standardized database, are fed into the model. These inputs translate into an adjustment to the net present value (NPV) of the investment in that country. Selecting a strategy (investing in Angola versus Nigeria) is facilitated because it is now possible to view both alternatives in terms of the same bottom line, adjusted for country risk.

Several other interfaces with strategy have already been mentioned in this chapter. The way strategic hedging programmes are thought about today is based on the perceived need to secure financing for investment in the future (strategy execution). All the various ways in which risk is optimized contribute to a better performance of the existing strategy (strategy performance). The ERM function is also involved in evaluating the consequences of significant changes to the strategy resulting from acquisitions or large greenfield investments under consideration (strategy selection). Equinor has also made progress in working with a risk radar, which aims to discover the risks in emerging trends that may not affect the company fully today but could do so in a number of years. The interest in the radar received a boost when the board of directors expressed a need for something that would help them to keep informed about the long-term trends (both threats and opportunities) that Equinor is facing. The radar takes a perspective beyond the three to five years covered in the normal risk maps, and has put a spotlight on issues such as the consequences of certain climate scenarios and possible developments of industry regulations. A related effort to understanding long-term strategic risk has been a project in which the ERM function has developed estimates as to how

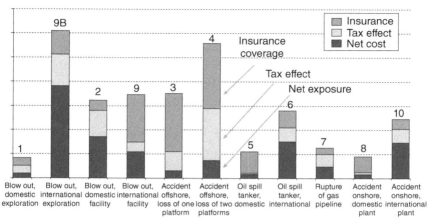

FIGURE 11.5 Catastrophic risk (net of insurance and tax, illustrative numbers)

different 'strategic paths' would contribute to different risk categories, such as reservoir risk, implementation risk, market risk, or risks related to health, safety, and the environment. Depending on which strategic path is taken, the composition of the company's overall portfolio of risks would gradually shift in a particular direction. Thorough investigations have also been made into catastrophic risks, the kind of tail risks that pose an existential threat to Equinor. These assessments have taken into account the extent to which insurance and tax deductions would mitigate the negative financial consequences, which has led to quite different risks being considered the most serious 'rock the boat risks' compared to the initial gross estimates. The discussions regarding tail risk have involved the board of directors, who actively supported the development of Equinor's capabilities in exploring the consequences of catastrophic risk. Figure 11.5 illustrates the transition from gross exposure to net for various identified catastrophic risks.

 ## FINAL THOUGHTS

In Equinor, understanding and managing risk is today considered a core value of the company, which is expressed in the corporate directives and widely communicated to employees. ERM is thoroughly embedded in the organization's work processes, and its ERM committee has managed the transition from a silo mentality to promoting Equinor's best interests in areas where risk needs to be considered. The company has introduced the concept of core risks, which are the risks exposures that the company needs to manage consistently vis-à-vis its investors and therefore require central management. In several areas where risk management used to be pursued in a silo fashion, based on incentives locally in the organization, risk is now optimized from the perspective of the company as a whole. ERM in Equinor is not a control function aimed at minimizing risk, but is dedicated to the goal of maximizing enterprise value given both downside risk and upside potential, while also enabling risk oversight through its independent voice and by being able to make its outputs available to the board of directors.

This chapter may give the impression that there has been a clear and straight path where things have been steadily progressing from one improvement to the other. This is not the actual experience. One should not expect that everything will run smoothly just because there has been an initial buy-in and the ball has been put in play. There have been intervals where the development of ERM was flat or even reversed, only to resume progress again. Organizations are fluid things and the ability to make progress within a specific area depends on many factors. A concept that challenges the organizational status quo and forces people to think and act differently will always face setbacks. In large firms, it takes persistence and patience over many years to reach full impact.

Achieving an impactful ERM that operates at the strategic level also requires proving one's mettle. It is not realistic to hope that one can jump to that level without first showing some kind of value added in various decision-making situations. When ERM professionals are in the room, it has to be felt that they contribute with something other than occasional remarks that maybe risk is too high. Acting as a gatekeeper who tries to limit risk-taking is a trap that risk managers often fall into. It is easy but not very constructive. This will stifle any demand for ERM to build up internally, as it will be unclear what this unit actually brings to the table. To get the virtuous cycle under way, ERM has to consist of people who are well versed in risk management principles but also capable of applying that in the context of a firm's value chain, so that the end result is not systematic risk avoidance but a more prosperous and effective organization.

CHAPTER TWELVE

Concluding Remarks

THE FATE OF AN enterprise risk management (ERM) programme is decided early on. It can take one of two main paths with very different destinations. If path one is followed, ERM becomes but an island, an isolated process that achieves little more than delivering a list of the firm's currently known risks to the board of directors who quickly check it off the agenda. If the other path is followed, ERM ends up becoming a force for change that brings about knowledge and behaviours that make a real difference to decision-making.

Choosing the second path will unlock ERM's full potential. In this case, ERM is arguably not a control function. The goal is instead to help generate better business decisions and increase firm value. As soon as value is accepted as the goal, the logical consequence is to always strive for the optimal balance between risk and return, which is a very different perspective from just keeping risks in check. In this empowered version of ERM, managing risk is elevated to something akin to a core value, something that is simply expected of all employees at all times.

There is a bargain involved, however. For this second path to be taken, executives must want to take it. If one thing is clear, it is that ERM cannot get off the ground unless the executive team is fully behind it. The bargain is that if they endorse it and commit the necessary resources, all the benefit of an empowered ERM stands a chance of materializing. There are many reasons why a chief executive officer (CEO) may not want to travel down this path, including lack of interest, understanding, resources, and so on. There is always that spurious aspect to things where it comes down to personal preferences on the part of key individuals. A more serious concern is when ERM is held back by a perception that the CEO's autonomy will decrease when the availability of information on risk and risk-taking increases. A CEO may prefer to keep their information advantage vis-à-vis the board of directors and thereby have more latitude to pursue their preferred agenda.

Choosing the first path may therefore seem like an attractive option to some executives. They will be seen to have acted responsibly by doing something about risk, and they will have a ready answer when somebody asks them 'What are your top 10 risks and what are you doing about them?' The executives get some degree of assurance, and peace of mind, that major risks receive appropriate attention. This means that their backs are covered, yet at the same time they can carry on largely as before. This low-impact version of ERM resembles a control function more than anything, as the main activity consists of making sure that the different business units and corporate functions report on their risks and have some response to them in place.

The number one hallmark of the 'success' of an ERM programme, in our view, is that the board of directors should, at all times, have full access to information about risk, both regarding the firm's major risk exposures and its aggregate risk profile. This is what allows them to carry out risk oversight in the best possible way. As we see it, a board of directors that is capable of high-level risk oversight is an asset, something that helps achieve better decision-making by engaging with the executives on actions taken with respect to risk. The point is not to overwhelm the directors with information or have them dig into almost every detail about risk. We are only proposing that the lines of communication between the board and the ERM function (or its most senior official) should be open and that information hoarding should be considered unacceptable.

Insisting on an independent risk management function might seem to be in opposition to its role as an enabler that supports executives in their decision-making process. Can it really be business oriented and still preserve its full integrity? We certainly believe so. To all intents and purposes, the kind of risk function we have in mind could equally be labelled a risk-and-return function because what it does is to facilitate the trade-off between risk and return with the goal of maximizing the value of the firm. It cannot get more 'business' than that. It is just that the board of directors have a legitimate request to know about the risks being taken. Where a tension could arise is when the executive team has committed to a strategy or transaction, yet the board hesitates due to the consequences it would have on the firm's risk profile based on assessments provided by the ERM function. In extreme cases, it could be construed as a vote of no confidence in the executives and lead them to withdraw their support for ERM.

Two things can be said about this. The ERM function is unlikely to achieve this level of capability and reach unless the executives initially thought that their firm genuinely benefits from incorporating risk management into its business pursuits. If they were primarily concerned with preserving degrees of freedom, they would have held back ERM implementation much earlier. The second thing is that bringing this kind of tension to the surface is in fact a good thing. There will always be elements pushing for grabbing opportunities and exploring the next big thing, perhaps in some cases fuelled by overconfidence and personal ambition. But there has to be resistance, something that checks for excesses and insists that the risks are proportionate to the reward. It is never good for the quality of the end product when things are too easy. That is just a recipe for sloppy execution. Much more likely than a breakdown, the tension will be resolved by a better thought-out proposal where risks are more clearly proportionate and within the company's ability to handle.

REVISITING THE ERM PUZZLES

Early on in this book we brought up several puzzling aspects of ERM. The inherent tension between the controlling and enabling roles just discussed was one of them. We now revisit some of the others to see if we are ready to conclude anything. One referred to the role of objectives and targets in ERM. The background for this was that the ERM frameworks tend to define risk in terms of deviations from such objectives. This is significant, because this concept has gone down well with executives and business units alike and has, to a fair extent, shaped the practice of ERM. It fits right into the model of management by objectives (MBO), in which everyone has targets to strive for (usually in the form of key performance indicators – KPIs), and it makes perfect sense for that manager to think of not achieving the target as risk. Because that resonates so well with managers, somebody who wants to 'sell' ERM to a firm could do worse than draw a dark picture of the threat of not meeting such targets

This framing of ERM has the strange effect of putting it at risk of becoming an elaborate apparatus for protecting KPIs. Targets, as we have seen, can induce many behaviours that pull the firm *away* from value-maximizing decisions. Firms may, for example, prefer not to spend resources on risk mitigation, even when it objectively would make sense, if that reduces their chance of meeting a profitability target. Or they may do just enough to beat the target and then mitigate risks to stabilize that outcome rather than pursue further upside potential. Even worse, performance pressure from KPIs may be a generator of risk, as people become increasingly willing to gamble or cut corners to improve the chance of meeting targets. Targets can thus become more a part of the problem than the solution.

There appears to be a fundamental and built-in conflict between target setting as part of MBO and a value-oriented ERM that seeks an optimization of risk and return. We are talking about essentially two different agendas within the same firm, and obviously these will not always lead to the same conclusion. The underlying cause of this situation is that KPIs are just rough proxies for value creation. If the targets are achieved, we can hope and surmise that value has been created in the process. In most cases, however, there is nothing magical about the targets themselves, as they are often aspirational rather than strongly connected to actual value creation. And the distortions the targets place on the incentives to manage risk in a responsible and proactive way can be real.

Yet none of this is to suggest that we do away with target setting. The targets establish aspirations that motivate, provide direction, and increase accountability. On the whole we must assume they bring more benefit than harm, because they provide incentives for performance improvements. And for cultural reasons, KPIs must be respected since they are 'official' and have been sanctioned by the board of directors. Highlighting the risk that KPIs are not met is not inherently wrong and can also lead to good discussions about what could be done better.

The conundrum is instead best solved by looking for cases where the targets cause obvious negative effects on risk management decisions from a corporate point of view; and doing something about them. The most promising way of achieving this is to make sure the analysis of major risks passes through ERM committee (or similar function) that sets out to identify the best risk response from the point of view of the firm as a whole. Important risk management decisions need to be lifted above any local agendas and short-term target chasing. KPIs can also, in some cases, be redesigned to better avoid any adverse effects they may have on optimal risk management, which happens when they too single-mindedly and ambitiously encourage the pursuit of 'more' performance without addressing the risk created by that pursuit.

Risk appetite presents us with another puzzle. The considerable confusion it has brought in practice is testimony to its inherent contradictions, yet it continues to be touted by many in the risk management community. It is an oxymoron that seems to invite our personal emotions, or preferences, about risk as a basis for decision-making. Given all the biases that we know affect peoples' decision-making with respect to risk, asking how we feel about the level of risk is not the preferred approach. While useful in that it helps bring attention to the *question* of how much risk we are willing to take, the notion of risk appetite is almost entirely unhelpful in producing an *answer* to the question. For specific risk exposures, a more robust approach is to ask what the cost of the risk is, which is a function of its probability and impact, and then weigh that against the cost of the measures that would be needed to mitigate it. This is a fact-based approach (in so far as one is willing to call subjective estimates of probability and impact facts) that simply asks whether the benefits outweigh the costs. Risk management, after all, is business. There has to be proportionality in the risk response: whenever the cost of risk mitigation is less than the reduction in the cost of risk, expected performance (and long-term firm value) goes up.

Then there is risk-*taking*, which is a different kind of decision-making situation than managing a specific exposure that already exists. By risk-taking we mean implementing investments and strategies that are expected to boost revenue growth and profitability, but that come with significant risk for the firm. Posing the question of risk appetite is only likely to generate confusion in this context as well. Instead, we should ask what kind of upside potential we can see in these ventures and compare that with the increase in the resulting aggregate risk. Aggregate risk, we have posited, is a function of critical thresholds of performance that imply costly disruptions to the value creation process, such as not being able to invest according to plan, or failing to protect loan covenants. So, instead of discussing risk appetite with respect to deviations from *targets*, we should develop a keen understanding of the distance to critical *thresholds*, and analyse to what extent various corporate policies bring us closer to (risk increases) or further away from (risk decreases) these thresholds. This provides a unified framework for evaluating the risk-return balance of a range of corporate polices like capital expenditure, acquisitions, hedging strategies, and capital structure.

The failure of ERM to conceptualize the risk of the firm as a whole, what we refer to as aggregate risk, is also puzzling given its stated ambitions of capturing the totality of risk and of taking place in a strategic setting. The distance-to-threshold framework allows firms to get a grip on aggregate risk and connect it to decision-making processes. But there is a catch: most of these critical thresholds are expressed in terms of financial performance, and many

ERM programmes seem unable or unwilling to pursue much in the way of financial analysis. Some, it seems, even hesitate to quantify things at all, preferring instead to rely on traffic light colours and verbal descriptions. This, we believe, is unfortunate and a factor in holding the impact of ERM back. Quantifying risk and connecting that with financial forecasts brings rigour, understanding, and comparability. This is an area where the ERM function could establish a clear relative advantage and make themselves useful to business units, executives, and the board of directors alike. The rest of the corporate world is deeply addicted to financial numbers and use them for much of their communication, yet ERM often chooses not to be part of that. As a result, many ERM functions remain unable to conceptualize and quantify risk in financial terms, predictably failing to connect with important decision-making processes. This leads to the greatest paradox of them all, namely that ERM, which is supposedly the most holistic of functions, becomes an isolated island. The lesson seems clear: ERM must become more financial before it can get fully strategic. Risk budgeting is a framework for closing this gap, and should be considered the second mainstay analytical output of an ERM programme, alongside the current workhorse of ERM, the risk register (or its summarized and visually rendered version, the risk map).

None of this is to suggest that things need to get complicated. Keeping it simple is always going to be a corporate virtue. We have tried to point to different keys, using the lessons learnt in Equinor, to unlock the potential of ERM. Most of the benefits of ERM can indeed be had from instilling a basic risk culture and risk governance. By raising risk awareness, opening lines of communication, and clarifying roles and responsibilities, major improvements can be made that lead to better decisions. As we have repeated throughout, much of the value lies in the conversations that these activities generate.

But for those who are willing to continue the journey, additional benefits can be realized. This could come, for example, from introducing risk budgeting or optimizing the risk-return balance in various ways by applying the principles of integrated risk management. As for that ultimate 'prize' of interacting with strategic decision-making, we certainly subscribe to the view that ERM can and should contribute in this setting. We have demonstrated several ways in which it can mesh with the strategy process and support decision-making. What ERM can bring is generally better methodology for trading off risk and return, and being adept at understanding dynamics – that is, hidden risks and contingent opportunities that all depend on variability in performance and are not obvious from just looking at forecasted numbers. But that presumes that it is staffed by the right kind of people, those who have the required skills and can make a difference. Bringing in a financial controller who has been in that position in the firm for fifteen years to head the ERM effort is unlikely to do that. This again goes back to the bargain. Are you prepared to recruit the right people for the job and empower them by unequivocally supporting ERM?

At the end of the day, empowered ERM is about improving the willingness and ability *of the entire firm* to make risk-conscious decisions that balance risk and return in the best possible way, on all levels of the organization and for all kinds of decision-making situations. It empowers the board of directors to do risk oversight; it empowers the executive team to understand the firm's risk profile and how it is impacted by corporate policies; and it empowers operating units to make better business decisions. When the culture is such that all these levels of the organization work together in an earnest effort to continuously detect, evaluate, and discuss risks in a climate of openness, ERM is empowered. This kind of ERM in turn enables the firm to take on the future more assuredly and to pursue its business opportunities with greater confidence and force.

Bibliography

Alviniussen, A., and H. Jankensgård, 2009. Enterprise risk budgeting: Bringing risk management into the financial planning process. *Journal of Applied Finance* 19.

Alviniussen, A., and H. Jankensgård, 2018. The risk-return trade-off: A six-step guide to ending the curse of risk appetite. Available on ssrn.com.

Aven, E., and T. Aven, 2015. On the need for rethinking current practice that highlights goal achievement risk in an enterprise context. *Risk Analysis – An International Journal,* 35.

Barney, J., 1991. Firm resources and sustained competitive advantage. *Journal of Management* 17.

Basel Committee on Banking Supervision, 2013. "Principles for effective risk data aggregation and risk reporting". Bank for International Settlements, Basel.

Beck, U., 1992. *Risk society: Towards a new modernity.* Sage: New Delhi.

Bernstein, P. L., 1996. *Against the gods: The remarkable story of risk.* John Wiley & Sons: Hoboken, NJ.

COSO, 1992. Internal control: Integrated framework. New York, NY.

COSO, 2004. Enterprise risk management: Integrated framework. New York, NY.

COSO, 2017. Enterprise risk management: Aligning risk with strategy and performance. June edition.

Culp, C.L., 2001. *The risk management process: Business strategy and tactics.* John Wiley & Sons: Hoboken, NJ.

Doherty, N.A., and C. Smith, 2020. Corporate insurance strategy: The case of British Petroleum. *Journal of Applied Corporate Finance,* 32.

Economides, M., 2010. BP culture made Gulf spill inevitable. *Forbes.* Available at https://www.forbes.com/sites/greatspeculations/2010/11/22/bp-culture-made-gulf-spill-inevitable/#70bf9c222c2e. Last accessed 4 August 2020.

European Central Bank (2018), "Report on the thematic review on effective risk data aggregation and risk reporting", European Central Bank, Frankfurt am Main.

Ferguson, A.D., and C.W. Smith, 1993. Corporate insurance strategy: The case of British Petroleum. *Journal of Applied Corporate Finance* 3.

Fraser, J.R.S., 2014. Building enterprise risk management into agency processes and culture. In Stanton, T., and D.W. Webster (Eds.), *Managing risk and performance: A guide for government decision makers.* John Wiley & Sons: Hoboken, NJ.

Fraser, J.R.S., 2010. The role of the board in risk management oversight. In Fraser, J.R.S., and B. Simkins (Eds.), Enterprise risk management: Today's leading research and best practices for tomorrow's executives. John Wiley & Sons: Hoboken, NJ.

Friedman, D., 2018. Culture by design. Infinity Publishing: W. Conshohocken, PA.

Froot, K.A., D.S. Scharfstein, and J.C. Stein, 1993. Risk Management: Coordinating Corporate Investment and Financing Policies. *Journal of Finance,* 48.

Gates, S., 2006. Incorporating strategic risk into enterprise risk management: A survey of current corporate practice. *Journal of Applied Corporate Finance,* 18.

Gigerenzer, G., 2013. *Risk Savvy: How to make good decisions.* Penguin Books: New York.

Graham, J.R., C. Harvey, and S. Rajgopal, 2005. The economic implications of corporate financial reporting. *Journal of Accounting and Economics,* 40.

IIA, 2017. International Professional Practices Framework®. IIA: Florida. Available at https://global.theiia.org/standards-guidance/Pages/Standards-and-Guidance-IPPF.aspx. Last accessed 5 August 2020.

ISO, 2018. ISO Risk Management: Principles and guidelines. International Organization for Standardization: Geneva.

Jankensgård, H. 2019. A theory of enterprise risk management. *Corporate Governance,* 19.

Jankensgård, H., A. Alviniussen, and L. Oxelheim, 2020. *Corporate foreign exchange risk management.* John Wiley & Sons: Hoboken, NJ.

Kahneman, D., and A. Tversky, 1979. Intuitive prediction: biases and corrective procedures. *TIMS Studies in Management Science* 12.

Kahneman, D., 2011. *Thinking fast and slow.* Farrar, Straus and Giroux: New York, NY.

Kaplan, J. 2010. Why corporate fraud is on the rise. *Forbes.* Available at https://www.forbes.com/2010/06/10/corporate-fraud-executive-compensation-personal-finance-risk-list-2-10-kaplan.html#44ccb8ba3aeb. Last accessed 4 August 2020.

Kay, J., 2010. *Obliquity: Why our goals are best achieved indirectly.* Profile Books Ltd: London.

Knight, F.H., 1921. *Risk, uncertainty, and profit.* Hart, Schaffner & Marx: New York, NY.

Kunreuther, H., and M. Useem, 2018. *Mastering Catastrophic Risk: How Companies Are Coping with Disruption.* Oxford University Press: Oxford.

Lipton, M., S.V. Niles, and M.L. Miller, 2018. Risk management and the board of directors. Harvard Law School Forum on Corporate Governance, 20 March. Available at https://corpgov.law.harvard.edu/2018/03/20/risk-management-and-the-board-of-directors-5/. Last accessed 5 August 2020.

Lynch, G., 2008. *At your own risk: How the risk-conscious culture meets the challenge of business change.* John Wiley & Sons: Hoboken, New Jersey.

Markowitz, H.,1952. Portfolio selection. *Journal of Finance, 7.*

Mikes, A., and R. Kaplan, 2015. When one size doesn't fit all: Evolving directions in the research and practice of Enterprise risk management. *Journal of Applied Corporate Finance, 27.*

Modigliani, F., and M. Miller, 1958. The cost of capital, corporation finance and the theory of investment. *American Economic Review, 48.*

Plous, S., 1993. *The psychology of judgment and decision making.* McGraw-Hill: New York, NY.

Power, M., 2007. *Organized uncertainty: Designing a world of risk management.* Oxford University Press: New York, NY.

Power, M., 2009. The risk management of nothing. *Accounting, Organizations and Society, 34.*

Prahalad, C. K., and G. Hamel, 1990. The core competence of the corporation. *Harvard Business Review, 68.*

Pulvino, T. C., 1998. Do asset fire-sales exist? An empirical investigation of commercial aircraft transactions. *Journal of Finance, 53.*

Quail, R., 2012. Defining your taste for risk. Corporate Risk Canada.

Rappaport, A., 2011. *Saving capitalism from short-termism: How to build long-term value and take back our financial future.* McGraw Hill: New York, NY.

Rampini, A. A., A. Sufi, and S. Viswanathan, 2014. Dynamic risk management. *Journal of Financial Economics, 111.*

Shleifer, A., and R.W. Vishny, 1992. Liquidation values and debt capacity: A market equilibrium approach. *Journal of Finance, 47.*

Shefrin, H., 2008. *Ending the management illusion: How to drive business results using the principles of behavioral finance.* McGraw-Hill: New York.

Simon, H.A.,1956. Rational choice and the structure of the environment. *Psychological Review, 63.*

Stulz, R.M., 1996. Rethinking Risk Management. *Journal of Applied Corporate Finance,* Fall issue.

Taleb, N.N., 2007. *The Black Swan: The impact of the highly probable.* Random House: New York.

Taleb, N.N., 2012. *Antifragile: Things that gain from disorder.* Random House: New York.

Tett, G., 2015. *The silo effect: Why putting everything in its place isn't such a bright idea.* Little, Brown: London.

Viscelli, T.R., D.R. Hermanson, and M.S. Beasley, 2017. The integration of ERM and strategy: implications for corporate governance. *Accounting Horizons, 31.*

Acknowledgements

I N WRITING A BOOK like this, one draws on the indefatigable work and hard-won insights of so many people. Enterprise risk management (ERM) is almost impossibly ambitious in scope, touching on nearly every facet of the firm. Taken literally, it has designs for several of its most important processes and functions. In taking on such a dynamic and all-encompassing subject, one must obviously count on the expertise of others to navigate many of the thorny issues that present themselves. Here we express our gratitude to the individuals who have blessed us with their thoughts and feedback on this book, or otherwise shaped our thoughts on the subject in major ways.

Our first thank you goes to Eyvind Aven, Petter's long-time co-builder of ERM in Equinor, who has provided us with many valuable suggestions.

We thank Martin Stevens for generously sharing his knowledge and experience in internal audit and risk management with us. This has significantly enhanced our understanding of this important function and its role in the value-creation process.

Thanks go to Frederik Lundtofte for educating us on probabilities and giving us insights into the wondrous world of mathematical analysis and its closely related philosophy.

We thank Ulrich Adamheit for bringing his many years of practical experience in overseeing risk management programmes to bear on this manuscript.

Thank you to Jennie Wallin for valuable feedback and for challenging us on risk appetite.

We thank John Fraser for his generosity of spirit and careful review of the manuscript. John is one of the true pioneers of ERM and a beacon of clarity with respect to its role in organizations.

We also thank Nicoletta Marinelli for her sharp observations that have helped this book in many ways. Authors accept responsibility for any errors errors that remain in the text.

Index